CHARLES SPURGEON

DISCOVERING THE POWER OF CHRIST'S PRAYER LIFE

COMPILED AND EDITED BY
LANCE WUBBELS

Emerald Books

P.O. BOX 635, LYNNWOOD, WA 98046

Scripture quotations are taken from the King James Version of the Bible.

About the Author

CHARLES HADDON SPURGEON (1834–1892) was the remarkable British "Boy Preacher of the Fens" who became one of the truly greatest preachers of all time. Coming from a flourishing country pastorate in 1854, he accepted a call to pastor London's New Park Street Chapel. This building soon proved too small and so work on Spurgeon's Metropolitan Tabernacle was begun in 1859. Meanwhile his weekly sermons were being printed and having a remarkable sale—25,000 copies every week in 1865 and translated into more than twenty languages.

Spurgeon built the Metropolitan Tabernacle into a congregation of over 6,000 and added well over 14,000 members during his thirty-eight-year London ministry. The combination of his clear voice, his mastery of language, his sure grasp of Scripture, and a deep love for Christ produced some of the noblest preaching of any age. An astounding 3,561 sermons have been preserved in sixty-three volumes, *The New Park Street Pulpit* and *The Metropolitan Tabernacle Pulpit*, from which the chapters of this book have been selected and edited.

During his lifetime, Spurgeon is estimated to have preached to 10,000,000 people. He remains history's most widely read preacher. There is more available material written by Spurgeon than by any other Christian author, living or dead. His sixty-three volumes of sermons stand as the largest set of books by a single author in the history of Christianity, comprising the equivalent to the twenty-seven volumes of the ninth edition of the *Encyclopedia Britannica*.

About the Editor

LANCE WUBBELS is the managing editor of Bethany House Publishers. His interest in the writings of Charles Spurgeon began while doing research on an editorial project that required extensive reading of Spurgeon's sermons. He discovered a wealth of sermon classics that are filled with practical, biblical insight for every believer and written in a timeless manner that makes them as relevant today as the day they were spoken. His desire is to select and present Spurgeon's writings in a way that will appeal to a wide audience of readers and allow one of the greatest preachers of all time to enrich believers' lives.

Wubbels is the author of *The Gentle Hills* fiction series and a heartwarming short novel, *One Small Miracle*, with Bethany House Publishers. A naturally gifted storyteller, he captures readers with a warm, homey style filled with wit and insight that appeals to a wide readership.

Contents

Introduction

THE EULOGIES OF Charles Spurgeon's preaching are almost endless. It is a preaching legacy that can never be forgotten; it may never be surpassed. Considered by his peers then and now as "The Prince of Preachers,"Charles Spurgeon will stand for many years to come as the epitome of pulpit mastery. Joseph Parker, another of London's famous preachers of the second half of the nineteenth century, wrote: "Mr. Spurgeon's career has proved that evangelical teaching can draw around itself the greatest congregation in the world and hold it for a lifetime.... The great voice has ceased. It was the mightiest voice I ever heard."

Recognized as one of the greatest expository preachers of all time, Charles Spurgeon built London's Metropolitan Tabernacle into the world's largest independent congregation during the nineteenth century. While many factors have been noted that help explain his stunning preaching legacy, the greatest secret that empowered Spurgeon was his devotion to prayer—both personal and congregational. When people would walk through the Metropolitan Tabernacle, Spurgeon would take them to a basement prayer room where people were always on their knees interceding for the church. Then the pastor would declare, "Here is the powerhouse of the church." Add to these words his burden, "If I could impress my heart on every syllable and baptize every word with my tears, I could not too earnestly entreat you to be above all things earnest in prayer,"and you get a profound sense of the importance Spurgeon placed on prayer.

Join the legendary Charles Spurgeon as he marvels at the power of Christ's prayer life. If we discover in the life of Christ, the perfect Son of God, an intense devotion to maintain a consistent prayer life, what of us? Spurgeon tells us: "Christ rose up early and went alone in the dark to pray because He loved to put prayer first of all. He would go nowhere till He had prayed. He would attempt nothing till He had prayed. He would not cast out a devil, He would not preach a sermon, He would work no cure, however necessary, however profitable, until first of all He had drawn near to God. Take heed to yourself that you follow the same rule. Look no man in the face till you have seen the face of God. Speak with no one till you have spoken with the Most High. Take not to running till you have in prayer laid aside every weight, lest you lose the race. Let us attempt nothing without Him."

Spurgeon paints masterful and passionate word pictures of Christ the intercessor—at daybreak, through whole nights, at Gethsemane, praying for sinners, for His people's sanctification and unity, for Peter, for those who are bowed down. All are marvelously instructive for us.

But what transformed Spurgeon most about Christ's prayer life was this scripture: "He ever liveth to make intercession *for us*." Not only did Christ lay down His life for us through His death, but the whole life of Christ throughout eternity—His boundless, endless, glorified existence—is still for us! Spurgeon says: "You have sat down at the foot of Calvary, your eyes filled with tears, and you have said, 'How delightful it is to behold His love written out in crimson characters in yonder streams of blood, that His very heart pours out for our redemption.' I want you to sit at the foot of His throne, and, as far as your eyes will permit, behold His splendor, and see how He spends His glory-life in perpetual intercession for you. He is as much ours on the throne as on the tree. He is ever living to apply to us with His own hands what He purchased by the nailing of those hands and the piercing of His heart upon the cross of our redemption."

What a life-changing message to read about! Well over one hundred years have gone by since Spurgeon's voice echoed through his great London church, but time has in no way diminished the powerful effect of Spurgeon's words. I invite you to read these twelve insightful chapters on Christ's prayer life as you would listen to a trusted and skilled pastor. Carl F.H. Henry wrote of Charles Spurgeon what is so applicable to this theme: "Multitudes of Christians still draw deeply at the well of Spurgeon's refreshing and victorious messages. The world will stop, look, and listen when it hears such a voice, and it is no surprise that even in the late twentieth century the good this has done lives on to bless our generation."

Careful editing has helped to sharpen the focus of these sermons while retaining the authentic and timeless flavor they undoubtedly bring.

*W*hereas Christ, by His death, provided all that was necessary for your salvation, He, by His life, applies that provision that He made in His death. He lives on purpose to see brought home to you and enjoyed by you all those blessed privileges that He purchased upon the tree when He died in your place. Had He not lived for you, His death for you would have miscarried. He would then have begun the work and provided all the materials for its completion, but there would have been none to render those materials available and to complete the building whose foundation had been laid in so costly a manner. We are pardoned by the death of Christ, but we are justified by His resurrection. We are saved because He died, but that salvation is brought home and secured to us because He sits at the right hand of God and continually makes intercession for us. I want you to think as much of a living Christ as you have ever thought of a dead Christ. You have sat down at the foot of Calvary, your eyes filled with tears, and you have said, "How delightful it is to behold His love written out in crimson characters in yonder streams of blood, that His very heart pours out for our redemption! I want you to sit at the foot of His throne and, as far as your dim eyes will permit, behold His splendor and see how He spends His glory-life in perpetual intercession for you. He is as much ours on the throne as on the tree. He is ever living to apply to us with His own hands what He purchased by the nailing of those hands and the piercing of His heart upon the cross of our redemption.

Chapter One

The Ever-Living Priest

*And they truly were many priests, because they were not suffered
to continue by reason of death: But this man, because he contin-
ueth ever, hath an unchangeable priesthood. Wherefore he is able
also to save them to the uttermost that come unto God by him,
seeing he ever liveth to make intercession for them*
—Hebrews 7:23–25.

THE APOSTLE PAUL is very much at home
with his theme whenever he is extolling his Master. When handling
the Jewish types and figures, with which he was so familiar, Paul
was charmed to point out how far superior the Lord Jesus Christ is
to any and all the priests of the Old Testament dispensation. In this
case, he is dwelling upon the special honor of our Lord, because
His priesthood is without end, seeing He Himself is not put forth
from the priesthood by reason of death. A common priest served
from thirty to fifty years of age, and then his work was done.
Priests of the house of Aaron, who became high priests, held their
office through life. Sometimes a high priest would thus continue in
his office for a considerable length of time, but in many cases he
was cut off as other men are by premature death. Hence, there was
priest after priest of the order of Aaron to go within the veil for the
people. Our Lord is of another race, being a priest according to the
order of Melchizedek, "having neither beginning of days, nor end
of life" (Heb. 7:3). He was made a priest not after the law of Moses
but after the power of an endless life. He continues to make intercession for the people of God by virtue of His eternal life and perpetual priesthood. In this respect, the true Messiah, the Lord Jesus

Christ, rises above all former priests. They were indeed but types and shadows of Jesus.

The superiority of our Lord Jesus Christ will not interest everyone. To many people it will seem a piece of devotional rapture, if not an idle tale, yet there will ever be a remnant according to the election of grace to whom this meditation will be inexpressibly sweet. They are indicated in the text: they who come to God by Jesus Christ. The people who are in the habit of using Christ as their way of access to God are those who value Him beyond all price, and such persons will delight to hear Him extolled in the highest terms.

We will begin our study, then, by the inquiry: Do we come unto God by Jesus Christ? Hearken, and answer for yourself. Do we come to God at all? Do we recognize the Lord our God as a person who should be approached? Are we not approaching Him? Are we among those who are always coming to God, to whom at the last the great Judge shall say, "You have long been coming, continue to come. Come ye blessed of my Father, inherit the kingdom prepared for you"? Or are we departing from God by forgetting Him or rebelling against Him, so that we shall be among that number to whom the Judge shall say, "You have long been departing, continue to do so. Depart, ye cursed, into everlasting fire in hell, prepared for the devil and his angels"?

Are we coming to God? That is the question. Is the direction of our lives *toward* God? We are going either to God or away from God, and by this we may forecast our everlasting destiny. The direction in which the arrow is flying prophesies the target in which it will be fixed. The way the tree is leaning foretells the place of its fall, and where the tree falls, there it will lie. So let us judge ourselves this day. Which way are we drifting? Have we ever come to God by sincere repentance of our wanderings? Have we come to Him by faith, and are we reconciled to Him? Do we come to Him in prayer? Do we come to Him day by day, speaking with Him and desiring to walk with Him? Do we come to God by communion with Him, having fellowship with the Father and with His son Jesus Christ? Do we, in fact, know the meaning of what it is to draw near to God? Blessed are they who know the name of the Lord and walk with Him, rejoicing in the light of His countenance (Ps. 89:15). It is to such that Jesus is precious as their way of access to the Father.

In the description there is a little word of distinction, for the people who are said to be saved by the great Intercessor are those who come to God *by Him*. Certain persons talk of coming to God as Creator, and Ruler, and even as Father, but they do not think of His dear Son as their way of approach. They forget or else deny the declaration of our Lord Jesus: "No man cometh unto the Father, but by me" (John 14:6). Yet this saying is true. There is no true way of approach to God except through Jesus Christ, the one Mediator between God and man. A deep abyss divides us from God, and only the ladder that Jacob saw can bridge the gulf. Our Lord Jesus, being God and man in one person, reaches from side to side of the chasm. Coming near to us, this ladder stands at our foot in the human nature of our Lord, and it reaches right up to the infinite Majesty by reason of the divine nature of our Redeemer. God and man, in one person, unites God and man in one league of love. We come to God by Jesus Christ. Prayers in which Christ is forgotten are insults to the God of revelation. Faith in which Jesus is not the foundation of our hope is mere delusion. God cannot accept us if we will not accept His Son. O sinner, God has opened one door in heaven. If you will not go in by that door, you shall never enter within the walls of the new Jerusalem. God bids you come to Him by One in whom He is well-pleased; and if you will not be pleased with Jesus, you cannot come to the Father. O you who are daily users of this royal way to God, you will forgive me if I hide myself behind my Lord and seek to do nothing more than, in all simplicity, to set forth His unchangeable priesthood and endless life. Pray the Lord to help me to extol the Great High Priest of our profession and also to help you to join in the praise of Jesus in the power of His Holy Spirit.

An Endless Life

I want you to think earnestly upon this very simple theme, for it is in complicities that we find our greatest consolations. Our Lord Jesus is not as Aaron, who had to be stripped of his garments on the top of Mount Hor and to die in the mount. Neither is He like to any of the sons of Aaron who in due time suffered the infirmities of age and at last bowed their heads to inevitable death. Jesus died once, but death has no more dominion over Him; it is witnessed of Him that He lives.

We clearly perceive that our Lord Jesus possesses endless life *as*

God, for how shall Godhead expire? It is not possible for the Godhead to cease or to suspend its existence. Our Lord God "is over all,... blessed for ever" (Rom. 9:5), and in this respect, He is necessarily everlasting as to His life.

But our Lord ever lives also in respect to *His manhood.* Though He died unto sin once, He soon rose again from the dead, His body never having seen corruption. He died *in* His priesthood and *for* His priesthood, but never *from* His priesthood. By His resurrection His manhood was fully restored to a life that dies no more. We speak of Him as "he that liveth, and was dead; and...[is] alive for evermore" (Rev. 1:18). This is a very sweet truth to those who are in Christ Jesus. The Lord Jesus Christ had lived one life as a man: Why did He not end that life as a man when He died on the cross? It shows His deep attachment to our manhood that He retained the human nature after His great sacrifice had been presented and accepted. The fact that He again appeared as a man among men and carried human nature to His glorified estate is clear evidence of His deep attachment to our humanity. If some glorious angel or archangel had loved a race of rabbits and had condescended for the salvation of these creatures to assume their nature, and if in that nature he had died for them, you would naturally expect that at the conclusion of his labors and sufferings he would lay aside the form of his humiliation and return to the greatness of his former estate. But our Lord Jesus Christ, whose stoop of condescension when He assumed our nature was greater than any archangel could have achieved, having taken our human nature and having bled and died in it, continued to wear it after He had said, "It is finished," after He had risen from the dead, and after He had taken his seat at the divine right hand! He has become so wedded to us, so truly one flesh with us, that He will not be divided from us in nature. He sits upon the throne of God, not in His pure Godhead but as one who has been slain, clothed in a body like our own. What manner of love is this! What bliss to know that my kinsman lives! Truly many waters could not quench His love to manhood, nor could death itself destroy it. The Son of God is still the Son of Man. He whom angels worship is not ashamed to call us brethren, for as partaker of our nature He lives and will live forever.

He ever lives, then, as God and as man, and I prolong the blended thoughts by saying that He ever lives *in His relationship to us.* This you have already seen to be the case, because He lives in our nature. But now I beg you to note that He lives as God and man *for us.* I love to read these words: "He ever liveth to make intercession for them" (Heb. 7:25). This is one great object for which He lives. To make intercession for those who come to God by Him is the business of His life. Is not this wonderful? If some influential and powerful person should say to you, "I live to promote your interest. Wherever I go and whatever I do, whatever I seek and whatever I obtain, I live for you," it would show great friendship and excite in us great expectations, would it not? Yet here is the Lord Jesus declaring that He lives for us. For us He appears in the presence of God, and for us He has gone to the many mansions of the Father's house, and for us He constantly intercedes with God. Oh, the deep debt of gratitude we owe to this glorious One, who having died for us now lives for us!

It is more than if a brother should say, "I live my whole life for you." For remember, this might be said to be the second life that our Lord gives to us. He lived for us here below a whole lifetime! He laid down that life for us, and now He lives again for us. I know not how to speak what I feel concerning the surpassing greatness of His love. He could not be content to give His life once for us, but He must take it again and then give it over again for us. See how He loves us: He died for us! See how He loves us: He lives again for us! He lives for sinners, for He lives to intercede, and for whom is intercession but for those who need an advocate? "If any man sin, we have an advocate" (1 John 2:1). May I say that Jesus lives two lives for us?

Yet more, it is said, "He ever liveth to make intercession for us." The whole life of Christ throughout eternity—His boundless, endless, glorified existence—is still for His people. He glorifies the Father and makes glad the hosts of heaven, but still this is the set purpose of His heart—to live for us. "[He] loved me, and gave himself for me" (Gal. 2:20) is true, but we may read it in the present tense if we like and it is still true: "He loves me, and He gives Himself for me." Christ loved His Church and gave Himself *for* it, and now He loves His Church and gives Himself *to* it. What inspiration lies in the endless life of Christ for us! Let our lives be lived wholly for Him since He lives wholly for us.

This truth of the living Christ should be remembered in our greatest need. Dear friend, there is an almighty and divine One in heaven who ever lives for our highest benefit. Let us adore Him most lovingly. This should show us how great our need is, that we always want a living Savior to interpose for us. A dying Savior was not enough; we still require every moment of our lives a living Savior engrossed with the care of our spirits, interposing on our behalf in all manner of ways, and delivering us from all evil. Our hour of necessity is ever present, for Jesus is ever guarding us, and His work is never a superfluity. Herein lies the great comfort that we should fall back upon whenever our burden presses too heavily upon our shoulders. Jesus, my great Redeemer, lives for me in all fullness of power and glory and devotes that life, with all that pertains to it, to the preservation of my soul from every evil. Can I not rest in this? With such a keeper, why should I be afraid? Must I not be safe when One so vigilant and so vigorous devotes His life to my protection? What innumerable blessings must come to those for whom Jesus spends the strength of His endless life!

Endless Priesthood

Our Lord is ordained to an unchangeable priesthood, or rather, to a priesthood that "passeth not from one to another." His office cannot be taken up by a successor. It is not transferable but belongs to Jesus alone, seeing He ever lives to carry it out in His own person. We have only one priest, and that one priest we have forever.

In this *we are not like the Israel of old*, for as we have already seen, a high priest would die. I can imagine that to many Jewish believers the death of a priest was a great affliction. I can hear an Israelite saying, "And so he is dead. He was a good man, a tender-spirited minister, a gentle and affectionate shepherd. I have told him all my heart, and now he is taken from me. I went to him in my youth in deep distress of conscience. He offered a sacrifice for me when I was unclean and brought me near to the holy place. Since then I have gone to him when I have needed guidance. He consulted the oracle on my behalf, and my way has been made plain. He knows the secrets of my family. He knows those delicate griefs that I have never dared to tell anyone else. Alas, he is dead, and half my heart has perished! What a gap is made in my life by his decease!" The mourner would be told that the priest's son had become his successor, but I think I hear him say, "Yes, I am aware of it. But the young man does not know what his father knew about me. I could never again lay bare my heart." There would always be the feeling in some minds that the next high priest might not be quite so acceptable with God or so tender toward the congregation as he who had passed away. He might be superior in education but inferior in affection; he might be more austere and less tender; he might have greater gifts and less fatherliness.

At any rate, it would seem like having to begin again when one went for the first time to the new priest. It would be a break in the continuity of one's comfort. The quiet flow of life would be marred, as when a river comes to its rapids and an impassable fall causes a break in the navigation and a necessary unloading of the vessel and a laborious *portage* instead of an easy passage down a gently flowing stream. "Oh," says one good Israelite, "the venerable high priest who has just fallen asleep was my friend. We took sweet counsel together and walked to the house of God in company. He was in my house when my beloved child died. He was with me when the partner of my bosom, the light of my eyes, was taken away from me at a stroke. His long experience he used for my instruction and comfort. But, alas, it is all gone, for the saint of God is dead!"

Beloved, here is our comfort: We have only *one* priest, and He ever lives. He had no predecessor and He will have no successor because He ever lives personally to exercise the office of high priest on our behalf. My soul rests in the faith of His one sacrifice, offered once and no more. There is but one presenter of that one sacrifice, and never can there be another, since the One is all sufficient and He never dies. Jesus reads my heart and has always read it since it began to beat. He knows my griefs and has carried my sorrows from of old, and He will bear both them and me when old age shall shrivel up my strength. When I shall fall asleep in death, He will not die but will be ready to receive me into His own undying blessedness. Do we not rejoice in the unbroken continuity and everlasting perpetuity of the priesthood of Christ!

Again, *we are not as Israel is at this moment*. Alas, poor Israel! After all her privileges of the past, where is she now? She is without a high priest. She does not dare even to think of anointing one of her Cohens to that office. She is without an altar or a sacrifice. Once a year on the day of atonement she has something that bears the shadow of sacrifice, but it is a worship of her own devising and not after the law of Moses or the ordinances of God. She is left without priest, altar, temple, or sacrifice. And the outlook of her sons and daughters as to the future life is for the most part exceedingly dark and dismal. I am assured that nothing is more unwelcome to a Jew than the thought of death, and it may well be so. Beloved, we are not without a priest. Our faith beholds Jesus passed into the heavens and abiding there in the glory of His once offered sacrifice, ever living to intercede for us. Jesus is to my soul at this moment as living a person as I am myself, and even more so. I have come to look on friends and dear ones as passing shadows. I see written across their brows the word *mortal,* but Jesus is the one friend who only has immortality and therefore can never be lost to me. His sacrifice is forever effectual, and His priesthood is forever in exercise. Christ's priesthood remains without end. What bliss it is to be a believer in Jesus and thus to have one priest and never to desire another!

We are not, as some perceive, Catholic priests. Some say that these priests are substitutes for Christ. If so, the assertion is a flat blasphemy against Him who is a priest forever and needs no substitute. Others say they are the vicars of Christ, carrying on His work now that He is gone by presenting the unbloody sacrifice of the mass. This also is clean contrary to the teaching of the apostle in this passage, wherein he proves that this man, because He continues forever, has a priesthood that cannot be passed from one to another. In this he shows that our Lord is different from the Aaronic priests who had their office taken up by those who followed them, whereas Jesus, like Melchizedek, has no successor but exercises His office in His own proper person according to the power of an endless life. We know no priests on earth now, except that in a secondary sense the Lord Jesus has made all believers to be kings and priests unto God (Rev. 1:6). We have now no special order of persons set apart to represent their fellows before God. Under the Christian dispensation we have only one priest, who continues ever in an untransferable priesthood; this is the apostle's argument. But this is not true if bishops and presbyters are priests in the sense in which some claim. I count the very thought of our having other sacrificing priests than the Lord Jesus to be derogatory to the one unique, completely accomplished sacrifice of our Great High Priest who abides alone in His personal office forever and ever. Our Lord Jesus walks in that supreme, solitary majesty that was foreshadowed in Melchizedek—and in that spirit He fulfills a priesthood that renders all other priests a superfluity and a mockery. What have we to do with more sacrifices when the one Sacrifice is offered once for all? Brethren, hold fast this precious truth and rejoice in it.

Endless Intercession

If I were to read this passage, "Seeing he ever liveth to interpose for them," it would not be an incorrect reading. The Lord Jesus Christ in His perpetual priesthood lives on purpose to be the Advocate, Defender, Patron, Mediator, and Interposer for His people. You who come to God by Him will highly esteem this constant service rendered to you by your Lord. Whereas Christ, by His death, provided all that was necessary for your salvation, He, by His life, applies that provision that He made in His death. He lives on purpose to see brought home to you and enjoyed by you all those blessed privileges that He purchased upon the tree when He died in your place. Had He not lived for you, His death for you would have miscarried. He would then have begun the work and provided all the materials for its completion, but there would have been none to render those materials available and to complete the building whose foundation had been laid in so costly a manner. We are pardoned by the death of Christ, but we are justified by His resurrection. We are saved because He died, but that salvation is brought home and secured to us because He sits at the right hand of God and continually makes intercession for us. I want you to think as much of a living Christ as you have ever thought of a dead Christ. You have sat down at the foot of Calvary, your eyes filled with tears, and you have said, "How delightful it is to behold His love written out in crimson characters in yonder streams of blood, that His very heart pours out for our redemption! I want you to sit at the foot of His throne and, as far as your dim eyes will permit, behold His splendor and see how He spends His glory-life in perpetual intercession for you. He is as much ours on the throne as on the tree. He is ever living to apply to us with His own hands what He purchased by the nailing of those hands and the piercing of His heart upon the cross of our redemption.

Why is it so needful that Jesus ever-living should always be interceding for us? I answer, first, it is most becoming *God-ward*. The great principle that God would teach men is this—that sin is so hateful to Him that the sinner can approach His justice only through a Mediator. This truth is most clearly set forth in the fact that even now that we are washed in the blood of the Lamb, there is no approach to God except through the intercession of Christ. Does not this teach the grand principle of the evil of sin, and teach it in the plainest manner? The distance that sin puts between the sinner and God, and the necessity of mediation so that a just God may commune with the imperfect—are not these fully taught by the institution of the perpetual intercession of the Son of God? This is as much a declaration of the righteousness of God as was the substitutionary death on Calvary.

Moreover, the intercession of Christ is needful God-ward to illustrate the union, cooperation, and intercommunion of the divine Trinity in the work of our salvation. The Son of God intercedes in heaven, and the Holy Spirit intercedes on earth. If Jesus intercedes, it is of necessity that the Father be there with whom He may intercede. The Son pleads and the Father hears and answers, and in consequence conveys to us by the Holy Ghost the blessings purchased by His Son. Thus, Father, Son, and Holy Spirit are brought before our minds as all concurring in the believer's salvation. A mediator who is not only man but also one person of the blessed Trinity continues to intercede for us, and thus we see how God remembers us.

Once again, our own communion with God is openly declared, while there sits on the throne of God a man who is also God, pleading with the Godhead. Man is always standing in glory in connection with God. The perpetual intercession of Christ is a perpetual recognition of the communion that now exists between God and once fallen but now restored manhood. We should look upon Christ pleading in glory as the sign, token, and evidence that man is reconciled to God, that man speaks with God, that God speaks with man, and that once again the old dominion is restored to man. For we see Jesus, who was made a little lower than the angels, for the suffering of death crowned with glory and honor.

The perpetual intercession is necessary God-ward. But it is even more necessary *man-ward.* Though we have been forgiven through the precious blood, yet we in many things offend, and therefore we need every day a fresh application of the blood of sprinkling. Conscience accuses us for daily flaws and faults, and it is therefore well for us that it is written that he "made intercession for the transgressors" (Isa. 53:12). Where would our hope of continual preservation from the weaknesses and sins of our nature be if Jesus did not constantly plead for us? The way is rough, the world is sinful, our wanderings are many, our desires are incessant, and therefore we need the eternal intercession. We are never out of danger and therefore always need the guardian prayer. We are never above weakness and folly and therefore require the perpetual patronage of our protector. What man is there who is not full of desires? What woman is there who does not need to come to the mercy seat many times a day? Jesus is always there, waiting to present our petitions, ever making our persons, our petitions, and our praise acceptable with God. Brethren, we are daily pressed, with either conflict with sin or suffering in the body, or service of our Lord or sympathy for our brethren. For all these we need help out of the holy place, help that can come only by way of the throne of the heavenly grace. We need an interposer, at whose feet we may lay down our burdens, into whose ears we may tell our sorrows. Therefore Jesus ever lives to make intercession for us.

Our great Intercessor also obtains for us those precious gifts and graces that are needful for our growth and usefulness. His is the hand that leads us onward to those attainments of the spiritual life that are needful for our usefulness in this world and for our preparation for the life to come. The higher virtues would be beyond our reach if His prayers did not bring us more and more of the Spirit of God to make us perfect in every good work to do His will.

Have you forgotten also that there is an enemy who is always alive and always full of malice? He acts as the accuser of the brethren who accuses them day and night before God. Were it not for our glorious Advocate, who for Zion's sake does never hold His peace, what would become of us? This accuser is also a tempter, who subtly contrives plots for our overthrow. It is at times true of us as it was of Peter: "Simon, Simon, behold, Satan hath desired to have you, that he may sift you as wheat: But I have prayed for thee" (Luke 22:31–32). How often are we hidden from evil by the prayers of Jesus! We do not know how many poisoned arrows are caught upon the shield of our Lord's intercession. The intercession of Christ as with ten thousand hands is always scattering benedictions. Job asks, "Hast thou entered into the springs of the sea?" (Job 38:16). Surely our Lord's intercession is the source of an ocean of blessedness. If we had but eyes enlightened of the Holy Spirit we should see the mountain full of horses of fire and chariots of fire round about the people of God. Who guides those horses? Who directs those chariots? Who is the captain of the hosts of spirits that encompass the camp of God? Who, but the Prince Emmanuel, who by His all-powerful intercession rules all things for us.

The Lord Jesus by His unceasing pleas keeps all the powers of darkness in check and moves all the powers of light for our rescue. His prayers form an atmosphere of blessing in which we live and move. We do not know, we cannot begin to calculate, the depths of our obligation to the ceaseless care of our unwearied Intercessor. Even when time shall be no more and all the saints shall be saved, their continuance in bliss will be due to His endless intercession.

Think of it—Jesus always praying, never ceasing! His very appearance in heaven is a plea. The memory of His finished work is a plea. His constant thought of us is a pleading with God. Not with tears and cries will He pray as He did in the days of His flesh; nor perhaps even with words will He plead, for His spirit speaks to the spirit of God without such vocal instrumentality as creatures require. This much we know: He is always praying, always prevailing, and consequently always showering down upon us blessings beyond all count, the most of which we scarcely recognize. And yet if they were withheld, we should perish miserably. Lord Jesus, Your dying blood is well matched by Your living plea, and our hearts rejoice in this because of these two sure proofs of Your love and grace.

Endless Salvation

"He is able to save without end, or to the uttermost, them who come unto God by Him." That word *uttermost* includes within it *a reference to time*. Because our Lord Jesus never dies, He is endlessly able to save. At all times His power to save remains. He was able to save some of you forty years ago, but you would not come to Him that you might have life. He is able to save you now though you have passed your fortieth years in impenitence. If you come to God by Him, He will save you however multiplied your sins. Beloved, many years ago, some of us put our trust in the Redeemer, and He forgave us our trespasses. Happy day! Happy day! We are much further advanced in life at this time, and our strength grows less as the shadows lengthen; but Jesus is evermore the same and is still able to save to the full. No diminution has taken place as to His ability to save. He who helped us in the seven struggles of our youth and the seventy burdens of our manhood will help us to seventy times seven, if need be. We need not fear old age or death, seeing He always has the dew of His youth and is always our friend, laying out His life for us, even as once He laid it down for us.

He is abundantly able to save *from the uttermost of evil to the uttermost of good.* As He ever lives in the fullness of life, so He can save to the fullness of salvation. His name is Jesus—the Savior— and as Jesus the Savior, He lives. He has not renounced His office or allowed any part of His life to run to another purpose. He lives to save.

The Lord Jesus Christ is now, "seeing he ever liveth," able to save to the uttermost *in point of our sin.* Whatever the sin of anyone, if he comes to God by Jesus Christ, it shall be forgiven. God forbid I should try to make a list of human crimes. What purpose would it serve? The reading of the details of vice is very defiling. I will not therefore attempt a catalogue of crimes into which mortals sink. But whatever the sin, the text draws a circle of hope around you, as it says: "He is able to save them to the uttermost that come unto God by him." Whatever your offense, if you will come to God and confess it and ask mercy through the name of Jesus, He is able to save you to the extreme limit of your need. If you have gone as far in sin as is possible and are forced to confess that if you could have gone further you would have, yet there is forgiveness. O my reader, though your hand is red with murder, yet the blood of Christ could wash it clean. "All manner of sin and blasphemy shall be forgiven unto men" (Matt. 12:31). Yes, let the silver trumpet sound it out! You chief of sinners, hear the news! The Savior lives that to the uttermost He may save such as you. Come, then, to your living Lord, you who groan under the load of deadly guilt, for He can take it all away.

So, too, He saves to *the uttermost of our need and misery.* One old divine says that if we were to climb a great hill from which we could see wide fields of spiritual distress and poverty, and if all this represented our experience, yet the Lord is able to spread salvation all round the far-off horizon and encompass all our needs. Come, poor trembler, climb the mountain and look far over this terrible wilderness. As far as ever you can see, or foresee, of dreaded need in years to come, so far and much further can the salvation of Jesus reach. As far as with the telescope of apprehension you can spy out trials in life and woes in death, so far is Jesus able to save you. The uttermost will never be reached by you, but it has long ago been provided for by Him. Though like the sea that swallows up a navy and is not full, your soul should never cease its cravings, yet Jesus can make you content. All you can require He can surely give you, since He ever lives by the power of an endless life to be the fullness of every emptied soul.

Jesus can save you *to the uttermost of your desires*. I want you to think of all you would like to be in righteousness and true holiness. All that you desire Jesus will do for you before He is finished with you. I asked a young convert the other day, "Are you perfect yet?" "Oh dear, sir," she said, "no." I asked, "Would you not like to be?" Her eyes twinkled, as well they might, and she said, "That is what I long for." It will be heaven to be perfect. Jesus is able to make us perfect, and He has resolved to do it, as it is written, "I shall be satisfied, when I awake, with thy likeness" (Ps. 17:15). In that likeness He will cause us to awake if we come to God through Him. Jesus will save us to the highest degree.

The Lord Jesus Christ will also save us *entirely*. He will work out the salvation of the whole man—body, soul, and spirit. He ever lives to save His people to the utmost, that is to say, all His people and all of every one of His people. Nothing essential to manhood shall be left to perish in the case of those whom He redeems. All that the first Adam ruined the second Adam shall restore. The Canaan of manhood from Dan to Beersheba shall be conquered by our Joshua. As yet the body is dead because of sin, though the spirit is alive because of righteousness; but the day comes when the body also shall be delivered from the bondage that sin has brought upon it. Not a bone, nor a piece of a bone, of a redeemed one shall be left in the hands of the enemy. God's deliverances are always complete. When the Lord sent His angel to bring Peter out of prison, He said to the slumbering apostle, "Cast thy garment about thee, and follow me" (Acts 12:8). That garment might be only a fisherman's cloak, but it must not be left in Herod's hands. He said also, "Bind on thy sandals," for when the angel of the Lord sets a man free, He will not leave even a pair of old shoes behind him. The redemption of Christ is perfect: It reaches to the uttermost. He seems to say to sin and Satan and death, as the Lord said to Pharaoh: "[T]here shall not an hoof be left behind" (Exod. 10:26). All that He has redeemed by price He will also redeem by power, and to that end He makes ceaseless intercession before God.

"To the uttermost"—from all our doubts and fears and follies and failures, Jesus will bring us by His endless intercession. "To the uttermost"—from every consequence of the fall and personal sin and actual death, Jesus by His intercession will save us. "To the uttermost." Think of it! To the resurrection life, to clearance at the judgment seat, to the highest glories of heaven, to boundless bliss throughout the ages He will save us. Right on while thou endurest, O eternity, the pleading of the High Priest shall save the chosen company, who forever rising into something higher and yet higher shall prove more and more the heights and depths of everlasting bliss! Because He lives we shall live also, and because He ever intercedes we shall forever be glorified.

There I leave my subject, only coming back to the one inquiry, *Do you come to God by Jesus Christ?* If so, the text speaks comfortably to you. It speaks not only of the Church as a whole but also of each individual believer. Jesus intercedes for each of those who "come unto God by him." You, dear friend, though unknown to fame are known to Jesus. You, dear sister, hidden away in obscurity, are not hidden from the all-seeing eye of the divine Mediator. His breast-plate bears your name, yea, He has graven it upon the palms of His hands, and He will never forget those whose memorials are thus perpetually with Him. May the living blessing of the ever-living Savior be with you today and forever! Amen.

There is always a connection, even if we do not see it, between that great crowd on Sunday and the pleadings of the saints. There is always a most intimate connection between the flocking converts of the ministry and those secret prayers that follow and precede them. There is such a connection that the two cannot be parted. God will not send great blessings in the way of open conversion if secret prayer is neglected. Let the preacher or the church forbear to pray, and God will forbear to bless. Ay, and after conversions, unless there is special prayer presented by the Lord's servants, much that looked like blessing may turn out to have been but the semblance of it, and future blessing may be withheld. If I could impress my heart on every syllable and baptize every word with my tears, I could not too earnestly entreat you to be above all things earnest in prayer.

Chapter Two

Before Daybreak
with Christ

And in the morning, rising up a great while before day, he went out, and departed into a solitary place, and there prayed. And Simon and they that were with him followed after him. And when they had found him, they said unto him, All men seek for thee. And he said unto them, Let us go into the next towns, that I may preach there also: for therefore came I forth. And he preached in their synagogues throughout all Galilee, and cast out devils"—Mark 1:35–39.

A WONDERFUL DAY WAS closed and crowned by a wonderful evening. Capernaum had been exalted to heaven that day, for deeds worthy of heaven had been wrought in her. Within the synagogue the power and authority of the new Teacher had been seen. But at the close of the Sabbath, when the people felt more free to lay their sick before Him, His divine majesty was glorified of all in the open streets of the little town. Galilee had never before seen such a day of preaching or such an eventide of healing. "And at even, when the sun did set, they brought unto him all that were diseased, and them that were possessed with devils. And all the city was gathered together at the door. And he healed many that were sick of divers diseases, and cast out many devils" (Mark 1:32–34).

Surely this day was worthy to take a front rank among "the days of the Son of man" (Luke 17:22). A very wonderful evening!

Did not they think it so who had long lain on their beds but suddenly found themselves walking and leaping and praising God? Those must have thought it so who saw their suffering relatives restored to health and vigor. Even devils must have felt it to be so as they fled pell-mell into the deep. Assuredly, the people of the city must have been greatly excited. On the housetops, in the market, and in every lane and alley, the one theme of talk must have been the new Rabbi, His strange teaching, and His unrivaled miracles. After our Lord's sermon in the synagogue, He held an inquiry meeting in the street, for He had no other assembly room. There He led them to look to Him and obtain healing. As this went on, crowds of persons were present confessing what the Lord had done for them. One might be content to die after being present at such a scene.

After that evening was over and people went home, they said, "It was a very extraordinary occasion. What new teaching is this? What power is this? We have never seen its like." It was a day from which to date an era. Heaven and earth and hell were all affected by it. That pure teaching opening the mystery of the kingdom, that healing energy setting forth the power of the redeeming King! No wonder that all tongues were fluent and all lips eloquent, when there was so divine a subject to enlarge upon. Children and peasants could repeat the chronicle of that day of grace. They needed not to expatiate, much less to exaggerate, for in truth it was a heavenly day and grew even brighter as the shadows fell. Those evening hours were as the hands of mercy, all bedecked with rings and jewels of heavenly charity: Love was then in her bridal attire, and miracles were the bespangled ornaments of her beauty.

Do you not think that the wonderful evening was followed by an equally wonderful morning? That Sunday morning, as we now call the first day of the week, was it not equally notable? Remember that grand excitement of the day and its long eventide, and then observe the hallowed devotion of the coming dawn. The Preacher and Miracle Worker had been worked up to a high pitch, and we should not have wondered had He needed a long rest. But instead, we read, "Rising up a great while before day, he went out, and departed into a solitary place, and there prayed."

Jesus has taken such necessary sleep as He desired, and He wakes. It is still dark, and all those in the house are asleep. He very quietly and noiselessly steals out of the chamber and finds His way into the street. You see Him go along alone till He has left the narrow roadway and reached the open fields. The gloaming of the morning has hardly come; the dawn is scarcely gray. It is "a great while before daylight," and the darkness hangs all around with its friendly veil. But He knows His way. He had been down those streets healing the sick, and out in the open He is at home, for He is acquainted with solitude, and the lines upon the face of sleeping nature are familiar to Him. He turns to the most solitary hillside. Yonder is a hollow recess that is quite out of sight. Jesus passes into that hidden place, and there, in the darkness, He kneels, He cries, He supplicates, He speaks with God, He prays. Is this His rest after a toilsome day? Is that His preparation for coming labor? It is even so. That early morning of prayer explains the evening of power. As a man, He had not possessed that wonderful power over human minds if He had not perpetually communed with God. And now that His day's work is done and the marvelous evening is over, all is not ended—a lifework still remains before Him, and therefore He must pray. He feels a need that there should be more marvelous evenings, that there should be further displays of power, and therefore the Great Worker draws nigh again to the source of strength, that He may refresh for that which lies before Him.

There is always a connection, even if we do not see it, between that great crowd on Sunday and the pleadings of the saints. There is always a most intimate connection between the flocking converts of the ministry and those secret prayers that follow and precede them. There is such a connection that the two cannot be parted. God will not send great blessings in the way of open conversion if secret prayer is neglected. Let the preacher or the church forbear to pray, and God will forbear to bless. Ay, and after conversions, unless there is special prayer presented by the Lord's servants, much that looked like blessing may turn out to have been but the semblance of it, and future blessing may be withheld. If I could impress my heart on every syllable and baptize every word with my tears, I could not too earnestly entreat you to be above all things earnest in prayer.

I delight to think of our Lord as praying before He did a great thing. It was His custom so to do. Perhaps the early morning prayer of our text preceded the Sermon on the Mount. I am not quite sure about that fact, though certain writers are assured of it. But I am quite certain that this special supplication followed an evening of miracles. And it seems to teach us that when God is with us, we should have more concern than ever to keep Him with us. When the blessing has really come and souls are being saved on all sides, then we are to double our cries to heaven, that the merciful presence may be retained and enjoyed to a still higher degree. Fresh from the wonderful successes of that miraculous night, the Christ of God goes on the Sunday morning to open the gates of the day with the uplifted hands of His prayer. Prayer should be our companion at all times. Pray when you are seeking a blessing; pray when you have newly obtained it.

Now, we shall look at four points of our Savior's character as we see them in these few verses. Let us hear the melody of those golden bells that adorn the garments of our Great High Priest. First, we are caused to observe that *prayer by Christ was intensely esteemed.* Second, *popularity is weighted in the balances and lightly valued.* Third, *practical duty followed out,* for when they said, "All men seek for thee," He said to them, "Let us go into the next towns that I may preach there also: for therefore came I forth." We shall put the four things altogether, seeing how the prayer and the preaching hang upon one another and how the despising of popularity is fitly joined with the intense purpose to carry out His lifework.

Prayer—How Intensely It Was Esteemed by Jesus!

He rose up that weekday morning early and retired to a solitary place to pray, *to teach us not to keep our religiousness for Sabbath days* or retain our prayerfulness for one day of the week. Many Jews in Christ's day said, "We have been to synagogue"; and when going to synagogue was over, their religion was over, too. Today we are surrounded by persons whose godliness is circumscribed within the four walls of their synagogue, their church, their tabernacle, or whatever else they like to call it. Religion means to many the observance of certain ceremonials at stated times. They put on different clothes and tread another floor, and then their religion begins. Do they put on different garments on the Sabbath because they are different men, or because they wish to be thought so? There is such a thing as a Sunday religion, and he who has it will be lost. The religion that lives only in our religious assemblies, how can it serve us? Prayer on Sunday is well enough, but better far is the supplication that continually waits upon God. Our Sabbath prayer should abound, but the weekdays equally need prayer and should be saturated with it. Grace is for streets and shops as well as for sanctuaries. It is well when God rules our thoughts as much in the shop as in the prayer meeting. We are as much under the governance of our Lord Jesus Christ when we are busy in the family as when we are sitting in the church of God. Oh, let us see to this! Our Master gives us a good example here. It was not upon the Sabbath morning that He woke so early. It was on the first day of the week, not yet rendered sacred by His resurrection, that our Lord rose early and made His way through the shadows to find a place of fellowship with the Father.

You observe that in His prayer *He desired very much to be alone.* He was anxious that His prayer might not be seen of men. Woe to the man whose devotion is observed by everybody and who never offers a secret supplication. Secret prayer is the secret of prayer, the soul of prayer, the seal of prayer, the strength of prayer. If you do not pray alone, you do not pray at all. I care not whether you pray in the street or in the church or in your room or in the cathedral, but your heart must speak with God in secret or you have not prayed. "But thou, when thou prayest, enter into thy closet, and when thou hast shut thy door, pray to thy Father which is in secret; and thy Father which seeth in secret shall reward thee openly" (Matt. 6:6). The less prayer is observed on earth, the more it is observed in heaven. That which is carefully concealed from men is seen of the Father.

I suppose, too, that our Lord loved to be alone *that He might pray aloud.* It is not necessary to pray with the voice, and it is sometimes highly undesirable that you should pray aloud. But, as a rule, you will find it greatly advantageous to use your voice as well as your mind in prayer. I speak what I have often proved. I am accustomed to pray without uttering a single sound, but I find a relief and a stimulus in occasionally "crying aloud." In a lone spot where I shall not be heard, I find it an intense delight to pour out my heart aloud, using words and exclamations whereby the spirit expresses itself with freedom and force. I think that the Savior, who was intensely human, felt much rest in the unrestrained pouring out of His heart and soul before His Father. He was supremely human as He was certainly divine; and I do not doubt that it was a comfort to Him to arouse the hills with His praises, startle the glens with His groans, and put a tongue into every bush and tuft by His strong cryings and tears. All nature was akin to Him, and the desert places were fitting chambers for His great soul, wherein as in His own house "the holy child Jesus" might speak with the Father face to face. I commend to you who would attain to high communion with the Eternal that, as often as you can, you get so far afield as to be able to pray aloud and use the unrestrained voice in prayer. "My voice shalt thou hear in the morning, O LORD" (Ps. 5:3). David continually speaks of crying with his voice unto God. It is not essential, but it is often helpful.

Our blessed Master desired to get alone because there He would feel free to express Himself—*to tell out His very secrets to the great Father.* His prayers in solitude! They must have been marvelous communications. How familiar with God, and yet how lowly! How simple, yet how spiritual! How full! How deep! How intense! Perhaps you have desired that they had been recorded, but I need not remind you that the world itself could not have contained all the books that might have been written. Be grateful for those that are written, and believe that infinite wisdom is as much displayed in the concealment of a part of our Lord's life as in the publication of the rest of it. Perhaps those prayers of His were such as we might not hear. Every saint pleads at times in forms of passionate petition that nobody else should hear but God. When we are quite alone, we may dare to say things that might seem too venturesome for any other. I am glad that we have not many of Luther's prayers, for I conceive that the great bold German often said things to his God that a common Christian might not dare to say. That which was perfectly reverent in him might have savored a presumption if you or I had ventured upon it. That which the Lord accepted from Luther, whom He had placed in so singular a position and constituted in so remarkable a way for His work, might have been offensive if spoken by another. The Master's prayers were a free, outspoken talk with the Most High. His heart was open to the Lord as yonder river to the shining of the moon above it.

Certainly, our Lord Jesus Christ rose up early and went alone in the dark to pray because *He loved to put prayer first of all.* He would go nowhere till He had prayed. He would attempt nothing till He had prayed. He would not cast out a devil, He would not preach a sermon, He would work no cure, however necessary, however profitable, until first of all He had drawn near to God. Take heed to yourself that you follow the same rule. Look no man in the face till you have seen the face of God. Speak with no one till you have spoken with the Most High. Take not to running till you have in prayer laid aside every weight, lest you lose the race. We cannot, we must not, think of entering upon a day or upon an enterprise without our God; let us attempt nothing without Him. So the Savior rises a great while before day and gets alone with His God, that for Him prayer might perfume the morning's dew and sweeten the first breath of the dawn.

There was about the Savior an intense desire to meet with God—to commune with the Father. Herein there is a living likeness between His prayers and ours. Yet His devotions must have been very different from ours because He had no sin to confess as we have. A large part of our communion with God must lie in our confession of sin, in our expression of personal weakness, and in our pleading the righteousness of our divine Redeemer. But this blessed One had no sins to own before the Most High and no weakness to lament, for in Him was neither sin nor tendency thereto. I can conceive that much of His devotion was shown in converse with the Father, when His blessed mind, forever in agreement with the mind of God, spoke to God, and God revealed Himself to Him. Intimate communication must have been the main ingredient of the Savior's prayers. Some of the sweetest devotion Christians ever enjoy does not lie in asking anything of the Father but lies in the enjoyment of the Father Himself. Two friends in closest fellowship do not spend their time in mutual explanations and setting things straight, nor even in asking favors of each other. They proceed to heart-to-heart converse, known only to those who have enjoyed the like.

We are always in need, and therefore our daily devotion must consist largely of petitions. But yet we are by divine grace the children of the Lord, and the child says many things to his father beside that which takes the form of a request. Have we not with joyful reverence told our heavenly Father how we love Him? How we long to be more like Him? How we desire to serve Him? That is how we talk with God alone. Our heart is to the heart of God as the echo to the living voice that calls to it. The Savior would tell out to the Father all His love to Him, how He desired nothing but the salvation of those whom the Father gave Him, how He was surety for them. All that the divine Jesus could and would say to His Father we may not endeavor to imagine. We could not be permitted to stand by and hear those solitary prayers, but they must have been something unique, worthy of the Sacred Persons who there held solemn dialogue. Yes, the great heart of Jesus swam in supplication as in its element, and in proportion as we become like Him we shall be of His mind as to private prayer.

Someone said to me the other day, "I am so conformed to the mind and will of God that I do not need to pray." I answered in sad surprise, "I pray God open your eyes to see the delusion under which you are laboring, for the holy Lord Jesus Christ abounded in prayer notwithstanding His absolute perfection." That kind of perfection that leads a man to think that he does not need to pray is damnable. I will use no softer word. I believe that the doctrine of perfection, as it is frequently taught in these fanatical days, will be the ruin of many a soul that holds it. Could you cease to pray, you would cease to live spiritually. It is the very breath of your nostrils if you are a child of God. As to your being so perfect as to need no more prayer and watchfulness, you lie to your own soul, as surely as you live. Instead of believing in your perfection, I pray God deliver you from so terrible a delusion. If you were perfect, you would still need to pray. Nay, you would pray more than ever, and your life, like that of Jesus, would be steeped and saturated in prayer. Our Lord, because He was perfect, longed perpetually to draw nigh unto God.

"Oh," says one, "I live in the spirit of prayer, and therefore I do not need times and seasons for prayer." And do you think that Christ did not live in the spirit of prayer? Yet He must have His special time and place to pray. Do not fall under the injurious notion that because your spirit cries to God in prayer all day long, therefore there must not be some season for more immediately coming into God's presence. If you imagine this, I am afraid that it will prove a snare to your feet. The Lord Jesus Christ, who knew better than you do that the main thing is the spirit of prayer rather than the act of prayer, yet Himself retired into desert places to maintain the act and exercise of prayer. Be spiritual. Be baptized into the spirit of prayer. But do not be deceived by the enemy, who can spirit a duty away while we dream that we only spiritualize it. We had better preserve the very bones of prayer—the posture, the time, place—rather than let it all ooze away into an impalpable mental condition. God keep us prayerful. He will do so if He makes us like His dear Son.

Further, I want you to notice concerning our Lord's prayer that there can be no doubt that *in His prayer He prayed for Himself.* Much of His prayer belonged to Himself, and to Himself alone. He was, we know, in one great instance, "heard in that he feared" (Heb. 5:7), and He was heard in many other things known only to Himself. But our Lord also much abounded in *prayer for His disciples*. He took their cases one by one and pleaded with the Father for them. Remember how He prayed for Peter—supplicating for him before he came into danger. He said, "Simon, Simon, behold Satan hath desired to have you" (Luke 22:31). The enemy had reached only as far as the desire, but the Good Shepherd was quicker than the wolf and had already interceded: "but I have prayed for thee" (Luke 22:32). Christ had outstripped the devil by praying before the temptation came. Here on earth, as a father in the midst of his children, He took care that none of them should be in danger through the lack of His loving intercession.

And do you not think that He was praying, too, at that time, *for the sinners who were round about Him?* As He looked into those faces in the streets of Capernaum, He read the stories of their sin, and these came back to His memory amid those lone hills. He knew more about men than we do, for He could search their thoughts. He knew how foolish they were and how far they had gone aside from God; and so in the silence of the desert He prayed with wide knowledge and profound sympathy, and He spoke with the Most High in eager pleadings for those whose sins He measured and whose doom He foresaw. To do His people and the world the grandest service in His power till He should lay down His life, our Lord stole away amid the heathery hills or the stony heaps of the shores of Galilee.

Dear friends, take care that you pray. Need I say it? Take care that you use all aids to prayer, such as being alone and rising early to pray. If your Lord needed prayer, you do much more require it. Take care that you pray much in the time of your success. Do not think that because of the wonders God did for you last night you are not to pray in the morning. Set a double guard over your spirit in the moment of rejoicing lest you be carried away by pride.

"Oh," you say, "but my prayers are so often disturbed!" I know it. The devil is sure to send somebody to knock at the door when you want to be quiet in prayer. Your Lord can sympathize with you in that, for Simon and they who were with him followed after Him and disturbed the solitude that He had sought with so much care. Simon was always to the front, and sometimes mischievously so.

Here he is leading the way in disturbing his Master. Do not wonder whether Satan finds a Simon to worry *you*. But as your Lord knows what it is to be disturbed, He can help you to bear up under disturbances, He can cheer you when these interruptions distress you, and He can aid you to renew your pleadings when the chain of your prayer has been broken.

Popularity Properly Weighed by the Savior

The disturbance that came to the Savior's prayer arose out of the desire of His disciples to tell Him that everybody was after Him. According to Luke's account in his fourth chapter, the people of the town were close on the heels of the disciples, to beg him not to go away but to stop and be their Prophet and heal their sick.

Our Lord's popularity was of the best kind. It had not been gained by any arts or tricks, nor by pandering to their pride, nor by yielding to their prejudices. He had preached nothing but the truth, and He had wrought no miracle among them for the mere sake of display but only for their good. Yet He did not care for the best of popularity. He did not think it worth the having for its own sake, and therefore He shunned it to the utmost. His popularity could be used, and He did use it, for when the people came together, He preached the gospel to them. But applause had no charms for Him. He knew what poor stuff it is—of what gas it is made. He knew how uncertain it is—how like the wind it will veer round in no time. He knew that it might prove dangerous; and it did prove dangerous, for they sought by and by to make Him a king.

Even His disciples would, if they could, have turned Him from His spiritual purpose. Poor hearts! They wished to see Him honored, but they did not know that honor from men would have brought no honor to Him. When they told our Lord, "All men seek for thee," He did not take notice of it but proposed to go elsewhere and preach the gospel. If ever you succeed in Christ's kingdom, bless God for your spiritual success, but do not think much of the popularity that follows upon it. Pass it over in silence, as though you heard it not. What is human approval? What can it do for you? "We are unprofitable servants: we have done that which was our duty to do" (Luke 17:10). If we have done anything good, no credit is due to us but only to the Lord, whose grace has made us to be His workmanship. If the Lord Jesus Christ, who preached by His own authority and power and who wrought miracles really by His own might, yet fled away as much as He could from the applause of men, much more let each of us do so. Oh, to walk before the Lord and be blind and deaf to all the censures and the plaudits of the poor creatures around us! I have seen men whom God has greatly blessed, who have been highly honored by their brethren, and yet they have been cast down and have therefore been made to lie low in their own esteem. God will not greatly bless us if we grow great. We may soon become too big to be used to win souls. I notice that soul winning is generally accomplished by humble instruments. It is a delicate task, and the Lord who does it will not use those who are great and strong and mighty in their own esteem. When the Lord finds His servants lowly, like the Lord Jesus Christ, then they shall be used. The longer I live the more do I see that as a rule, pride is the death of all true spiritual usefulness. As you love God and would desire to honor Him by a useful life, put far from you the temptation to sip of the intoxicating cup of human honor. Draughts of worldly glory are not for the priests of the Most High.

Though not in the Savior's case, yet in ours there is a close connection between our prayers and our being kept humble before the Lord. It is remarkable how kindly our neighbors watch over our vineyards in that respect. They are all in a fraternal flutter for fear we should grow vain. It is very good of them, but we do not wish them to rob themselves for our advantage. "Ah, sir," said a good lady to me one day, "I pray for you every day that you may be kept humble!" She was a fine-looking woman and splendidly dressed, and therefore I replied, "Thank you much. But you remind me of a failure in my duty. I have never prayed *for you* that you might be kept humble." "Dear sir," she cried, "there is no need for such prayers, for I am not tempted to be proud." How proud she was to have attained to such a delusion! When anybody says, "I am not tempted to be proud," shrewd common sense suggests that it is time to wake up lest the enemy get a fatal advantage of the vain spirit. When there is much prayer, abundant prayer, and drawing near to God, the greatest success can be borne without risk. Prayer ballasts the ship, and so when God fills the sails with a prosperous wind, the vessel is not overborne.

Practical Duty Followed Out

They said, "All men seek for thee." I think that most of us would have replied, "Well, then, let us go down and talk to them."

But Jesus cries, "Let us go into the next towns, that I may preach there also." Instead of desiring honor, He shuns it. Yes, He leaves no space for it, for He occupies each hour with a new labor. *He will break up new soil:* Old harvests only serve to fill the basket for sowing new seed. He will go *to encounter other trials* as soon as the first are overcome. When He enters a place for the first time, there is opposition, and Jesus is eager to face it. For Him there remained no love of ease, no resting upon laurels already won. His nobly impatient spirit cries, "We have done something for Capernaum; let us seek fresh fields and pastures new." He will also *enlist assistance* and rouse others to share in the holy war. How condescendingly the Master puts it! He says, "Let *us* go." "O divine Master, all men seek for *thee.*" And the answer is, "Let *us* go into the next towns." He lifted his poor disciples into the *us* with Himself. They will feel how unworthy they are to be in such high fellowship. They will admire His condescension in putting them there. And they will be the more ready to go on with Him, taking their full part in evangelizing the other villages and towns.

Our Lord is thinking of the whole business. It is all before His mind's eye, what He is to do personally and what He is to do through each one of them. The practical duty of doing His part of the work and using them for their part of the work is strong upon Him. With a quick eye He sees, not what has been done but what is to be done, not what God has given but what God will still give in answer to the prayer that He has prayed. And He expects that it will be so large that He will want all His followers to help Him in the process of ingathering it. So He says, "Let *us* go into the next towns." He does not say, "Let us rest and be thankful," but He obeys the secret instinct that drives Him forward to be doing more and more of good to the sons of men. He feels within His soul that imperial *must* that every now and then crops up in His story as it is told by the evangelists. He is under a necessity to do the Father's will in blessing the sons of men, and all else is as nothing to Him: "Therefore came I forth," says He. The errand for which He came forth evidently presses Him, constrains Him, impels Him, and He must go forward till all His baptism is accomplished. His disciples cry, "All men seek thee, stay in Capernaum," but He thinks of the myriads who do *not* seek Him but need Him more than those who do. Let His zeal for the unseeking multitudes inflame our hearts, and let us in enthusiastic chorus sing concerning the lost sheep:

O, come, let us go and find them!
In the paths of death they roam;
At the close of the day 'twill be sweet to say,
"I have brought some lost one home."

Jesus seemed to say, "Come with Me, and I will lead the way, for therefore am I sent, that all over Galilee and Judea I may wander after wandering souls and give them health of body and salvation of spirit." This absorption in His life purpose is one great evidence and accompaniment of our Lord's perfect spiritual sanity. He could not repose in work done, for the work that remained drove Him ever onward. The Master never gloried with any sinful pride, but in your case and mine, the way to keep from ever glorying in what we have done is to think of what we have yet to do.

Forget the steps already trod,
And onward urge thy way.

You know what the general said when one of his officers rode up and cried, "Sir, we have taken a standard." "Take another," cried he. Another officer salutes him and exclaims, "Sir, we have taken two guns." "Take two more," was the sole reply. This way lies the reward of holy service: You have done much, you shall do more. Have you won a soul? Win another. Did you bring fifty to Christ? Bring fifty more. If you have been faithful in little you shall be entrusted with much. What is all we have accomplished compared with the needs of our nation, compared with the desolated condition of the world? Brethren, in the hour of success, resolve on wider labor. Go forward. Press on. Go to other cities. Attempt other methods of service, for therefore came you forth from God.

Preaching Put to the Front

He says, "Let us go into the next towns, *that I may preach* there also: for therefore came I forth." It is refreshing to hear preaching spoken of without a sneer. "The pulpit is a worn-out piece of furniture," so they say. Writers have quite annihilated preachers: The few of us who survive may as well go home to our beds. I am not going to speak of any excellence in preachers or stand up for my brethren as though we were the wisest of all men. Suppose I confess that we are a set of fools? This is nothing remarkable, we always have been so. But it remains still written in Scripture, "It pleased God by the foolishness of preaching to save them that believe" (1 Cor. 1:21). Such is our folly that we are fools enough to go on preaching after our critics have decided that we belong to the dead past. Notwithstanding all that the wise men tell us about our day being over, we shall keep to our marching orders: "Go ye into all the world, and preach" (Mark 16:15). In that day when stock shall be taken of results and judgment shall be according to equity, it will be found that the preachers of the gospel have, after all, with all their imperfections, been the great instruments in the hands of God for bringing in His people to eternal salvation. I reckon that the most of you who have been converted to God will say that it was what you heard that was used of the Holy Ghost for your conversion. When heart speaks to heart with accents of emotion, it is somehow powerful.

When a warm heart speaks to an earnest ear, it proves itself a suitable means for the transmission of blessing. The man speaks what he does know, and he throws a tone, a force, a light, a vigor into what he says. I know you grumble at the dullness of preachers, and I do not wonder at it, but I believe that the improvement of that matter lies much with yourselves. You shall find, I believe, that when more attention has been paid to the ministry, when you have prayed more for students, and when more care has been exercised in churches that only the right kind of men shall be helped into the ministry, the preachers of the Word will rise into higher rank in your esteem. When, instead of a man's being set apart for a minister because his father has a living to give him or because he cannot pick up a living any other way, only men who are really moved by the Holy Ghost shall be introduced into the ministry, then the dishonor will be wiped from the pulpit, and it shall be seen to be the tower of the flock, the castle of the truth. We preach Christ crucified and preach it because we are commanded to preach it, and we are well assured that wisdom is justified of her children. God's grand means of preaching the gospel, which the Lord Jesus followed so closely, is used for the sure accomplishment of eternal purposes.

I want to say this much more: It is the praying man who is the right preaching man, and if any of you long to do good to your neighbors, you must begin on your knees. You cannot have power with man for God until first you have power with God for man. Solitary prayer was the equipment for the Prince of preachers when He came forth among the crowds. It is the best equipment for you, also. In solitary vigil, buckle on the armor of light. Workers for God, I entreat you to be abundant in supplication, that if success comes you may not be elevated unduly by it, that if nonsuccess comes you may not be depressed unduly by it. Come what may, having prayed, it is yours to continue steadfast in present duty, still doing that for which you were sent, and still believing that the gospel of Jesus will prevail. O my comrade, may the Lord uphold us even to the end!

As for you who never pray, *what will become of you?* As for you who, instead of preaching, do not care to hear preaching, what can become of you? If the Lord Jesus Christ went out to pray so early in the morning, do you know what He was praying for? Why, for the salvation of sinners like you, that you might be saved. His cries and tears were for those who neither plead nor weep for themselves. When Jesus stood up to preach, what had He on His mind but the salvation of sinners like you? Shall He think of you, and will you not think of Him? Look to Him! See how He loves sinners! Now that He has been dead and buried and has risen again and gone into His glory, He still lives to save sinners! Look to Him! Trust Him! Seek Him in solitary prayer, and He will meet with you. Rise up early, "a great while before day," if you have no other means of being alone, and cry to Him for mercy, and He will set heaven's gate open before you and answer you even as His Father answered Him.

The Lord bless you, for Christ's sake. Amen.

But I will not confine your thoughts to that incident because, as I have already said, the prophet's words had a wider range. To me it is marvelous that He, being pure, should plead for transgressors at all, especially for you and for me. Let the wonder begin there. Sinners by nature, sinners by practice, willful sinners, sinners who cling to sin with a terrible tenacity, sinners who come back to sin after we have paid for it, and yet the Just One has espoused our cause and become a suitor for our pardon. We are sinners who omit duties when they are pleasures and follow after sins that are known to involve sorrows. We are sinners of the most foolish kind, wanton, willful sinners, and yet He who hates all sin has deigned to take our place and plead the causes of our souls. Our Lord's hatred of sin is as great as His love for sinners. His indignation against everything impure is as great as that of the thrice holy God who is furious when He comes into contact with evil. And yet this divine Prince, of whom we sing, "Thou lovest righteousness, and hatest wickedness" (Ps. 45:7), espouses the cause of transgressors and pleads for them. Oh, matchless grace! Surely angels wonder at this stretch of condescending love. Brethren, words fail me. I ask you to adore!

Chapter Three

Jesus Interceding
for Transgressors

And made intercession for the transgressors—Isaiah 53:12.

OUR BLESSED LORD made intercession for transgressors in so many words while He was being crucified, for He was heard to say, "Father, forgive them; for they know not what they do" (Luke 23:34). It is generally thought that He uttered this prayer at the moment when the nails were piercing His hands and feet and the Roman soldiers were roughly performing their duty as executioners. At the very commencement of His passion, He begins to bless His enemies with His prayers. As soon as the Rock of our salvation was smitten, there flowed forth from it a blessed stream of intercession.

Our Lord fixed His eye upon that point in the character of His persecutors that was most favorable to them, namely, that they knew not what they did. He could not plead their innocence, and therefore He pleaded their ignorance. Ignorance could not excuse their deed, but it did lighten their guilt, and therefore our Lord was quick to mention it as in some measure an extenuating circumstance. The Roman soldiers, of course, knew nothing of His higher mission. They were the mere tools of those who were in power, and though they "mocked him, coming to him, and offering him vinegar" (Luke 23:36), they did so because they misunderstood His claims and regarded Him as a foolish rival of Caesar, only worthy to be ridiculed. No doubt the Savior included these rough Gentiles in His supplication, and perhaps their centurion, who "glorified God, saying, Certainly this was a righteous man" (Luke 23:47), was converted in answer to our Lord's prayer. As for the Jews, though they had some measure of light, yet they also acted in the dark. Peter, who would not have flattered any man, yet said, "And now, brethren, I wot that through ignorance ye did it, as did also your rulers" (Acts 3:17). It is doubtless true that had they known, they would not have crucified the Lord of glory, though it is equally clear that they should have known Him, for His credentials were clear as noonday. Our Redeemer, in that dying prayer of His, shows how quick He is to see anything that is in any degree favorable to the poor clients whose cause He has undertaken. He spied out in a moment the only fact upon which compassion could find foothold, and He secretly breathed out His loving heart in the cry, "Father, forgive them; for they know not what they do." Our great Advocate will be sure to plead wisely and efficiently on our behalf. He will urge every argument that can be discovered, for His eye, quickened by love, will allow nothing to pass that may tell in our favor.

The prophet, however, does not intend to confine our thoughts to the one incident that is recorded by the evangelists, for the intercession of Christ was an essential part of His entire lifework. The mountain's side often heard Him, beneath the chilly night, pouring out His heart in supplications. He might as fitly be called the man of prayers as "the man of sorrows" (Isa. 53:3). While He was teaching and working miracles by day, He was silently communing with God and making supplication for men; and His nights, instead of being spent in seeking restoration from His exhausting labors, were frequently occupied with intercession. Indeed, our Lord's whole life is a prayer. His career on earth was intercession wrought out in actions. Since "he prayeth best who loveth best," He was a mass of prayer, for He is altogether love. He is not only the channel and the example of prayer but also the life and force of prayer. The greatest plea with God is Christ Himself. The argument that always prevails with God is Christ incarnate, Christ fulfilling the law, and Christ bearing the penalty. Jesus is the reasoning and logic of prayer, and He is an ever living prayer to the Most High.

It was part of our Lord's official work to make intercession for the transgressors. He is a Priest, bringing His offering and presenting prayer on the behalf of the people. Our Lord is the Great High Priest of our profession, and we read that in fulfilling this office He offered up prayers and supplications with strong crying and tears (Heb. 5:7). And we know that He is now offering up prayers for the souls of men. This, indeed, is the great work that He is carrying on today. We rejoice and rest in His finished work, but that relates to His atoning sacrifice. His intercession springs out of His atonement, and it will never ease while the blood of His sacrifice retains its power. The blood of sprinkling continues to speak better things than that of Abel. Jesus is pleading now and will be pleading till the heavens shall be no more. For all who come to God by Him, He still presents His merits to the Father and pleads the causes of their souls. He urges the grand argument derived from His life and death and so obtains innumerable blessings for the rebellious sons of men.

Admiration for His Grace

Come, gather up your scattered thoughts and meditate upon Him who alone was found able to stand in the gap and turn away wrath by His pleading. If you will consider His intercession for transgressors, I think you will be struck with the love and tenderness and graciousness of His heart. Remember that *He offered intercession verbally while He was standing in the midst of their sin.* Sin heard of and sin seen are two very different things. We read of crimes in the newspapers, but we are not at all so horrified as if we had seen them for ourselves. Our Lord actually saw human sin, saw it unfettered and unrestrained, saw it at its worst. Transgressors surrounded His person and by their sins darted ten thousand arrows into His sacred heart, and yet while they pierced Him He prayed for them. The mob surrounded Him, yelling, "Crucify him, crucify him," and His answer was "Father, forgive them" (Luke 23:21, 34). He knew their cruelty and ingratitude but answered them only with a prayer.

The great ones of the earth were there, too, sneering and jesting—Pharisee and Sadducee and Herodian. He saw their selfishness, conceit, falsehood, and bloodthirstiness, and yet He prayed. Strong bulls of Bashan had beset Him round, and dogs had compassed Him (Ps. 22:12, 16), yet He interceded for men. Man's sin had stirred up all its strength to slay God's love, and therefore sin had arrived at its worst point, and yet mercy kept pace with malice and outran it, for He sought forgiveness for His tormentors. After killing prophets and other messengers, the wicked murderers were now saying, "This is the heir; come, let us kill him, and the inheritance shall be ours" (Mark 12:7). And yet that heir of all things, who might have called fire from heaven upon them, died crying, "Father, forgive them." He knew that what they did was sin, or He would not have prayed "forgive them," but He set their deed in the least unfavorable light and said, "they know not what they do."

He set His own Sonship to work on their behalf, appealing to His Father's love to pardon them for His sake. Never was virtue set in so fair a frame before, every goodness came so adorned with abundant love as in the person of the Lord Jesus, and yet they hated Him all the more for His loveliness and gathered round Him with the deeper spite because of His infinite goodness. He saw it all and felt the sin as you and I cannot feel it, for His heart was purer and therefore tenderer than ours. He saw that the tendency of sin was to put Him to death, yes and to slay God Himself if it could achieve its purpose. Yet, though His holy soul saw and loathed all this tendency and atrocity of transgression, He still made intercession for the transgressors. It seems beyond measure wonderful that He should know sin so thoroughly, understand its heinousness, and feel it so wantonly assailing Himself when He was doing nothing but deeds of kindness. And yet with all that vivid sense of the vileness of sin upon Him, even there and then He made intercession for the transgressors, saying, "Father, forgive them; for they know not what they do."

Another point of His graciousness was also clear on that occasion, namely, that He should *intercede while in agony*. It is marvelous that He should be able to call His mind away from His own pains to consider their transgressions. You and I, if we are subject to great pains of body, do not find it easy to command our minds, and especially to collect our thoughts and restrain them, so as to forgive the person inflicting the pain and even to invoke blessings upon his head. Remember that your Lord was suffering while He made intercession, beginning to suffer the pangs of death, suffering in soul as well as in body, for He had just come from the garden where His soul was exceeding sorrowful, even unto death. Yet in the midst of the depression of spirit that might well have made Him forgetful of the wretched beings who were putting Him to death,

He forgets Himself and only thinks of them and pleads for them. I am sure that we should have been taken up with our pains even if we had not been moved to some measure of resentment against our tormentors. But we hear no complaints from our Lord, no accusations lodged with God, no angry replies to them such as Paul once gave: "God shall smite thee, thou whited wall" (Acts 23:3). Not even a word of mourning or of complaining concerning the indignities that He endured, but His dear heart all ascended to heaven in that one blessed petition for His enemies which there and then He presented to His Father.

But I will not confine your thoughts to that incident because, as I have already said, the prophet's words had a wider range. To me it is marvelous *that He, being pure, should plead for transgressors at all,* especially for you and for me. Let the wonder begin there. Sinners by nature, sinners by practice, willful sinners, sinners who cling to sin with a terrible tenacity, sinners who come back to sin after we have paid for it, and yet the Just One has espoused our cause and become a suitor for our pardon. We are sinners who omit duties when they are pleasures and follow after sins that are known to involve sorrows. We are sinners of the most foolish kind, wanton, willful sinners, and yet He who hates all sin has deigned to take our place and plead the causes of our souls. Our Lord's hatred of sin is as great as His love for sinners. His indignation against everything impure is as great as that of the thrice holy God who is furious when He comes into contact with evil. And yet this divine Prince, of whom we sing, "Thou lovest righteousness, and hatest wickedness" (Ps. 45:7), espouses the cause of transgressors and pleads for them. Oh, matchless grace! Surely angels wonder at this stretch of condescending love. Brethren, words fail me. I ask you to adore!

Further, it is to me a very wonderful fact that *in His glory He should still be pleading for sinners.* There are some men who, when they have reached to high positions, forget their former associates. They knew the poor and needy friend once, but when they have risen out of such conditions, they are ashamed of the people whom once they knew. Our Lord is not thus forgetful of the degraded clients whose cause He espoused in the days of His humiliation. Yet though I know His constancy, I marvel and admire. The Son of Man on earth pleading for sinners is very gracious, but I am overwhelmed when I think of His interceding for sinners now that He reigns yonder, where harps unnumbered tune His praise and cherubim and seraphim count it their glory to be less than nothing at His feet, where all the glory of His Father is resplendent in Himself and He sits at the right hand of God in divine favor and majesty unspeakable. How can we hear without amazement that the King of kings and Lord of lords occupies Himself with caring for transgressors—caring indeed for you and me. It is condescension that He should commune with the bloodwashed before His throne and allow the perfect spirits to be His companions, but that His heart should steal away from all heaven's felicities to remember such poor creatures as we are and make incessant prayer on our behalf, this is like His own loving self—it is Christlike, Godlike. I can almost see at this moment our Great High Priest pleading before the throne, wearing His jeweled breastplate and His garments of glory and beauty, wearing our names upon His breast and His shoulders in the most holy place. What a vision of incomparable love! It is a fact, and no mere dream. He is within the holy of holies, presenting the one sacrifice. His prayers are always heard and heard for us, but the marvel is that the Son of God should condescend to exercise such an office and make intercession for transgressors. This matchless grace well nigh seals my lips, but it opens the floodgates of my soul, and I would fain pause to worship Him whom my words fail to set forth.

Again, it is gloriously gracious *that our Lord should continue to do this.* Ever since He has gone into His glory, yet He has never ceased to make intercession for transgressors. Never on heaven's most joyous holiday, when all His armies are marshaled and in their glittering squadrons pass in review before the King of kings, has He forgotten His redeemed ones. The splendors of heaven have not made Him indifferent to the sorrows of earth. Though He may have created myriads of worlds, and though assuredly He has been ruling the courses of the entire universe, never once, I say, has He suspended His incessant pleading for the transgressors. Nor will He, for the holy Scriptures lead us to believe that as long as He lives as Mediator He will intercede: "[H]e is able also to save them to the uttermost that come unto God by him, seeing he ever liveth to make intercession for them" (Heb. 7:25). He lived and lives to intercede, as if this were the only reason for His living. Beloved, as long as the great Redeemer lives and there is a sinner still to come to Him, He will still continue to intercede.

O my Master, how shall I praise You! If You had undertaken such an office now and then, going into the royal presence once in a while to intercede for some special cases, it would have been divinely gracious on Your part, but that You should never cease to intercede surpasses all our praise. Wonderful are His words as written in prophecy by Isaiah: "For Zion's sake will I not hold my peace, and for Jerusalem's sake I will not rest, until the righteousness thereof go forth as brightness, and the salvation thereof as a lamp that burneth" (Isa. 62:1). As the lamp in the temple never went out, so neither has our Advocate ceased to plead day or night. Unwearied in His labor of love, without a pause He has urged our suit before the Father's face.

Beloved, I cannot enlarge upon this, for adoration of such love quite masters me. But let your heart be enlarged with abounding love to such an Intercessor as this, who made, who does make, and who will make intercession for the transgressors. I have said, *"will make,"* and indeed this is no bare assertion of mine, for my text may be read in the future tense as well as in the past. Indeed, it must have been meant to be understood in the future, since the prophecy was written some seven hundred years before our Lord had breathed His intercessory prayer at the cross. Although the prophet, to make his language pictorial and vivid, puts it in the past tense, it was actually in the future to him, and therefore we cannot err in reading it in the future, as I have done: "he *shall* make intercession for the transgressors." Constant love puts up a ceaseless plea. Endless compassion breathes its endless prayer. Till the last of the redeemed has been gathered home, that interceding breath shall never cease to prevail.

Confidence in Christ

I have called you to feel admiration for His grace, and now I earnestly pray that we may be led of the Holy Spirit to view His intercession for transgressors as to put our confidence in Christ. There is ground for a sinner's confidence in Christ, and there is abundant argument for the believer's complete reliance in Him, from the fact of His perpetual intercession.

Let me show you this first because, beloved, *His intercession succeeds.* God hears Him, of that we do not doubt. But what is the basis of this intercession? Read carefully the verse: "[B]ecause he hath poured out his soul unto death: and he was numbered with the transgressors; and he bare the sin of many" (Isa. 53:12). See, then, the success of His plea arises out of His substitution. He pleads and prevails because He has borne the sin of those for whom He intercedes. The main strength of His prevalence in His intercession lies in the completeness of the sacrifice that He offered when He bore the sin of many. Come, then, my soul, if Christ's prayer prevails because of this, so will your faith. Resting on the same foundation, your faith will be equally secure of acceptance. Come, my heart, rest on that truth: "he bare the sin of many." Throw yourself with all your sin upon His substitution and feel that this is a safe resting place for your believing because it is a solid basis for your Lord's intercession. The perfect sacrifice will bear all the strain that can possibly come upon it. Test it by the strongest faith and see for yourself. Plead it with the boldest requests and learn its boundless prevalence. You may urge the plea of the precious blood with the Father, seeing the Lord Jesus has urged it and has never failed.

Again, *there is reason for transgressors to come and trust in Jesus Christ, seeing He pleads for them.* You need never be afraid that Christ will cast you out when you can hear Him pleading for you. If a son had been disobedient and left his father's house and yet were to come back again, if he had any fear about his father's receiving him, it would all disappear if he stood listening at the door and heard his father praying for him. Whenever a soul comes to Christ, it need have no hesitancy, seeing Christ has already prayed for it that it might be saved. I tell you, Christ prays for you when you *do not* pray for yourself. Did He not say of His believing people, "Neither pray I for these alone, but for them also which shall believe on me through their word" (John 17:20)? Before His elect become believers, they have a place in His supplications. Before you know yourself to be a transgressor and have any desire for pardon, while as yet you are lying dead in sin, His intercession has gone up even for such as you are. "Father, forgive them" was a prayer for those who had never sought forgiveness for themselves. And when you *dare not* pray for yourself, He is still praying for you. When under a sense of sin you dare not lift so much as your eyes toward heaven, when you think "Surely it would be in vain for me to seek my heavenly Father's face," He is pleading for you. Ay, and when you *cannot* plead, when through deep distress of mind you feel choked in the very attempt to pray, when the language of supplication seems to blister your lip because you feel yourself to be so unworthy, when you cannot force even a holy groan from your despairing heart, He stills pleads for you. Oh, what encouragement this should give you! If *you* cannot pray, *He* can; and if you feel as if your prayers must be shut out, yet His intercession cannot be denied. Come and trust Him! He who pleads for you will not reject you. Do not entertain so unkind a thought, but come and cast yourself upon Him. Has He not said, "[H]im that cometh to me I will in no wise cast out" (John 6:37)? Venture upon the assured truth of that word, and you will be received into the abode of His love.

I am sure, too, that if Jesus Christ pleads for transgressors as transgressors, while as yet they have not yet begun to pray for themselves, *He will be sure to hear them when they are at last led to pray.* When the transgressor becomes a penitent, when he weeps because he has gone astray, let us be quite sure that the Lord of mercy who went after him in his sin will come to meet him now that he returns. There can be no doubt about that. I have known the power of this text when I have been heavy in heart. I have seen my sinfulness, and I have been filled with distress, but I have blessed the Lord Jesus Christ that He makes intercession *for the transgressors,* for then I may venture to believe that He intercedes for me, since I am a transgressor beyond all doubt. Then again, when my spirit has revived and I have said, "But yet I am a child of God, and I know I am born from above," then I have drawn a further inference: If He makes intercession for transgressors, I can depend upon it that He is even more intent upon pleading for His own people. If He is heard for those who are out of the way, assuredly He will be heard for those who have returned unto the Shepherd and bishop of their souls. For them above all others He will be sure to plead, for He lives to intercede for all who come unto God by Him.

So that our confidence may be increased, *consider the effect of our Lord's intercession for transgressors.* Remember first that many of the worst transgressors have been *preserved in life* in answer to Christ's prayer. Had it not been for His pleading, they would have been dead long ago. You know the parable of the fig tree that cumbered the ground, bearing no fruit and impoverishing the soil (Luke 13:6–9). The master of the vineyard said, "Cut it down," but the vine dresser said, "Let it alone this year also, till I shall dig about it, and dung it: And if it bear fruit, well." Need I say who He is that stays the axe that otherwise long ago had been laid at the root of the barren tree? I tell you that you owe your very life to my Lord's interference on your behalf. You did not hear the intercession, but the great owner of the vineyard heard it, and in answer to the gracious entreaties of His Son, He has let you live a little longer. Is there no ground for faith in this gracious fact? Can you not trust in Him through whose instrumentality you are yet alive?

Remember next that *the gift of the Holy Spirit*, which is needful for the quickening of transgressors, was the result of Christ's intercession. I do not doubt but that between the prayer of Christ for His murderers and the outpouring of the Holy Ghost at Pentecost there was an intimate connection. As the prayer of Stephen brought Saul into the Church and made him an apostle, so the prayer of Christ brought in three thousand at Pentecost to become His disciples. The Spirit of God was given "to the rebellious also" in answer to the pleadings of our Lord. It is a great blessing thus to have the Spirit of God given to the sons of men, and if this comes through Jesus' prayers, let us trust in Him, for what will not come if we rely upon His power? Upon sinners He will still display His power, for they will be pricked in their hearts and will believe in Him whom they have pierced.

It is through Christ's intercession that *our poor prayers are accepted with God*. John, in the Revelation, saw another angel standing at the altar, having a golden censer, to whom there was given much incense, that he should offer it with the prayers of all saints upon the golden altar that was before the throne (Rev. 8:3). Where does the much incense come from? What is it but Jesus' merits? Our prayers are accepted only because of His prayers. If, then, the intercession of Christ for transgressors has made the prayers of transgressors to be accepted, let us without wavering put our trust in Him, and let us show it by offering our supplications with a full assurance of faith and an unstaggering confidence in the promise of our covenant God. Are not all the promises yea and amen in Christ Jesus? Let us remember Him and ask in faith, nothing wavering.

It is through the prayers of Christ, too, that we are *kept in the hour of temptation*. "[Father],...keep them from the evil" (John 17:15) is a part of our Lord's supplication, and His Father hears Him always. Surely, if we are kept in the midst of temptation from being destroyed because Christ pleads for us, let us never fear to trust ourselves in His kind, careful hands. He can keep us, for He has kept us. If His prayers have delivered us out of the hand of Satan, His eternal power can bring us safely home, though death lies in the way.

Indeed, it is because He pleads *that we are saved* at all. He is "able also to save them to the uttermost that come unto God by him, seeing he ever liveth to make intercession for them" (Heb. 7:25). This, also, is one grand reason why we are able to challenge all the accusations of the world and of the devil, for "Who is he that condemneth? It is Christ that died, yea rather, that is risen again, who is even at the right hand of God, who also maketh intercession for us" (Rom. 8:34). Satan's charges are all answered by our Advocate, who defends us at the judgment seat when we stand there like Joshua in filthy garments, accused of the devil; and therefore the verdict is always given in our favor: "Take away the filthy garments from him" (Zech. 3:4) Oh you who would bring slanderous accusations against the saints of God, they will not damage us in the court of the great King, for "if any man sin, we have an advocate with the Father, Jesus Christ the righteous" (1 John 2:1). Think of what the intercession of Jesus has done, and you will clearly perceive great inducements to place your sole reliance in your Lord. Come, weary heart, take the Lord Jesus to be your confidence— what more do you want? Can you desire a better friend than He is, a more prevalent Advocate before the throne? Come, leave all other trusts and yield yourself to Him. I pray you accept this advice of love. And if you are foolish enough to have doubts and fears, come, see how Jesus pleads for you. Give Him your burden to bear, leave with Him your anxieties at this moment that He may care for you. He will carry on your petition before the eternal throne and carry it through to success. He who engages a lawyer to manage his legal business among men leaves his affairs in his hands, and he who has such a pleader before God as Christ Jesus, the Wonderful, Counselor, has no need to torment himself with anxieties. Rather let him rest in Jesus and wait the result with patience.

Obedience to Christ's Example

I say obedience to His example, for I take the example of Christ to be an embodied precept as much binding upon us as His written commands. The life of Christ is a precept to those who profess to be His disciples. Now, may I put a few practical matters before you, and will you endeavor by the help of God's Spirit to carry them out?

First, then, your Lord makes intercession for the transgressors; therefore, *imitate Him by forgiving all transgressions against yourself.* Have any offended you? Let the very recollection of the offense as far as possible pass from your mind, for none have ever injured you as men injured Christ. They have not nailed you to a cross, nor pierced your hands and feet and side. Yet if *He* said, "Father, forgive them," well may you say the same. Ten thousand talents did you owe? Yet He forgave you all that debt, not without a grievous outlay to Himself. Your brother owes you but a hundred pence, will you take him by the throat (Matt. 18:28)? Will you not rather freely forgive him even to seventy times seven? Can you not forgive him? If you find it to be impossible, I will not speak to you any longer as a Christian, because I must doubt whether you are a believer at all. The Lord cannot accept you while you are unforgiving, since He says, "Therefore if thou bring thy gift to the altar, and there rememberest that thy brother hath ought against thee; Leave there thy gift before the altar, and go thy way; first be reconciled to thy brother, and then come and offer thy gift" (Matt. 5:23–24).

If peace is not made, you will not be accepted. God does not hear those in whose hearts malice and enmity find a lodging. Yet I would speak to you in tones of love rather than with words of threatening. As a follower of the gentle Christ, I beseech you to imitate Him in this, and you shall find rest and comfort to your own soul. From the day in which Christ forgives you, rise to that nobility of character that finds a pleasure in forgiving all offenses fully and frankly for Christ's sake. Surely, the atonement He offered, if it satisfied God, may well satisfy you and make amends for the sin of your brother against you as well as against the Lord. Jesus took upon Himself the transgressions of the second table of the law as well as of the first, and will you bring a suit against your brother for the sin that Jesus bore? You must forgive, for the blood has blotted the record! Let these words of Scripture drop upon your heart like gentle dew from heaven: "And be ye kind one to another, tenderhearted, forgiving one another, even as God for Christ's sake hath forgiven you" (Eph. 4:32).

Next, imitate Christ, dear friend, *in pleading for yourself.* Since you are a transgressor and you see that Jesus intercedes for transgressors, be bold to say, "If He pleads for such as I am, I will put in my humble petition and hope to be heard through Him. Since I hear Him cry, 'Father, forgive them,' I will humbly weep at His feet and try to mingle my faint and trembling plea with His all-prevalent supplication." When Jesus says, "Father, forgive them," it will be your wisdom to cry, "Father, forgive *me*." Dear reader, that is the way to be saved. Let your prayers hang like the golden bells upon the skirts of the Great High Priest; He will carry them within the veil and make them ring out sweetly there. As music borne on the breeze is heard afar, so shall your prayers have a listener in heaven because Jesus wafts them there.

Since your prayers are feeble, yoke them to the omnipotence of His intercession. Let His merits be as wings on which they may soar and His power as hands with which they may grasp the priceless blessings. What shall I say to those who refuse to pray when they have such an encouragement as the aid of Jesus? Tones of tenderness are suitable when addressing the ungodly, when we would persuade them to pray. But if they refuse the intercession of Jesus Christ Himself, we must add our solemn warnings. If you perish, your blood be on your own head. Rejecters of great mercy must expect great wrath. The intercession of your Savior, when refused, will be visited upon you most terribly in the day when He becomes your Judge.

Let us imitate our Lord in a third point, dear friend; namely, if we have been forgiven our transgressions, *let us now intercede for transgressors,* since Jesus does so. He is the great example of all His disciples, and if He makes it His constant business to supplicate for sinners, should not His people unite with Him? Therefore would I stir you up to pray. Never let the prayer meetings decline. Let us, as a Church, make intercession for transgressors and never rest from seeking the conversion of all around us. I trust that every day, so often as you bow the knee, you will make intercession for the transgressors. Many of them are sinning against their own souls, but they know not what they do. They think to find pleasure in sin. In this also they know not what they do. They break the Sabbath, they despise the sanctuary, they reject Christ, they go downward to hell with mirth, singing merry glees as if they were going to a wedding feast. They know not what they do.

But you do know what they are doing. By your humanity— scarcely shall I need to urge a stronger motive—by mere humanity, I beseech you, do all you can for these poor souls, and especially pray for them. You are not pointed to the cross and asked to bleed for sinners, you are only asked to make intercession. Intercession is an honorable service where you are allowed to entreat the King for others. If you could have permission to frequent the queen's courts, you would not think it a hardship to be asked to present a petition for another. It would be to you a delight to be enjoyed, a privilege to be snatched at eagerly, that you should be permitted to present requests for others. Stand where Abraham stood and plead for sinners: Sodom could scarce be worse than many portions of the world at this hour. Plead, then, with all your heart. Plead again, and again, and again with the Lord, though you are but dust and ashes, and cease not till the Lord says, "I have heard the petition, I will bless the city, I will save the millions, and my Son shall be glorified."

Let us take care, dear friend, that if we do plead for others *we mix with it the doing of good to them,* because it is not recorded that He made intercession for transgressors until it is first written, "he bare the sin of many." For us to pray for sinners without instructing them, without exerting ourselves to arouse them or making any sacrifice for their conversion, without using any likely means for their conviction, would be a piece of mere formality on our part. According to our ability, we must prove the sincerity of our petitions by our actions. Prayer without effort is falsehood, and that cannot be pleasing to God. Yield up yourself to seek the good of others, and then may you intercede with honest hearts.

Last, *if Christ appears in heaven for us, let us be glad to appear on earth for Him.* He owns us before God and the holy angels; let us not be ashamed to confess *Him* before men and devils. If Christ pleads with God for men, let us not be backward to plead with men for God. If He by His intercession saves us to the uttermost, let us hasten to serve Him to the uttermost. If He spends eternity in intercession for us, let us spend our time in intercession for His cause. If He thinks of us, we should also think of His people, and especially supplicate for His afflicted. If He watches our cases and adapts His prayers to our necessities, let us observe the needs of His people and plead for them with understanding. Alas, how soon do men weary of pleading for our Lord! If a whole day is set apart for prayer and the meeting is not carefully managed, it readily becomes a weariness of the flesh. Prayer meetings very easily lose their flame and burn low. Shame on these laggard spirits and this heavy flesh of ours that needs to be pampered with liveliness and brevity or we go to sleep at our devotions. "Forever" is not too long for *Him* to plead, and yet an hour tries us here. On, and on, and on through all the ages, still His intercession rises to the throne, and yet we flag and our prayers are half dead in a short season. See, Moses lets his hands hang down, and Amelek is defeating Joshua in the plain!

Can we endure to be thus losing victories and causing the enemy to triumph? If your ministers are unsuccessful, if your laborers for Christ in foreign lands make little headway, if the work of Christ drags, is it not because in the secret place of intercession we have but little strength? The restraining of prayer is the weakening of the Church. If we aroused ourselves to lay hold upon the covenant angel and resolutely cried, "I will not let thee go, except thou bless me" (Gen. 32:26), we should enrich ourselves and our age. If we used more of the strong reasons that make up the weapon of all-prayer, our victories would not be so few and far between. Our interceding Lord is hindered for lack of an interceding Church. The kingdom comes not because so little use is made of the throne of grace. Get to your knees, for on your knees you conquer. Go to the mercy seat and remain there. What better argument can I use with you than this: Jesus is there, and if you desire His company, you must ofttimes resort there. If you want to taste His dearest, sweetest love, do what He is doing: Union of work will create a new communion of heart. Let us never be absent when praying men meet together. Let us make a point of frequenting assemblies gathered for prayer, even if we give up other occupations. While we live, let us be above all things men of prayer, and when we die, if nothing else can be said of us, may men give us the epitaph that is also our Lord's memorial: "He made intercession for the transgressors." Amen.

Jesus, therefore, to prevent interruption, to give Himself the opportunity of pouring out His whole soul, and to avoid ostentation, sought the mountain. What a grand oratory for the Son of God! What walls would have been so suitable? What room would have worthily housed so mighty an intercessor? The Son of God most fittingly entered God's own glorious temple of nature when He would commune with heaven. Those giant hills and the long shadows cast by the moonlight were alone worthy to be His companions. No pomp of gorgeous ceremony can possibly have equaled the glory of nature's midnight on the wild mountain's side, where the stars, like the eyes of God, looked down upon the worshiper and the winds seemed as though they would bear the burden of His sighs and tears upon their willing wings. Samson, in the temple of the Philistines, moving the giant pillars, is a mere dwarf compared with Jesus of Nazareth moving heaven and earth as He bows Himself alone in the great temple of Jehovah.

Chapter Four

All Night in Prayer

And it came to pass in those days, that he went out into a mountain to pray, and continued all night in prayer to God
—Luke 6:12

IF ANY PERSON MIGHT have lived without prayer, it was surely the Lord Jesus Christ. To us poor weak, erring mortals, prayer is an absolute necessity. But it does not at first sight seem to be so to Him who was "holy, harmless, undefiled, separate from sinners" (Heb. 7:26). In some aspects of prayer, our Lord Jesus Christ could take no share. For instance, in that most important department, namely, personal confession of sin, He could take no portion. There were no slips in His outward life, there were no declensions in His inward heart. "[F]orgive us our debts, as we forgive our debtors" (Matt. 6:12) is a very suitable prayer for Him to teach us, but He could not use it Himself. Nor had He any need to pray against inward corruptions, seeing He was born without them. We wrestle hard each day with original sin, but Jesus knew no such adversaries. It is as much as we can do, with all the weapons of our holy war, to keep down the foes of our own household, but our Lord had no sinful nature to subdue. The inner life is a daily struggle with some of us, so that Paul's exclamation "O wretched man that I am!" (Rom. 7:24) is exceedingly familiar to our lips, but our Lord said truly of Himself, "[T]he prince of this world cometh, and hath nothing in me" (John 14:30).

Moreover, our Lord had not to seek some of the things that are exceedingly needful to His disciples. One desire that I trust is ever present with us is for growth in grace, for advancement in the divine life. But our Lord was always perfect in holiness and love. I see not how there could have been any advancement in purity in Him. He was always the spotless lily of innocence, incomparable, faultless, without spot or wrinkle or any such thing. Our Lord had no need to examine His life at the end of every day. When He retired for prayer, there would be no need to scan the actions of the day to detect shortcomings and flaws. There would be no necessity to investigate secret motives to see whether He might not have been actuated by sinister principles. The deep wellsprings of His being were not of earth but were altogether divine. When He bowed His knee in the morning, He had no need to pray to be protected from sin during the day. He went forth to His daily labor without the weaknesses that we bear within us and was free from the tendencies to evil that we bear about us. Tempted He was in all points like as we are, but the arrows that wound us glanced harmlessly from Him.

Yet notice carefully that although our glorious Master did not require to pray in some of those respects in which it is most needful to us, yet never was there a man who was more abundant in prayer and in supplication, nor one in whom prayer was exercised with so much intensity and importunity. He was the greatest of preachers, but His prayers made even a deeper impression than His sermons on His disciples, for they did not say, "Lord, teach us to preach," but they did exclaim, "Lord, teach us to pray" (Luke 11:1). They felt that He was Master of that heavenly art, and at His feet they desired to sit that they might learn how to move heaven and earth with sacred wrestlings. Since our sinless Lord was thus mighty in prayer, does not His example say to us with a voice irresistibly persuasive, "Watch and pray, that ye enter not into temptation" (Matt. 26:41)? You desire to be conformed to the image of Christ—be conformed in this respect, that you are a man of prayer. You desire to know the secret of His power with men—seek to obtain His power with God. You wish to obtain the blessings that were so copiously bestowed upon Him—seek them where He sought them and find them where He found them. If you would adorn His doctrine and increase His kingdom, use the weapon of all-prayer, which ensures victory to all who use it as the Captain did.

Although our Lord Jesus Christ was most constant in His perpetual devotions, yet devout men have been accustomed to set apart times for extraordinary supplication. A man who does not pray regularly is but a hypocrite when he pretends to pray specially. Who would care to live in a miser's house who starved you all the year round, except that now and then on a feast day he fed you well? We must not be miserly in prayer, neglecting it regularly and abounding in it only on particular occasions when a showy display rather than sincerity may influence us. But even he who keeps a bounteous table sometimes spreads a more luxurious feast than at other times; and even so must we, if we habitually live near to God, select our extraordinary seasons in which the soul shall have her fill of fellowship. Our Lord Jesus Christ in the text before us has set us an example of extraordinary devotion, supplying us with all the details of the exercise.

Notice *the place* that He selected for it. He sought the solitude of a mountain. He was so popular that He could not hope in any city or village to be free from innumerable followers. He was so great a benefactor that He could never be without sick folk entreating healing at His hands. He knew no leisure, no, not so much as to eat bread and therefore to obtain a little respite. He sought the hollow of some lofty hill, where foot of man could not profane His loneliness. If you would draw near to God in an extraordinary manner, you must take care to be entirely undisturbed. I know not why it is, but whenever one desires to approach very near to God, there is sure to be a knock at the door, or some matter of urgent business, or some difficult circumstance to tempt us from our knees. Is it so that Satan knows how soul-enriching retirement and devotion are and, therefore, if he can by any method stir up friend or foe to call us out of our closet, he will surely do so? Here our Lord was beyond call. The mountain was better than a closet with bolted doors. Far off was the din of the city and the noise of those who clamored with their merchandise. Neither the shout of triumph nor the wail of sorrow could reach Him there. Beloved friend, carefully seek if you can a perfect solitude, but if not, reach as near to it as you can, and as much as possible keep out the sound and thought of the outer world.

Did not our Lord resort to the mountain so that He might be able to pray aloud? I cannot speak for others, but I often find it very helpful to be able to speak aloud in private prayer. I do not doubt but that very spiritual minds can pray for a great length of time without the motion of the lips, but I think the most of us would often find it a spur and assistance if we could give utterance to our cries and sighs, no one being present to hear. We know that our Lord was accustomed to use strong cryings and tears, and these it would not have been desirable for a human ear to listen to. In fact, His natural modesty would have put Him under a restraint. He therefore sought mountains far away that He might, in His Father's presence and in the presence of no one else, pour out His entire soul—groaning, struggling, wrestling, or rejoicing, as His spirit might be moved at the time.

Did He not also seek the mountain to avoid a public display? If we pray to be seen of men, we shall have our reward, and a pitiful reward it will be. We shall have the admiration of shallow fools, and nothing more. If our object in prayer is to obtain blessings from God, we must present our prayers unspoiled by human observation. Get alone with your God if you would move His arm. If you fast, do not give the appearance to men that you are fasting. If you plead personally with God, tell none of it. Take care that this is a secret between God and your own soul; then shall your Father reward you openly. But if you parade about like a Pharisee, to sound your trumpet in the corner of the streets, you shall go where the Pharisee has gone, where hypocrites feel forever the wrath of God.

Jesus, therefore, to prevent interruption, to give Himself the opportunity of pouring out His whole soul, and to avoid ostentation, sought the mountain. What a grand oratory for the Son of God! What walls would have been so suitable? What room would have worthily housed so mighty an intercessor? The Son of God most fittingly entered God's own glorious temple of nature when He would commune with heaven. Those giant hills and the long shadows cast by the moonlight were alone worthy to be His companions. No pomp of gorgeous ceremony can possibly have equaled the glory of nature's midnight on the wild mountain's side, where the stars, like the eyes of God, looked down upon the worshiper and the winds seemed as though they would bear the burden of His sighs and tears upon their willing wings. Samson, in the temple of the Philistines, moving the giant pillars, is a mere dwarf compared with Jesus of Nazareth moving heaven and earth as He bows Himself alone in the great temple of Jehovah.

For purposes of extraordinary devotion, the time selected by our Master is also a lesson to us. He chose the silent hours of night. Now it may so happen that if we *literally* imitated Him, we might altogether miss our way, for no doubt He chose the night because it was most convenient, congenial, and in every way appropriate. To some of us, the night might be most inappropriate and unsuitable. If so, we must not follow it but must follow our Lord in the spirit rather than in the letter. We should give to spiritual things that part of the day when we can be most quiet, those hours when we can most fairly allot to it without neglecting our other duties of their proper proportion of time. By day, our Savior was preaching; He could not cease from preaching even to spend the day in prayer. By day, the multitude needed healing; our Lord would not suspend His benevolent work for His private communions. We are to take care never to present one duty to God stained with the blood of another, but to balance and proportion our different forms of service so that our lifework may be perfect and entire. Usually, however, night will be the favored season for wrestling Jacobs. When every man had gone to his own home to rest, the Man of Nazareth had a right to seek His solace where best He could, and if sleep refreshed others and prayer more fully refreshed Him, then by all means let Him pray. I recommend that you set apart for special intercessions times that answer to this description, when the time is your own, not your master's; your own, not your family's; not pilfered from family devotion or abstracted from public worship. It is the time of quiet when all around you is in repose, the time congenial to solemnity, and the awe of a spirit hushed into reverent subjection yet uplifted to rapt devotion. Such time, with many, may be the night; with others, it may be the day. Let sanctified common sense be your direction.

Again, our Lord sets us a good example in this matter of extraordinary seasons of devotion in *the protracted character of His prayer.* He continued all night in prayer. I do not think that we are bound to pray long as a general rule. I am afraid, however, there is no great need to make the remark, for most Christians are short enough, if not far too short, in private worship. By the aid of the Holy Spirit, it is possible to throw by holy energy and sacred zeal as much prayer into a few minutes as into many hours, for prevalent prayer is not measured by God by the yard or by the hour. Force is its standard rather than length. When the whole soul groans itself out in half a dozen sentences, there may be more real devotion in them than in hours of mere word spinning. True prayer is the soul's mounting up to God, and if it can ride upon a cherub or the wings of the wind, so much the better, yet in extraordinary seasons, when the soul is thoroughly caught up to an eminent intensity of devotion, it is well to continue it for a protracted season. We know not that our Lord was vocally praying all the time. He may have paused to contemplate. He may have surveyed the whole compass of the field over which His prayer should extend, meditating upon the character of His God, recapitulating the precious promises, remembering the needs of His people, and thus arming Himself with arguments with which to return to wrestle and prevail.

How very few of us have ever spent a whole night in prayer, and yet what blessings we might have had for such asking! We know little of what a night of prayer would do for us; its effect we can scarcely calculate. One night alone in prayer might make us new men, changed from poverty of soul to spiritual wealth, from trembling to triumphing. We have an example of it in the life of Jacob. Before, he was the crafty shuffler, always bargaining and calculating, unlovely in almost every respect; yet one night in prayer turned the supplanter into a prevailing prince and robed him with celestial grandeur. From that night he lives on the sacred page as one of the nobility of heaven. Could not we, at least now and then, in these weary earthbound years, dedicate single nights for such enriching traffic with the skies? What, have we no sacred ambition? Are we deaf to the yearnings of divine love? Yet, for wealth and for science, men will cheerfully give up their warm couches, and cannot we do it now and then for the love of God and the good of souls? Where is our zeal, our gratitude, our sincerity? I am ashamed while I thus upbraid both myself and you. May we often tarry at Jabbok and cry with Jacob as he grasped the angel, "I will not let thee go, except thou bless me" (Gen. 32:26). Surely, if we have given whole days to pleasure, we can afford a space of heavenly wisdom. Time was when we gave whole nights to the world's revelry and did not tire then. We chided the sun that he rose so soon and wished the hours would lag awhile that we might delight in wilder merriment and perhaps deeper sin. Why should we weary in heavenly employments? Why grow weary when asked to watch with our Lord? Up, sluggish heart, Jesus calls you! Rise and go forth to meet the heavenly Friend in the place where He manifests Himself.

Jesus has further instructed us in the art of special devotion by *the manner of His prayer.* Notice, He continued all night in prayer *to God.* How much of our prayer is really a muttering to the winds, a talking to the air, for the presence of God is not realized by the mind. "[H]e that cometh to God must believe that he is, and that he is a rewarder of them that diligently seek him" (Heb. 11:6). Do you know what it is mentally to lay hold upon the great unseen One and to talk with Him as really as you talk to a friend whose hand you grip? How heavenly to speak right down into God's ear, to pour your heart directly into God's heart, feeling that you live in Him as the fish live in the sea and that your every thought and word are discerned by Him. It is true pleading when the Lord is present to you and you realize His presence and speak under the power and influence of His divine o'ershadowing. That is to pray indeed, but to continue all night in such a frame of mind is wonderful to me, for I must confess that if for a while I get near to God in prayer, yet distracting thoughts will intrude, the ravenous birds will come down upon the sacrifice, the noise of archers will disturb the songs at the place of drawing of water. How soon do we forget that we are speaking to God and go on mechanically pumping up our desires, perhaps honestly uttering them but forgetting to whom they are addressed! Oh, were He not a gracious God, the imperfection of our prayers would prevent so much as even one of them reaching His ear! But He knows our frailty and takes our prayers, not as what they are but as what we mean them to be, and beholding them in Jesus Christ, He accepts both us and them in the Beloved. Do let us learn from our Master to make our prayers distinctly and directly appeals to God. That gunner will do no service to the army who takes no aim but is content so long as he does but fire; that vessel makes an unremunerative voyage that is not steered for a port but is satisfied to sail in any direction. We must direct our prayers to God and maintain soul fellowship with Him, or our devotion will become a nullity, a name for a thing that is not.

The Ethiopic translation reads "in prayer *with God.*" Truly this is the highest order of prayer, and though the translation may be indefensible, the meaning is correct enough, for Jesus was eminently with God all night. To pray with God, do you know what that is? To be the echo of Jehovah's voice! To desire the Lord's desires and long with His longings! This is a gracious condition to be in, when the heart is a tablet for the Lord to write upon, a coal blazing with celestial fire, a leaf driven with the heavenly wind. Oh, to be absorbed in the divine will, having one's whole mind swallowed up in the mind of God! This for a whole night would be blessed, this forever bliss itself.

Note, too, that some have translated the passage "in the prayer *of God*." This is probably an incorrect translation, but it brings out a precious meaning. The most eminent things were in the Hebrew language ascribed to God, so that by it would be meant the noblest prayer, the most intense prayer, the most vehement prayer, a prayer in which the whole man gathers up his full strength and spends it in an agony before the eternal throne. Oh, to pray like that! The great, deep, intense prayer of God! I am afraid that as a rule in our prayer meetings we are much too decorous, and even in our private prayers we feel too much the power of formality. How I delight to listen to a brother who talks to God simply and from his heart! I must confess I have a great liking for those rare old-fashioned Methodist prayers that are now quite out of date. Our Methodist friends, for the most part, are getting too fine and respectable nowadays, too genteel to allow of prayers such as once made the walls to ring again. Oh, for a revival of those glorious violent prayers that flew like hot ammunition against the battlements of heaven! Oh, for more moving of the posts of the doors in vehemence, more thundering at the gates of mercy! I would sooner attend a prayer meeting where there were groans and cries all over the place and cries and shouts of "Hallelujah!" than be in polite assemblies where everything is dull as death and decorous as the whitewashed sepulchre. Oh, for more of the prayer of God, the whole body, soul, and spirit working together, the whole man being aroused and stirred up to the highest pitch of intensity to wrestle with the Most High! Such, I have no doubt, the prayer of Jesus was on the cold mountain's side.

Once more, we may learn from Jesus our Lord *the occasion* for special devotion. At the time when our Master continued all night in prayer He had been upbraided by the Pharisees. He fulfilled the resolve of the man after God's own heart: "Let the proud be ashamed; for they dealt perversely with me without a cause: but I will meditate in thy precepts" (Ps. 119:78). So David did, and so did David's Lord. The best answer to the slanderers of the ungodly is to be more constant in communion with God. Has it been so with you? Have you been persecuted or despised? Have you passed through any unusual form of trial? Then celebrate an unusual season of prayer. This is the alarm bell that God rings. Hasten to Him for refuge. See to it that in this your time of trouble you go to the mercy seat with greater diligence.

Another reason is also noticed in the context. Christ had said to His disciples, "Pray ye therefore the Lord of the harvest, that he will send forth labourers into his harvest" (Matt. 9:38). What He told them to do He would be sure to do Himself. He was just about to choose twelve apostles, and before that solemn act of ordination was performed, He sought power for them from the Most High. Who can tell what blessings were vouchsafed to the twelve in answer to that midnight intercession? If Satan fell like lightning from heaven, Jesus' prayer did it rather than the apostles' preaching. So, if you enter upon a new enterprise or engage in something that is weightier and more extensive than what you have done before, select a night or a day and set it apart for special communion with the Most High. If you are to pray, you must work, but if you are to work, you must also pray. If your prayer without your work will be hypocrisy, your work without your prayer will be presumption, so see to it that you are specially in supplication when specially in service. Balance your praying and working, and when you have reached the full tale of the one, do not diminish the other.

To anyone who asks me, "When should I give myself especially to a protracted season of prayer?", I would answer that these occasions will frequently occur. You should certainly do this when about to join the church. The day of your profession of your faith publicly should be altogether a consecrated day. I recall rising before the sun to seek my Master's presence on the day when I was buried with Him in baptism. It seemed to me a solemn ordinance not to be lightly undertaken or flippantly carried out; a duty which, if done at all, should be performed in the most solemn and earnest manner. What is baptism without fellowship with Christ? To be buried in baptism, but not *with Him,* what is it? I say to young people who are joining the church, mind you do not do it thoughtlessly, but in coming forward to enlist in the army of Christ, set apart a special season for self-examination and prayer. When you arrive at any great change of life, do the same. Do not enter upon marriage or upon starting in business without having sought a benediction from your Father who is in heaven. Any of these things may involve years of pain or years of happiness to you. Seek, therefore, to have the smile of God upon what you are about to do. Should you not also make your times of peculiar trial to be also times of special prayer? Wait upon God now that your child is suffering. Wrestle with Him as David did about the child of Bathsheba. Draw near to God with fasting and prayer for a life that is specially dear to you if perhaps it may be preserved. And should death follow and the tree beneath which you found shelter be cut down, then again, before the grave is closed and the visitation is forgotten, draw near to God with sevenfold earnestness. And if you have been studying the Word of God and cannot master a passage of Scripture, if some truth of revelation staggers you, now again is a time to set yourself like Daniel by prayer and supplication to find out what is the meaning of the Lord in the book of His prophecy. Indeed, such occasions will often occur to you who are spiritual, and I charge you by the living God, if you would be rich in grace, if you would make great advances in the divine life, if you would be eminent in the service of your Master, attend to these occasions. Get an hour alone, an hour, ay, two hours a day if you can, and go not away from the Master's presence till your face is made to shine as once the face of Moses did when he had been long upon the mount alone with God.

And now having thus brought out the example of Christ as well as I can, I want to make an application of the subject to church life. My words shall be few, but I earnestly desire that God may make them weighty.

A church, to have a blessing upon its special times of prayer, must abound in constant prayer at other times. I do not believe in spasmodic efforts for revival. There should be special occasions, but these should be the outgrowths of ordinary, active, healthy vigor. To neglect prayer all the year round and then to celebrate a special week, is it much better than hypocrisy? To forsake the regular prayer meetings but to come in crowds to a special one, what is this? Does it not betray superficiality or the effervescence of mere excitement? The Church should always pray. Prayer is to her what salt and bread are to our tables. No matter what the meal, we must have salt and bread there, and no matter what the church's engagements, she must have her regular constancy of prayer. I think that in London our churches err in not having morning and evening prayer daily in every case where the church is large enough to maintain it. I am glad that our zealous brethren have here for some years maintained that constant prayer. But we must see to it that we keep this up, and moreover, those who are lax and lagging behind must ask forgiveness of their heavenly Father and endeavor henceforth to be more instant in supplication.

If, *men* ought always to pray and not to faint, much more *Christian men.* Jesus has sent His Church into the world on the same errand upon which He Himself came, and that includes intercession. What if I say that the Church is the world's priest? Creation is dumb, but the Church is to find a mouth for it. Ungodly men are dumb of heart and will, but we who have the will and the power to intercede dare not be silent. It is the Church's privilege to pray. The door of grace is always open for her petitions, which never return empty-handed. The veil was rent for her, the blood was sprinkled upon the altar for her, God constantly invites her. Will she refuse the privilege that angels might envy her? Is not the Church the Bride of Christ? May she not go in unto her King at any time, at every time? Shall she allow the precious privilege to be unused? The Church ever has need for prayer. There are always some in her midst who are declining and frequently those who are falling into open sin. There are the lambs to be prayed for that they may be carried in Christ's bosom. There are the strong to be prayed for lest they grow presumptuous, and the weak lest they become despairing.

In such a church as this is, if we kept up prayer meetings twenty-four hours in the day, three hundred and sixty five days in the year, we might never be without a special subject for supplication. Are we ever without the sick and the poor? Are we ever without the afflicted and the wavering? Are we ever without those who are seeking the conversion of their relatives, the reclaiming of backsliders, or the salvation of the depraved? With such congregations constantly gathering, with such a densely peopled neighborhood, with three million sinners around us, the most part of them lying dead in trespasses and sins, with such a country beginning to be benighted in superstition, in a world full of idols, full of cruelties, full of deviltries, if the Church does not pray, how shall she excuse her base neglect of the command of her loving Lord and covenant head? Let this church then be constant in supplication.

There should be frequent prayer meetings, constantly attended by all. Every man should make it a point of duty to come as often as possible to the place of prayer. I wish that all throughout this country the prayers of God's churches were more earnest and constant. It might make a man weep tears of blood to think that in so many cases the prayer meetings are so shamefully attended. I know towns where the prayer meeting is put off during the summer months, as if the devil would be put off during the summer! I know of agricultural districts where they are always put off during the harvest, and I make some excuses for them because the fruits of the earth must be gathered in, but I cannot understand large congregations where the prayer meeting and preaching are amalgamated because there will not be enough people coming out to make two decent services in the week. And then they say that God does not bless the Word. How can He bless the Word? They say, "Our conversions are not so numerous as they were," and they wonder why. Do you wonder that they have not a blessing when they do not seek it? Do you wonder that we have it when we do seek it? That is but a natural law of God's own government, that if men will not pray, neither shall they have; and if men will pray, and pray vehemently, God will deny them nothing. He opens wide His hand and says, "Ask, and it shall be given you" (Matt. 7:7). I wish our denomination of Baptists and other denominations of Christians were greater believers in prayer, for the mischief of ritualism and rationalism that is coming upon us, the curse that is withering our nation, the blight and mildew that are devouring the vineyard of the Lord, have all come upon us because public prayer has almost ceased in the land as to its constancy, intensity, and importunity. The Lord recover us from this sin!

But let the Church be as diligent in prayer as she may on regular occasions, she should still have her special seasons. A thing that is regular and constant is sure to tire, and a little novelty is lawful. A little speciality may often tend to revive those who otherwise would be given to slumber. The Church should have her special praying times because she has her special needs. There are times when spiritual epidemics fall upon churches and congregations. Sometimes it is the disease of pride, luxury, worldliness. At other times there are many falling into overt sin. Sometimes a black form of vice will break out in the very midst of a church of God. At other times it is a heresy, or a doctrine carried to excess, or ill will, or lack of brotherly love, or a general lethargy. At such special times of trial a church should have her extraordinary prayer meetings. She should also do so when she is engaging in new enterprises and is about to break up new ground. Let her call her members together, and with heart and soul let them commend the work to God. There should be special seasons of prayer because the Holy Spirit prompts us to it. "I believe in the Holy Ghost" is a sentence of the Apostle's Creed, but how few do really believe it! We seem to fancy that we have no motions of the Holy Spirit now among godly men as in old times. But I protest before the living God that such is not the case. The Holy Spirit at this day moves in those who are conversant with Him, and those who are content to regard His gracious monitions He prompts to special fellowship. We speak what we do know, we declare what we have tasted and handled. The Holy Ghost, at certain times, prompts us to come together with peculiar earnestness and special desires. And then, if this is not sufficient, and God has been pleased to set His seal to special seasons of prayer, they should be held. There have been more ingatherings under special efforts of a month than under ordinary efforts of eleven months.

Now, I must have just a word with you upon another matter, namely, that *it should be our endeavor to bring power into these special meetings.* They are lawful, they are necessary, and let us make them profitable. The way to do so is to draw near to God as Christ did. When He prayed, it was a Son talking to His Father, the Son of God talking with the Father God and unbosoming His heart in close communion. Come as children of God to your Father; speak to Him as to one who is very near akin to you. There will be no lack of power if such be the case. Jesus drew near to God in His prayer as a priest, the High Priest making intercession for the people. You are all priests and kings unto God if you believe in Christ. Come with your breastplates on; come that you may intercede before the throne, pleading the merit of the precious blood. There will be no flagging if every man put on his priestly mitre. Jesus came before God with a burning zeal for His Father's glory. He could say "The zeal of thine house hath eaten me up" (John 2:17). Burn and blaze with love to God. Wait upon Him. Let that be a special private season of prayer and ask Him to teach you how to love Him, show you how to reverence Him, and fire you with an intense ambition to spread abroad the savor of His name. Jesus Christ drew near to God in prayer with a wondrous love to the souls of men. Those tears of His were not for Himself but for others. Those sighs and cries were not for His own pangs but for the sorrows and the sins of men. Try to feel as Christ did. Get a tender heart, an awakened conscience, quickened sympathies, and then if you come up to the house of God, the prayer meetings cannot be dull.

Seek to be bathed in the blood of Christ. Go to the wounds of Christ and get life blood for your prayers. Sit you down at Golgotha and gaze upon your dying Lord and hear Him say, "I have loved you and given Myself for you." Then rise up with this resolve in your soul:

> *Now for the love I bear His name,*
> *What was my gain I count my loss,*

and go forward determined in His strength that nothing shall be lacking on your part to win for Him a kingdom, to gain for Him the hearts of the sons of men. If such shall be your state of mind, I am quite sure there will be power with God in prayer.

In closing, we have a special need and a special encouragement to make our prayers things of power. What a multitude my own church is! I often wish, though I beg to be pardoned of the Lord for it, that I had never occupied the position that I now fill, because of its solemn responsibilities. I tell you, when I feel them, they crush me to the ground, and I can only manage to sustain my spirits by endeavoring to cast them upon the Lord. With three thousand seven hundred members or thereabouts, what can *I* do? Somebody complains that this sick one is not visited or that that sinning one is not rebuked. How can I do it? How can one man, how can twenty men, how can a hundred men do the work? God knows I would, if I could, cut myself in pieces, that every piece might be active in His service. But how can we rule and minister fully in such a church as this? God has supplied my lack of service very wonderfully. Still there are things that make my heart ache day and night, as well as other matters that make my soul to leap for joy. Oh, pray for this great church! Where our power utterly fails us, let us implore the divine power to come in, that all may be kept right. We have need to pray, for some have fallen. We have to confess it with a blush that crimsons our cheek; some have fallen shamefully. Oh, pray that others may not fall and that the good men and true among us may be upheld by the power of God through faith unto salvation.

Think of all the works we are involved in. If we do not pray for them, they will be so much wasted effort. Pray that God's blessing may rest upon the Word being preached every week. Intercede for all the workers of the church. Forget not your own sons, turn not your hearts away from your own children whom God has sent forth to be heralds of the cross. In your Sunday schools, in your city missions, in your street preachings, in your orphanages, everywhere you are seeking to glorify Christ, do not, I beseech you, forget the one thing needful in all this. Do not be foolish builders who will buy marble and precious stones at great cost and then forget to lay the cornerstone securely. If it is worthwhile to serve God, it is worthwhile to pray that the service may be blessed. Why all this labor and cost? It is but offering to the Lord that which He cannot accept, except by prayer you sanctify the whole. I think I see you as a church standing by the side of your altar with the victims slain and the wood placed in order, but there is as yet still lacking the fire from on high. Intercede, you Elijahs, men of like passions with us but yet earnest men, upon whose hearts God has written prayer—intercede mightily! Until at last the fire shall come down from heaven to consume the sacrifice and to make all go up like a pillar of smoke unto the Most High.

I cannot write you as I desire. The earnestness of my heart prevents my writing what I feel, but if there are any bonds of love between us and Christ, by His precious blood, by His death sweat, by His holy life, and by His agonizing death, I do beseech you to strive together in your prayers that the Spirit of God may rest upon you, and to God shall be the glory. Amen and Amen.

Beloved, this sanctification is a work of God from its earliest stage. We go astray of ourselves, but we never return to the great Shepherd apart from His divine drawings. Regeneration, in which sanctification begins, is wholly the work of the Spirit of God. Our first discovery of wrong and our first pang of penitence are the work of divine grace. Every thought of holiness and every desire after purity must come from the Lord alone, for we are by nature wedded to iniquity. So also the ultimate conquest of sin in us and the making us perfectly like to our Lord must be entirely the work of the Lord God, who makes all things new, since we have no power to carry on so great a work of ourselves. This is a creation; can we create? This is a resurrection; can we raise the dead? Our degenerate nature can rot into a still direr putrefaction, but it never can return to purity or sweeten itself into perfection. This is of God and God alone. Sanctification is as much the work of God as the making of the heavens and the earth. Who is sufficient for these things? We go not even a step in sanctification in our own strength. Whatever we think we advance of ourselves is but a fictitious progress that will lead to bitter disappointment. Real sanctification is entirely from first to last the work of the Spirit of the blessed God, whom the Father has sent forth that He might sanctify His chosen ones. See, then, what a great thing sanctification is and how necessary it is that our Lord should pray to His Father, "Sanctify them through thy truth."

Chapter Five

Our Lord's Prayer for His People's Sanctification

Sanctify them through thy truth: thy word is truth—John 17:17.

OUR LORD JESUS PRAYED much for His people while He was here on earth. He made Peter the special subject of His intercession when He knew that he was in extraordinary danger. The midnight wrestlings of the Son of Man were for His people. In the sacred record, however, much more space is taken up by our Lord's intercessions as He nears the end of His labors. After the closing supper, His public preaching work being ended and nothing remaining to be done but to die, He gave Himself wholly to prayer. He was not again to instruct the multitude nor to heal the sick; and in the interval that remained before He should lay down His life, He girded Himself for special intercession. He poured out His soul in life before He poured it out in death.

In this wonderful prayer in John 17, our Lord, as our Great High Priest, appears to enter upon that perpetual office of intercession that He is now exercising at the right hand of the Father. Our Lord ever seemed in the eagerness of His love to be anticipating His work. Before He was set apart for His lifework, by the descent of the Holy Ghost upon Him, He had been about His Father's business (Luke 2:49). Before He finally suffered at the hands of cruel men, He had a baptism to be baptized with, and He was distressed till it was accomplished (Luke 12:50). Before He actually died, He was covered with a bloody sweat (Luke 22:44), and was exceeding sorrowful even unto death (Mark 14:34). And in this case, before He in person entered within the veil, He made intercession for us. He never delays when the good of His people calls for Him. His love has wings as well as feet. It is true of Him evermore, "And he rode upon a cherub, and did fly: yea, he did fly upon the wings of the wind" (Ps. 18:10). O beloved, what a friend we have in Jesus! So willing, so speedy to do for us all that we need. Oh, that we could imitate Him in this being quick of understanding to perceive our line of service and eager of heart to enter upon it.

John 17 should be universally known as the Lord's Prayer and may be called the holy of holies of the Word of God. There we are admitted to that secret place where the Son of God speaks with the Father in closest fellowship of love. Here we look into the heart of Jesus as He sets out in order His desire and requests before His Father on our behalf. Here inspiration lifts her veil, and we behold the truth face to face. Our text lies somewhere near the middle of the prayer; it is the heart of it. Our Lord's desire for the sanctification of His people pervades the whole prayer, but it is gathered up, declared, and intensified in the one sentence: "Sanctify them through thy truth: thy word is truth." How invaluable must the blessing of sanctification be when our Lord, in the highest reach of His intercession, cries, "Sanctify them"! In the sight of His passion on the night before His death, our Savior lifts His eyes to the great Father and cries in His most plaintive tones, "Father, sanctify them." The place whereon we stand is holy ground, and the subject demands our solemn thought. Come, Holy Spirit, and teach us the full meaning of this prayer for holiness!

First, I call your attention to *what it is the Savior asks:* "Sanctify them." Then, I will note *for whom He asks it:* He asks it for those whom His Father had given Him. Third, we shall note *of whom He asks it:* He asks this sanctification of God the Father Himself, for it is He alone who can sanctify His people. Last, we will enquire *how this blessing is to be wrought:* "Sanctify them through thy truth." And our Lord adds an explanatory sentence that was a confession of His own faith toward the Word of the Lord and an instruction to our faith in the same matter. "Thy word is truth."

What Jesus Asked

What is this inestimable blessing that our Savior so earnestly requests at the Father's hand? He first prays, "Holy Father, keep through thine own name those whom thou hast given me" (John 17:11). And He adds again: "Keep them from the evil" (John 17:15). But this negative blessing of preservation from evil is not enough. He seeks for them positive holiness, and therefore He cries, "Sanctify them." The word is one of considerable range of meaning. I am not able to follow it through all its shades, but one or two must suffice.

It means, first, *dedicate them to Your service.* That must be the meaning of the word further down, when we read, "And for their sakes I sanctify myself" (John 17:19). In the Lord's case, it cannot mean purification from sin, because our Savior was undefiled. His nature was unblemished by sin, and His actions were unspotted. No eye of man nor glance of fiend could discover fault in Him, and the search of God only resulted in the declaration that in Him God was well pleased. Our Lord's sanctification was His consecration to the fulfillment of the divine purpose, His absorption in the will of the Father. "Lo, I come to do thy will, O God" (Heb. 10:9). In this sense our interceding Lord asks that all His people may by the Father be ordained and consecrated to holy service. The prayer means: "Father, consecrate them to Yourself. Let them be temples for Your indwelling, instruments for Your use."

Under Jewish law, the tribe of Levi was chosen out of the twelve and ordained to the service of the Lord instead of the firstborn, of whom the Lord had said, "For all the firstborn of the children of Israel are mine:...on the day that I smote every firstborn in the land of Egypt I sanctified them for myself" (Num. 8:17). Out of the tribe of Levi, one family was taken and dedicated to the priesthood. Aaron and his sons are said to have been sanctified (Lev. 8:30).

A certain tent was sanctified to the service of God, and hence it became a sanctuary. And the vessels that were in the tent, whether they were greater, like the altar and the holy table and the ark of the covenant, or whether they were of less degree, like the bowls and the snuff-dishes of the candlestick, were all dedicated or sanctified (Num. 7:1). None of these things could be used for any other purpose than the service of Jehovah. In His courts there was a holy fire, a holy bread, and a holy oil. The holy anointing oil, for instance, was reserved for sacred uses. "Upon man's flesh shall it not be poured" (Ex. 30:32); and again, "Whosoever shall make like unto that, to smell thereto, shall even be cut off from his people" (Ex. 30:38).

These sanctified things were reserved for holy purposes, and any other use of them was strictly forbidden. Bullocks and lambs and sheep and turtledoves, and so forth, were given by devout offers, brought to the holy place, and dedicated unto God. Henceforth, they belonged to God and must be presented at His altar. This is one part of the meaning of our Lord's prayer. He would have each of us consecrated to the Lord, designated and ordained for divine purposes. We are not the world's, otherwise we might be ambitious; we are not Satan's, otherwise we might be covetous; we are not our own, otherwise we might be selfish. We are bought with a price, and hence we are His by whom the price was paid. We belong to Jesus, and He presents us to His Father and begs Him to accept us and sanctify us to His own purposes. Do we not most heartily concur in this dedication? Do we not cry, "Father, sanctify us to Your service"? I am sure we do if we have realized our redeemed condition.

Beloved, if the sprinkling of Jesus' blood has really taken effect upon us, we belong from this time forth to Him who died for us and rose again. We regard ourselves as God's people, the servants of the great King. We were as sheep going astray, but we have now returned to the great Shepherd and bishop of souls; and henceforth we are His people and the sheep of His pasture. If any should ask, "To whom do you belong?," we answer, "I belong to Christ." If any inquire, "What is your occupation?," we reply with Jonah, "I fear the LORD" (Jon. 1:9). We are not now at our own disposal, neither can we hire ourselves out to inferior objects, mercenary aims, or selfish ambitions. We are engaged by solemn contract to the service of our God. We have lifted up our hand to the Lord, and we cannot draw back. Neither do we wish to withdraw from the delightful covenant; we desire to keep it to the end. We seek no liberty to sin nor license for self; rather do we cry, "Bind the sacrifice with cords, even unto the horns of the altar. Sanctify us, O Lord. Let us know, and let all the world know, that we are Yours, because we belong to Christ."

In addition to this, those who belonged to God and were dedicated to His service were *set apart and separated from others*. There was a special service for the setting apart of priests. Certain rites were performed at the sanctifying of dedicated places and vessels. You remember with what solemn service the tabernacle was set up and with what pomp of devotion the temple itself was set apart for the divine service. The Sabbath day, which the Lord has sanctified, is set apart from the rest of time. The Lord would have those who are dedicated to Him to be separated from the rest of mankind. For this purpose, He brought Abraham from Ur of the Chaldees and Israel out of Egypt. "The people shall dwell alone, and shall not be reckoned among the nations" (Num. 23:9). The Lord says of His chosen, "This people have I formed for myself; they shall shew forth my praise" (Isa. 43:21). Before long this secret purpose is followed by the open call: "[C]ome out from among them, and be ye separate;...touch not the unclean thing; and I will...be a Father unto you, and ye shall be my sons and daughters" (2 Cor. 6:17-18). The Church of Christ is to be a chaste virgin, wholly set apart for the Lord Christ. His own words concerning His people are these, "[T]hey are not of the world, even as I am not of the world" (John 17:14).

By the election of grace from before the foundation of the world, this distinction commences and the names are written in heaven. Thereupon follows a redemption peculiar and special, as it is written: "These were redeemed from among men, being the first-fruits unto God and to the Lamb" (Rev. 14:4). This redemption is followed by effectual calling, wherein men are made to come forth from the old world into the kingdom of Christ. This is attended with regeneration, in which they receive a new life and so become as much distinguished from their fellowmen as the living are from the dead. This separating work is further carried on in what is commonly known as sanctification, whereby the man of God is removed further and further from all fellowship with the unfruitful works of darkness and is changed from glory unto glory, into an ever-growing likeness of his Lord, who was "holy, harmless, undefiled, separate from sinners" (Heb. 7:26). Those who are sanctified in this sense have ceased to be unequally yoked with unbelievers. They have ceased to run with the multitude to do evil. They are not conformed to this present evil world. They are strangers and pilgrims upon the earth. The more assuredly this is true of them, the better.

There are some, in these apostate days, who think that the Church cannot do better than to come down to the world to learn her ways, follow her maxims, and acquire her "culture." In fact, the notion is that the world is to be conquered by our conformity to it. This is as contrary to Scripture as the light is to the darkness. The more distinct the line between him who fears God and him who does not, the better all round. It will be a black day when the sun itself is turned into darkness. When the salt has lost its savor and no longer opposes putrefaction, the world will rot with a vengeance. The text is still true, "that we are of God, and the whole world lieth in wickedness" (1 John 5:19). The seed of the woman knows no terms with the serpent brood but continual war. Our Lord says that in this matter He came not to send peace on the earth but a sword. "[B]ecause ye are not of the world, but I have chosen you out of the world, therefore the world hateth you" (John 15:19). If the Church seeks to cultivate the friendship of the world, she has this message from the Holy Ghost by the pen of the apostle James: "Ye adulterers and adulteresses, know ye not that the friendship of the world is enmity with God? whosoever therefore will be a friend of the world is the enemy of God" (James 4:4). James charges all who would please the world with the black and filthy crime of spiritual adultery. The heart that should be given to Christ and purity must not wander forth wantonly to woo the defiled and polluted things of this present evil world. Separation from the world is Christ's prayer for us.

Put these two things together—dedication to God and separation unto Him—and you are nearing the meaning of the prayer. But note that it is not all separation that is meant. There are some who "separate themselves" and yet are sensual, not having the Spirit. Separation for separation's sake savors rather of Babel than of Jerusalem. It is one thing to separate from the world and another thing to be separate from the Church. Where we believe that there is living faith in Jesus and the indwelling of the Holy Ghost, we are called not to division but to unity. For actual and manifest sin we must separate ourselves from offenders. But we err if we carry on this separation where it is not authorized by the Word of God. The Corinthians and Galatians were far from being perfect in life, and they had made many mistakes in doctrine, yea, even upon vital points. But inasmuch as they were truly in Christ, Paul did not command anyone to come out of those churches and to be separate therefrom. He exhorted them to prove each man his own work, and he labored to bring them all back to the one and only gospel and to a clearer knowledge of it.

We are to be faithful to truth, but we are not to be of a contentious spirit, separating ourselves from those who are living members of the one and indivisible body of Christ. To promote the unity of the Church by creating new divisions is not wise. Cultivate at once the love of the truth and the love of the brethren. The body of Christ will not be perfected by being rent. Truth should be the companion of love. If we heartily love even those who are in some measure in error but who possess the life of God in their souls, we shall be the more likely to set them right. Separation from the world is a solemn duty; indeed it is the hard point, the crux and burden of our religion. It is not easy to be filled with love for men and yet for God's sake, and even for their own sake, to be separated from them. May the Lord teach us this.

At the same time, this word *sanctification* means what is commonly understood by it, namely, *the making of the people of God holy.* "Sanctify them," that is, work in them a pure and holy character. "Lord, make Your people holy," should be our daily prayer. I want you to notice that this word in the Greek is not that which is rendered *purify*, but it has another shade of meaning. Had it meant purify, it would hardly have been used in reference to our Lord as it is in the next verse.

It has a higher meaning than that. O brethren, if you are called Christians, there must be no room for doubt as to the fact that you are purged from the common sins and ordinary transgressions of mankind, else are you manifestly liars to God and deceivers of your own souls. Those who are not moral, honest, kind, or truthful are far from the kingdom. How can these be the children of God who are not even decent children of men? Thus, we judge, and rightly judge, that the life of God cannot be in that man's soul who abides willfully in any known sin, taking pleasure therein. No; purification is not all. We will take it for granted that you who profess to be Christians have escaped from the foul pollution of lust and falsehood. If you have not done so, humble yourselves before God and be ashamed, for you need the very beginnings of grace. "And they that are Christ's have crucified the flesh" (Gal. 5:24). But sanctification is something more than mere morality and respectability. It is deliverance not only from the common sins of men but also from the hardness, deadness, and carnality of nature. It is a deliverance from that which is of the flesh at its very best, and it is an admittance into that which is spiritual and divine. That which is carnal comes not into communion with the spiritual kingdom of Christ. We need that the spiritual nature should rise above that which is merely natural. This is our prayer—Lord, spiritualize us. Elevate us to dwell in communion with God. Make us to know Him whom flesh and blood cannot reveal or discern. May the Spirit of the living God have full sovereignty over us and perfect in us the will of the Lord, for this is to be sanctified.

Sanctification is a higher word than purification, for it includes that word and vastly more. It is not sufficient to be negatively clean. We need to be adorned with all the virtues. If you are merely moral, how does your righteousness exceed that of the scribes and Pharisees? If you pay your lawful debts, give alms to the poor, and observe the rites of your religion, what do you more than others whom you reckon to be in error?

Children of God should exhibit the love of God. They should be filled with zeal for His glory. They should live generous, unselfish lives. They should walk with God and commune with the Most High. Ours should be a purpose and an aim far higher than the best of the unregenerate can understand. We should reach a life and a kingdom of which the mass of mankind know nothing. I am afraid that this spiritual sense of the prayer is one that is often forgotten. Oh, that God's Holy Spirit might make us to know it by experimentally feeling it in ourselves! May "Holiness to the Lord" be written across the brow of our consecrated humanity!

Beloved, this prayer of our Lord is most necessary, for without sanctification how can we be saved, since it is written: "Follow...holiness, without which no man shall see the Lord" (Heb. 12:14). How can we be saved from sin if sin still has dominion over us? If we are not living holy, godly, spiritual lives, how can we say that we are redeemed from the power of evil?

Without sanctification we shall be unfit for service. Our Lord Jesus contemplated the sending of each of us into the world even as the Father sent Him into the world. But how can He give a mission to unsanctified men and women? Must not the vessels of the Lord be clean?

Without sanctification we cannot enjoy the innermost sweets of our holy faith. The unsanctified are full of doubts and fears; and what wonder? The unsanctified often say of the outward exercise of religion, "What a weariness it is!" and no wonder, for they know not the internal joys of it, having never learned to delight themselves in God. If they walk not in the light of the Lord's countenance, how can they know the heaven below that comes of true godliness? It is a prayer that needs to be prayed for me, for you, and for the whole Church of God! "Father, sanctify them through thy truth."

For Whom This Prayer Was Offered

It was not offered for the world outside. It would not be a suitable prayer for those who are dead in sin. Our Lord referred to the company of men and women who were already saved, of whom He said that they had kept God's Word: "thine they were, and thou gavest them me" (John 17:6). They were therefore sanctified already in the sense of being consecrated and set apart for holy purposes. And they were also sanctified in a measure already in the sense of being made holy in character, for the immediate disciples of our Lord, with all their errors and deficiencies, were holy men. It was for the apostles that Jesus thus prayed, so that we may be sure that the most eminent saints need still to have this prayer offered for them: "Sanctify them through thy truths." Though, my sisters, you may be Deborahs, worthy to be called mothers in Israel, yet you need to be made more holy. Though you may be true fathers in God, of whom the Scripture says truly that we have "not many," yet you still need that Jesus should pray for you: "Sanctify them through thy truth."

These chosen ones were sanctified, but only to a degree. Justification is perfect the moment it is received, but sanctification is a matter of growth. He who is justified is justified once for all by the perfect work of Jesus, but he who is sanctified by Christ Jesus must grow up in all things into Him who is the Head. To make us holy is a lifework, and for it we should seek the divine operation every hour. We would rise to the utmost pitch of holy living and never content ourselves with present attainments. Those who are most pure and honorable have yet their shortcomings and errors to mourn over. When the Lord turns the light strong upon us, we soon see the spots upon our raiment. It is indeed when we walk in the light as God is in the light that we see most clearly our need of the cleansing blood of Jesus. If we have done well, to God be the glory of it, but we might have done better. If we have loved much, to God's grace be the praise, but we should have loved more. If we have believed steadfastly, we should have believed to a far higher degree in our Almighty Friend. We are still below our capacities. There is a something yet beyond us. O ye sanctified ones, it is for you that Jesus prays that the Father may still sanctify you.

I want you to notice more particularly that these believers for whom our Lord prayed were to be the preachers and teachers of their own and succeeding generations. These were the handful out of whom would grow the Church of the future, whose harvest would gladden all lands. To prepare them to be sent out as Christ's missionaries, they must be sanctified. How shall a holy God send out unholy messengers? An unsanctified minister is an unsent minister. An unholy missionary is a pest to the tribe he visits. An unholy teacher in a school is an injury rather than a blessing to the class he conducts. Only in proportion as you are sanctified unto God can you hope for the power of the Holy Spirit to rest on you and to work with you so as to bring others to the Savior's feet. How much may each of us have been hampered and hindered by a lack of holiness! God will not use unclean instruments; nay, He will not even have His holy vessels borne by unclean hands. "But unto the wicked God saith, What hast thou to do to declare my statutes?" (Ps. 50:16). A whole host may be defeated because of one Achan in the camp, and this is our constant fear. Holiness is an essential qualification to a man's fitness for being used of the Lord God for the extension of His kingdom. Hence, our Lord's prayer for His apostles and other workers: "Holy Father, sanctify them."

Furthermore, our Lord Jesus Christ was about to pray, "That they all may be one" (John 17:21), and for this desirable result, holiness is needed. Why are we not one? Sin is the great dividing element. The perfectly holy would be perfectly united. The more saintly men are, the more they love their Lord and one another, and thus they come into closer union with each other. Our errors and our sins are roots of bitterness that spring up and trouble us, and many are defiled. Our infirmities of judgment are aggravated by our imperfections of character and our walking at a distance from our God. These breed coldness and lukewarmness, out of which grow disunion and division, sects and heresies. If we were all abiding in Christ to the full, we should abide in union with each other and with God, and our Lord's great prayer for the unity of His Church would be fulfilled.

Moreover, our Lord finished His most comprehensive prayer by a petition that we might all be with Him—with Him where He is, that we may behold His glory (John 17:24). Full sanctification is essential to this. Shall the unsanctified dwell with Christ in heaven? Shall unholy eyes behold His glory? It cannot be. How can we participate in the splendor and triumphs of the exalted Head if we are not members of His body? How can a holy Head have impure and dishonest members? No, brethren, we must be holy, for Christ is holy. Uprightness of walk and cleanness of heart are absolutely requisite for the purposes of Christian life, whether here or here-after. Those who live in sin are the servants of sin. Only those who are renewed by the Holy Ghost unto truth and holiness and love can hope to be partakers of holy joys and heavenly bliss.

To Whom This Prayer Is Directed

"Sanctify them through thy truth." No one can sanctify a soul but Almighty God, the great Father of Spirits. He who made us must also make us holy, or we shall never attain that character. Our dear Savior calls the great God "*holy* Father" in this prayer, and it is the part of the holy God to create holiness. A holy *Father* can only be the Father of holy children, for like begets like. To you who believe in Jesus, He gives power to become the sons of God, and a part of that power lies in becoming holy according to the manner and character of our Father who is in heaven. As we are holy, so do we bear the image of that Lord from heaven who, as the second man, is the firstborn to whom the many brethren are conformed. The holy Father in heaven will own those as His children upon earth who are holy. The very nature of God should encourage us in our prayers for holiness, for He will not be slow to work in us to will and to do according to His perfect will.

Beloved, this sanctification is a work of God from its earliest stage. We go astray of ourselves, but we never return to the great Shepherd apart from His divine drawings. Regeneration, in which sanctification begins, is wholly the work of the Spirit of God. Our first discovery of wrong and our first pang of penitence are the work of divine grace. Every thought of holiness and every desire after purity must come from the Lord alone, for we are by nature wedded to iniquity. So also the ultimate conquest of sin in us and the making us perfectly like to our Lord must be entirely the work of the Lord God, who makes all things new, since we have no power to carry on so great a work of ourselves. This is a creation; can we create? This is a resurrection; can we raise the dead? Our degenerate nature can rot into a still direr putrefaction, but it never can return to purity or sweeten itself into perfection. This is of God and God alone. Sanctification is as much the work of God as the making of the heavens and the earth. Who is sufficient for these things? We go not even a step in sanctification in our own strength. Whatever we think we advance of ourselves is but a fictitious progress that will lead to bitter disappointment. Real sanctification is entirely from first to last the work of the Spirit of the blessed God, whom the Father has sent forth that He might sanctify His chosen ones. See, then, what a great thing sanctification is and how necessary it is that our Lord should pray to His Father, "Sanctify them through thy truth."

The truth alone will not sanctify a man. We may maintain an orthodox creed, and it is highly important that we should do so, but if it does not touch our heart and influence our character, what is the value of our orthodoxy? It is not the doctrine itself that sanctifies, but the Father sanctifies by means of the doctrine. The truth is the element in which we are made to live in order to attain holiness. Falsehood leads to sin, truth leads to holiness; but there is a lying spirit, and there is also the Spirit of truth, and by these the error and the truth are used as means to an end. Truth must be applied with spiritual power to the mind, the conscience, and the heart, or else a man may receive the truth and yet hold it in unrighteousness. I believe this to be the crowning work of God in man, that His people should be perfectly delivered from evil. He elected them that they might be a peculiar people, zealous for good works. He ransomed them that He might redeem them from all iniquity and purify them unto Himself. He effectually calls them to a high and holy vocation, even to virtue and true holiness.

Every work of the Spirit of God upon the new nature aims at the purification, the consecration, the perfecting of those whom God in love has taken to be His own. Yea, more; all the events of Providence around us work toward that one end. Our joys and our sorrows, our pains of body and griefs of heart, our losses and our crosses—all these are sacred medicines by which we are cured for the disease of nature and prepared for the enjoyment of perfect spiritual health. All that befalls us on our road to heaven is meant to fit us for our journey's end. Our way through the wilderness is meant to try us and to prove us, that our evils may be discovered, repented of, and overcome, and that thus we may be without fault before the throne at the last. We are being educated for the skies, prepared for the assembly of the perfect. It does not yet appear what we shall be, but we are struggling up toward it. We know that when Jesus shall appear, we shall be like Him, for we shall see Him as He is (1 John 3:2). We are rising into holiness by hard wrestling and long watching and patient waiting. These tribulations thresh our wheat and get the chaff away. These afflictions consume our dross and tin to make the gold more pure. All things work together for good to them who love God, and the net result of them all will be the presenting of the chosen unto God, not having spot or wrinkle, or any such thing.

Thus I have reminded you that the prayer for sanctification is offered to the divine Father, and this leads us to look out of ourselves and wholly to our God. Do not set about the work of sanctification yourselves as if you could perform it alone. Do not imagine that holiness will necessarily follow because you listen to an earnest preacher or unite in sacred worship. God Himself must work within you. The Holy Ghost must inhabit you. And this can only come to you by faith in the Lord Jesus. Believe in Him for your sanctification, even as you have believed for your pardon and justification. He alone can bestow sanctification upon you, for this is the gift of God through Jesus Christ our Lord.

How Sanctification
Is to Be Accomplished in Believers

Sanctify them *through thy truth:* "thy word is truth." Beloved, observe how God has joined holiness and truth together. There has been a tendency of late to divide truth of doctrine from truth of precept. Men say that Christianity is a life and not a creed. This is a part truth and very near akin to a lie. Christianity is a life that grows out of truth. Jesus Christ is the way and the truth as well as the life, and He is not properly received except He is accepted in that threefold character.

No holy life will be produced in us by the belief of falsehood. Sanctification in visible character comes out of edification in the inner faith of the heart, or otherwise it is a mere shell. Good works are the fruit of true faith, and true faith is a sincere belief of the truth. Every truth leads toward holiness; every error of doctrine, directly or indirectly, leads to sin. A twist of the understanding will inevitably bring a contortion of the life sooner or later. The straight line of truth drawn on the heart will produce a direct course of gracious walking in the life. Do not imagine that you can live on spiritual garbage and yet be in fine moral health, or that you can drink down poisonous error and yet lift up a face without spot before God. Even God Himself only sanctifies us by the truth. Only that teaching will sanctify you that is taken from God's Word. Any teaching that is not true or the truth of God cannot sanctify you. Error may puff you up, it may even make you think that you are sanctified. But there is a very serious difference between boasting of sanctification and being sanctified, and a very grave difference between setting up to be superior to others and being really accepted before God. Believe me, God works sanctification in us by the truth and by nothing else.

But what is the truth? There is the point. Is the truth that which I imagine to be revealed to me by some private communication? Am I to fancy that I enjoy some special revelation, and am I to order my life by voices, dreams, and impressions? Brethren, fall not into this common delusion. God's Word to us is in Holy Scripture. All the truth that sanctifies men is in God's Word. Do not listen to those who cry, "Lo here!" and "Lo there!" I am pestered almost every day by crazy persons and pretenders who have revelations. One man tells me that God has sent a message to me by him. I reply, "No, sir, the Lord knows where I dwell, and He is so near to me that He would not need to send to me by you." Another man announces in God's name a dogma that on the face of it is a lie against the Holy Ghost. He says the Spirit of God told him so-and-so, but we know that the Holy Ghost never contradicts Himself.

If your imaginary revelation is not according to this Word, it has no weight with us. And if it is according to this Word, it is no new thing. This Bible is enough if the Lord does but use it and quicken it by His Spirit in our hearts. Truth is neither your opinion nor mine. Jesus says, "Thy word is truth." That which sanctifies men is not only truth but also the particular truth that is revealed in God's Word: "Thy word is truth." What a blessing it is that all the truth that is necessary to sanctify us is revealed in the Word of God, so that we have not to expend our energies upon discovering truth but may to our far greater profit use revealed truth for its divine ends and purposes! There will be no more revelations; no more are needed. The canon is fixed and complete, and he who adds to it shall have added to him the plagues that are written in this Book (Rev. 22:18). What need of more when here is enough for every practical purpose? "Sanctify them through thy truth: thy word is truth."

This being so, the truth that is needful for us to receive is evidently fixed. You cannot change Holy Scripture. You may arrive more and more accurately at the original text, but for all practical purposes, the text we have is correct enough. Scripture itself cannot be broken; we cannot take from it or add to it. The Lord has never rewritten or revised His Word, nor will He ever do so. *Our* teachings are full of errors, but the Spirit mistakes not. We have the "Retractations" of Augustine, but there are no retractations with prophets and apostles. The faith has been delivered once for all to the saints, and it stands fast forever. "Thy word is truth." The Scripture alone is absolute truth, essential truth, decisive truth, authoritative truth, undiluted truth, eternal, everlasting truth. Truth given us in the Word of God is that which is to sanctify all believers to the end of time. God will use it to that end.

Learn, then, how earnestly you should search the Scriptures! See how studiously you should read this Book of God! If this is the truth, and the truth with which God sanctifies us, let us learn it, hold it, and stand fast in it. To Him who gave us the Book, let us pledge ourselves never to depart from His testimonies. To us, at any rate, God's Word is truth. "But they argue differently in the schools!" Let them argue. "But oratory with its flowery speech speaks otherwise!" Let it speak: Words are but air and tongues but clay. O God, "Thy word is truth." "But philosophers have contradicted it!" Let them contradict it. Who are they? God's Word is truth. We will go no farther while the world stands. But then let us be equally firm in our conviction that we do not know the truth aright unless it makes us holy. We do not hold truth in a true way unless it leads us to a true life. If you use the back of a knife, it will not cut. Truth has its handle and its blade, so see that you use it properly. You can make pure water kill a man. You must use every good thing aright or it will not be good. The truth, when fully used, will daily destroy sin, nourish grace, suggest noble desires, and urge to holy acts. I do pray that we may by our lives adorn the doctrine of God our Savior in all things. Some do not so. I say this to our shame and to my own hourly sorrow.

The one point of failure to be most deeply regretted would be a failure in the holiness of our church members. If you act as others do, what witness do you bear? If your family is not graciously ordered, if your business is not conducted upon principles of the strictest integrity, if your speech is questionable as to purity or truthfulness, if your life is open to serious rebuke—how can God accept you or send a blessing on the church to which you belong? It is all falsehood and deceit to talk about your being the people of God when even men of the world shame you. Your faith in the Lord Jesus must operate upon your life to make you faithful and true. It must check you here and excite you there. It must keep you back from this and drive you on to that. It must constantly operate upon thought and speech and act, or else you know nothing of its saving power. How can I speak more distinctly and emphatically? Do not come to me with your experiences and your convictions and your professions unless you sanctify the name of God in your life.

We had better quit our professions if we do not live up to them. In the name of Him who breathed this prayer just before His face was encrimsoned with the bloody sweat, let us cry mightily to the Father, "Sanctify us through Your truth; Your Word is truth." As a people, we have stuck to the Word of the Lord, but are we practically obeying it? We have determined to keep God's ways. Oh, that we might commend it by our holiness! Nothing is truth to me but this one Book, this infallibly inspired writing of the Spirit of God. It is incumbent upon us to show the hallowed influence of this Book. The vows of God are on us, that by our godly lives we should show forth His praises who has brought us out of darkness into His marvelous light. This Bible is our treasure. We prize each leaf of it. Let us bind it in the best fashion, in the finest leather of a clear, intelligent faith; then let us put a golden clasp upon it and gild its edges by a life of love, and truth, and purity, and zeal. Thus shall we commend the volume to those who have never looked within its pages. Brethren, the sacred roll, with its seven seals (Rev. 5:1), must not be held in hands defiled and polluted. But with clean hands and pure heart we must hold it forth and publish it among men. God help us so to do for Jesus' sake! Amen.

*B*efore my astonished gaze, there seems to me to rise up as from a great sea of confusion a wondrous building. I see the first stone sunk into the depths of that sea dyed with blood, and I see the top of it just emerging above lofty waves of strife and confusion. Now I see other stones built on that, all of them dyed with blood—the first apostles, all of them martyrs. I see stone rising upon stone as age succeeds age. At first, nearly all the foundations are laid in the fair vermilion of martyrdom, but the structure rises. The stones are very different, coming from Asia, Africa, America, and Europe. They are taken from among princes and from among peasants. These stones are very diverse. Perhaps while they were here they scarcely recognized that they belonged to the same building, but there they are, and for thousands of years that building goes on and on and on building, every stone being made ready. We know not how many more years that masterly edifice will take, but at the last, despite all the frowns of hell and all the power of devils, that edifice will be completed, not a single stone being lost, not one elect child of God being absent, and not one of those stones having suffered any injury or been put out of its place. And the whole so fair, so matchless, such a display of power and wisdom and love that even the hateful ones whose hearts are hard as adamant against the Most High will be compelled to say God must have sent Christ. They cannot restrain that confession when all the Church shall be one as the Father is one with Christ. Oh, happy day! Dawn on our eyes and make us to be blessed.

Chapter Six

Our Lord's Prayer
for His People's Unity

Neither pray I for these alone, but for them also which shall
believe on me through their word; That they all may be one; as
thou, Father, art in me, and I in thee, that they also may be one
in us: that the world may believe that thou hast sent me.
                                        —John 17:20–21

FOR SEVERAL YEARS I have thankfully re-
ceived the text of the first Sabbath in the year from a venerable cler-
gyman of a church in the suburbs of our city. Spared by a gracious
Providence, my good brother has sent me these two verses for my
subject with his Christian greetings. I can only hope that as we have
enjoyed together for several years a true communion of spirit in the
things of God, until one or the other of us shall be taken up to dwell
above we may walk together in holy service, loving each other fervently with a pure heart.

The most tender and touching prayer of the Master contained
in John 17 opens up to us His inmost heart. He was in Gethsemane,
and His passion was just commencing. He stood like a victim at the
altar, where the wood was already laid in order and the fire was
kindled to consume the sacrifice. Lifting up His eyes to heaven,
with true filial love gazing upon His Father's throne and resting in
humble confidence upon heaven's strength, He looked away for a
moment from the strife and resistance unto blood that was going
on below. He asked for that upon which His heart was most fully
set. This prayer, I take it, not only was the casual expression of the

Savior's desire at the last but also is a sort of model of the prayer that is incessantly going up from Him to the eternal throne. There is a difference in the mode of its offering—with sighs and tears He offered up His humble petition below, but with authority He pleads enthroned in glory now. But the plea is the same. That which He desired while still below is that which His soul pants after now that He is taken up and is glorified above.

It is significant, beloved, that the Savior should in His last moments not only desire the salvation of all His people but also plead for the unity of the saved ones, that being saved they might be united. It was not enough that each sheep should be taken from the jaw of the wolf. He would have all the sheep gathered into one fold under His own care. He was not satisfied that the members of His body should be saved as the result of His death. He must have those members fashioned into a glorious body. Unity lying so very near the Savior's heart at such a time of overwhelming trial must have been held by Him to be priceless beyond all price. It is of this unity that we study. First of all, we will have a little to say upon *the unity desired*. Then we will note *the work that was necessary—namely, that the chosen be gathered in*. That will be followed by a study of *the prayer offered, the result anticipated*, and *the question suggested*.

The Unity Desired

These words of the Savior have been perverted to the doing of a world of mischief. Ecclesiastics have fallen asleep, and while asleep they have dreamed a dream—a dream founded upon the letter of the Savior's words of which they discern not the spiritual sense. They have proved in their own case, as has been proved in thousands of others, that the letter kills and only the spirit gives life. Falling asleep, these ecclesiastics have dreamed of a great confederation, presided over by a number of ministers, these again governed by superior officers, and these again by others, and these topped at last by a supreme visible head who must be either a person or a council. This great confederacy contains within itself kingdoms and nations and becomes so powerful as to work upon states, to influence politics, to guide councils, and even to gather together and to move armies. The shadow of the Savior's teaching, "My kingdom is not of this world" (John 18:36), must have caused an occasional nightmare in the midst of their dream, but they dreamed on. And what is worse, they turned the dream into a reality, and the time was when the professed followers of Christ were all one, when looking north, south, east, and west from the center at the Vatican, one united body covered all Europe.

And what was the result? Did the world believe that God had sent Christ? The world believed the very opposite. The world was persuaded that God had nothing to do with that great crushing, tyrannous, superstitious, ignorant thing that called itself Christianity. All professors were one, but the world believed not. The fact was that this was not the unity that Jesus had so much thought of. It was never His intention to set up a great united body to be called a Church that should domineer and lord everywhere over the souls of men and comprehend within its ranks kings, princes, and statesmen who might be worldly, ungodly, hateful, sensual, devilish. It was never Christ's design to set up a conscience-crushing engine of uniformity. And so the great man-devised machine, when it was brought to perfection and set to work with the greatest possible vigor, instead of working out that the world should believe that the Father had sent Christ, wrought out just this—that the world did not believe anything at all but became infidel, licentious, and rotten at the core. The system had to be abated as a common nuisance and something better brought into the world to restore morality.

Yet people dream that dream still: Even good people do so. The Puritans, after they had been hunted and haled to prison in this country, fled to New England, and no sooner had they seated themselves upon the shore than they began to say, "We must all be one. There must be no schism." And the big whip was brought out for the Quaker's back and the manacles for the Baptist's bleeding wrists, because these men, somehow or other, would not be one after this kind of fashion but would think for themselves and obey God rather than man. Nowadays is the dream that once more all may be one. A mere dream! A mere chimera of a kindly but whimsied brain! If it should ever come to be a reality, it would prove to be a upas tree, at the roots of which every honest man must at once lay his axe.

But what did the Savior mean, "That they all may be one; as thou, Father, art in me"? We must begin at the beginning. *What were the elements of this unity that Christ so anxiously desired?* The answer is very distinctly given us in this chapter. The unity was to be composed of the people who are here called "they"—"that *they* all may be one." Will you let your eye run down the chapter to see who they are? Look in the second verse: "that he should give eternal life to as many as thou hast given him." The unity then proposed is of persons specially given to Jesus by the Father. Not, then, of all men who happen to dwell in any particular province, district, or city, but a unity of persons who have received life eternal. Special persons, then, who have been quickened by God the Holy Ghost and brought into vital union with the person of the Lord Jesus are to be one. Further, they are described in the sixth verse as persons to whom God's name has been manifested—people who have seen what others never saw and beheld what others cannot know. They are men given out of the world, so the verse tells us—chosen men, taken out from the ordinary mass. Not kingdoms, states, empires, but selected persons. They are persons who have been schooled and have learned unusual lessons: "Now they have known that all things whatsoever thou hast given me are of thee" (vs. 7). And they have learned their lesson well, for we find it written: "[T]hey have kept thy word....they have believed that thou didst send me" (vv. 6, 8). They are described in the ninth verse as being prayed for by Christ in a sense in which He never prays for the world at all. They are people, according to the tenth verse, in whom Christ is glorified, in whom the name of Jesus shines with resplendent luster. Look the whole chapter through, and you will discover that the unity that the Master intended was that of chosen persons who by the Holy Spirit conferring life upon them are led to believe in Jesus Christ. These are spiritual-minded men who live in the realm of spirit, prize spiritual things, and form a confederacy and a kingdom that is spiritual and not of this world.

Here is the secret. Carnal minds hear that Jesus is to wear a crown of pearls, so they find pearls in shells and they try to join the oyster shells together, and what a strange thing they make! But Jesus will have no union of the shells, for the shells must be struck off as worthless things. The jewels, and the jewels only, are to be joined together. It is rumored that the King is to wear a crown and that pure gold is to form that brilliant circlet. Straightway men bring their huge nuggets and would fashion the diadem of masses of rock, earth, quartz, and I know not what. But it must not be. The King wears no such crown as that. He will refine the gold, He will melt away the earth, the crown is to be made of the pure gold, not of the material with which the gold happens to be united.

The one Church of God, of what is it composed then? Is it composed of the Church of England, the Congregational Union, the Wesleyan Conference, and the Baptist body? No, it is not. Is not then the Church of England a part of the body of Christ, the Baptist denomination a part? No; I deny that these bodies as such, unrefined and in the dross, are a part of the great unity for which Jesus prayed. But there are believers united with the Church of England who are a part of the body of Christ, and there are believers in all denominations of Christians, ay! and many in no visible church at all, who are in Christ Jesus, and consequently in the great unity. The Church of England, or any other denomination as such, is not a part of Christ's true body. The spiritual unity is made up of spiritual men, separated, picked out, cleared away from all the mass with which they happen to be united. I have spoken very boldly, perhaps, and may be misunderstood; but this I mean, that you cannot take out any visible church, however pure, and say that as it stands it belongs to the spiritual unity for which Jesus prayed. There are in the visible churches a certain number of God's elect ones, and they are of the body of Jesus Christ. But their fellow professors, if unconverted, are not in the mystical unity. Christ's body is not made up of denominations or of presbyteries or of Christian societies. It is made up of saints chosen of God from before the foundation of the world, redeemed by blood, called by His Spirit, and made one with Jesus.

But now, passing on, *what is the bond that keeps these united ones together?* Among others, there is the bond of the *same origin.* Every person who is a partaker of the life of God has sprung from the same divine Father. The Spirit of God has quickened all the faithful alike. No matter that Luther may be very dissimilar from Calvin. Luther is made and created a new creature in Christ Jesus by that same fiat that created Calvin. We discover the same life in each— they have been quickened by the same Spirit and made to live by the same energy. And though they knew it not, they were still one. Nay more, all true believers are supported by the *same strength.* The life that makes vital the prayer of a believer today is the same life that quickened the cry of a believer two thousand years ago. If this world shall last so long as another thousand years, the selfsame Spirit that shall make the tear trickle from the eye of a penitent, then, is that which this day bows us before God Most High. Moreover, all believers have the *same aim* and object. Every true saint is shot from the same bow and is speeding towards the same target. There may be, there will be, much that is not of God about the man, much of human infirmity, defilement, and corruption; but still the inward spirit within him that God has put there is forcing its way to the same perfection of holiness and is meanwhile seeking to glorify God.

Above all, *the Holy Spirit,* who indwells every believer, is the true fount of oneness. Christians in this land of ours two hundred years ago were strangely different in outward manners from us, but when we talk with them through their old writings and music, we find, if we are the Lord's people, that we are quite at home with them. Though the manifestation may vary, yet the same Spirit of God works the same graces, the same virtues, the same excellencies, and thus helps all saints to prove themselves to be of one tribe. I meet an Englishman anywhere the wide world over, and I recognize in him some likeness to myself, and there is some characteristic or other about him by which his nationality is betrayed. And so I meet a Christian five hundred years back in the midst of Romanism and darkness, but his speech reveals him. If my soul shall traverse space in one hundred years to come, although Christianity may have assumed another outward garb and fashion, I shall still recognize the Christian. I shall detect the Galilean brogue still, there will be something that will show to me that if I am an heir of heaven I am one with the past and one with the future, yea, one with all the saints of the living God. This is a very different bond from that which men try to impose upon each other in order to create union. They put straps round the outside, they tie us together with many knots, and we feel uneasy. But God puts a divine life inside us, and then we wear the sacred bonds of love with ease. If you get the limbs of a dead man, you can tie them together, and then if you send the body on a journey and the carriage jolts, a leg will slip out of its place and an arm be dislocated. But get a living man and you may send him where you will, and the bandages of life will prevent his dropping asunder. In all the truly elect children of God who are called and chosen and faithful, there is a bond of divine mysterious love running right through the whole, and they are one and must be one, the Holy Ghost being the life that unites them.

There are tokens that evidence this union and prove that the people of God are one. We hear much moaning over our divisions. There may be some that are to be deplored among ecclesiastical confederacies, but in the spiritual Church of the living God, I really am at a loss to discover the divisions that are so loudly proclaimed. It strikes me that the tokens of union are much more prominent than the tokens of division. But what are they? First there is a union *in judgment* upon all vital matters. I converse with a spiritual man, and no matter what he calls himself, when we talk of sin, pardon, Jesus, the Holy Spirit, and such themes, we are agreed. We speak of our blessed Lord. My friend says that Jesus is fair and lovely; so say I. He says that he has nothing else to trust to but the precious blood; nor have I anything beside. I tell him that I find myself a poor, weak creature; he laments the same. I live in his house a little while; we pray together and you could not tell who it was that prayed, Calvinist or Arminian, we pray so exactly alike; and when we open the hymn book, very likely if he happens to be a Wesleyan he chooses to sing, "Jesus, lover of my soul." I will sing it, and the next morning he will sing with me, "Rock of ages, cleft for me." If the Spirit of God is in us, we are all agreed upon great points. Let me say that among true saints the points of union even in matters of judgment are ninety-nine, and the points of difference are only as one.

In *experimental points,* as face answereth to face, so does the heart of man to man. Only get upon experimental topics concerning soul dealings with God, leave the letter and get to the spirit, crack the shells and eat the kernel of spiritual truth, and you will find that the points of agreement between genuine Christians are something marvelous. But this union is to be seen most plainly in union of *heart.* I am told that Christians do not love each other. I am very sorry if that is true, but I rather doubt it, for I suspect that those who do not love each other are not Christians. Where the Spirit of God is, there must be love, and if I have once known and recognized any man to be my brother in Christ Jesus, the love of Christ constrains me no more to think of him as a stranger or foreigner but as a fellow citizen with the saints. Now I hate High Churchism as my soul hates Satan, but I love George Herbert, although George Herbert is a desperately High Churchman. I hate his High Churchism, but I love George Herbert from my very soul, and I have a warm corner in my heart for every man who is like him. Let me find a man who loves my Lord Jesus Christ as George Herbert did, and I do not ask myself whether I shall love him or not. There is no room for question, for I cannot help myself. Unless I can leave off loving Jesus Christ, I cannot cease loving those who love Him. Here is George Fox, the Quaker, a strange sort of body, it is true, going about the world making much noise and stir. But I love the man with all my soul because he had an awful respect for the presence of God and an intense love for everything spiritual. How is it that I cannot help loving George Herbert and George Fox, who are in some things complete opposites? Because they both loved the Master. I will defy you, if you have any love for Jesus Christ, to pick or choose among His people. You may hate as much as you will the shells in which the pearls lie and the dross with which the gold is mixed, but the true, the precious blood-bought gold, the true pearl, heaven-dyed, you must esteem. You must love a spiritual man, find him wherever you may. Such love does exist among the people of God, and if anybody says it does not, I can only fear that the speaker is unfit to judge. If I come across a man in whom there is the Spirit of Christ, I *must* love him, and if I did not I should prove I was not in the unity at all.

Oneness in judgment, in experience, and in heart are some of the evidences of this union, but if you want more plain and palpable union, which even carnal eyes can see, note the unity of Christian *prayer.* Oh, how slight the difference there! Well-taught believers address the throne of grace in the same style, whatever may be the particular form that their church organization may have assumed. So is it with *praise.* There, indeed, we are as one, and our music goes up with sweet accord to the throne of the heavenly grace. Beloved, we are one in *action.* True Christians anywhere are all doing the same work. Here is a brother preaching; I do not care about what white thing he has on, but if he is a genuine Christian, he is preaching Christ crucified. And here am I, and he may not like me because I have not that white rag on, but still I delight to preach Christ crucified. When you come to the real lifework of the Christian, it is the same in every case, it is holding up the cross of Christ. "Oh," say you, "but there are many Christians in the world preaching this and that and the other." I am saying nothing of them or about them, about their ecclesiastical belongings, about those who merely cling to the church. I am speaking of the elect, the precious ones, the simpleminded, Christ-taught men and women, and their motive of action is the same, and there is among them a true union that is the answer to our Lord's prayer. He did not plead in vain, what He sought He has obtained. The truly quickened are this day one and shall evermore remain so.

I think I hear someone saying, "But I cannot see this unity." One reason may be because of your lack of information. I saw a large building the other day being erected, and I was puzzled about how that would make a complete structure. It seemed to me that the gables would come in so very awkwardly. But I dare say if I had seen a plan, there might have been some central tower or some combination by which the wings, one of which appeared to be longer than the other, might have been brought into harmony, for the architect doubtless had a unity in his mind that I had not in mine. So you and I have not the necessary information as to what the Church is to be. The unity of the Church is not to be seen by you today. The plan is not worked out yet. God is building over yonder, and you see only the foundation. In another part, the topstone is all but ready, and you cannot comprehend it. Shall the Master show you His plan? Is the Divine Architect bound to take you into His studio to show you all His secret motives and designs? Not so; wait awhile and you will find that all these diversities and differences among spiritually minded men, when the master plan comes to be worked out, are different parts of the grand whole, and you with the astonished world will then know that God has sent the Lord Jesus. I go into a great factory and see a wheel spinning away in a manner completely different from every other wheel; there are all sorts of motions concentric and eccentric; and I say, "What an extraordinary muddle this all seems!" Just so! I do not understand the machinery. So when I go into the great visible Church of God, if I look with the eyes of my spirit, I can see the inner harmony. But if with these eyes I look upon the great outward Church, I cannot see it, nor will it ever be seen till the hidden Church shall be made manifest at the appearing of the Lord.

The reason you do not see the unity of the Church may be because of the present roughness of the material. See yonder a pile of stones and a cluster of trees; I cannot see the unity. Of course not. When these trees are all cut into planks, when these stones are all squared, then you may begin to see them as a whole. The various stones of the divine building of the Church are all out of shape at present; they are not polished. We shall never be one till we are sanctified. The unity of Christ is a unity of holy, not unholy, beings. And as we each grow more and more prepared by the work of Christ for our own place, we shall discover more and more the unity of the Church.

Perhaps, too, let me remark, we cannot see the unity of the Church because we ourselves cannot see anything. Is that a hard saying? Who can bear it? There are thousands of professors who cannot see anything. Do not suppose, dear friends, that the unity of the Church is a thing that is to be seen by these eyes of ours. Never! Everything spiritual is spiritually discerned. You must get spiritual eyes before you can see it. Many people say there is no unity. I should be astonished if there were any that they could see or feel. They are not in Christ themselves. Their hearts have never felt what spiritual life means. How should they be able to understand that into which they have never entered? Jesus says, "That they all may be one; as thou, Father, art in me." "I know what that means," says Carnal-mind. "They are all to worship after the same fashion and use the same ritual." That is all poor Carnal-mind knows about it. He confounds the outward with the inward and misses the Lord's meaning. But, beloved, you know better than this. You do know, I trust, and feel that the true saints of the living God are one with each other at this very moment and that they recognize and discover this unity in proportion as they become like their Lord and Master, being conformed to His image and made fit for the place that they are to occupy. Just as a professor can take up a bone and from that one bone discover the whole structure of the entire animal, I do not doubt but what there is a mutual dependence and consistency between every Christian and his fellows, so that if we understood the science of spiritual comparative anatomy, as we may do in heaven, we should be able to form from any one Christian the fashion of the entire Church of God, from the mutual dependence of one upon the other.

The Work That Is to Be Done

There are many chosen ones who have not yet believed in Jesus Christ, and the Church cannot be one till they are saved. Here is work to be done by other chosen instruments. These chosen ones are to believe—that is a work of grace—but they are to believe through our word. Brethren, if you would promote the unity of Christ's Church, look after His lost sheep, seek out wandering souls. If you ask what is to be your word, the answer is in the text— it is to be concerning Christ. They are to believe in Him. Every soul that believes in Christ is built into the great gospel unity in its measure, and you will never see the Church as a whole while there is one soul left unsaved for whom the Savior shed His precious blood. Go out and teach His Word. Declare the doctrines of grace as He has given you ability. Hold up Christ before the eyes of men, and you will be the means in God's hand of bringing them to believe in Him, and so the Church shall be built up and made one. Here is work for the beginning of the year that lasts till the end of the year. Do not sit down and scheme and plot and plan how this denomination may melt into the other. Let that alone. Your business now is to go and "tell to sinners round what a dear Savior you have found," for that is God's way of using you to complete the unity of His Church. Unless these sinners are saved, the Church is not perfect. That is to say, saints in heaven cannot be perfect unless *we* get there. What! The blessed saints in heaven not perfect except the rest of believers come there? So the Scripture tells us, for they would be a part of the body and not a whole body. They cannot be perfect as a flock unless the rest of the sheep come there. They beckon us from the battlements of heaven and say to us, "Come up hither, for without you we cannot be one as Jesus Christ is one with His Father. We are an imperfect body till you come." And we from our position of grace turn round to the sinful world and say to the chosen of God from among that sinful world, "Come to Jesus! Trust Jesus! Believe in Him! For without you we cannot be perfect, nor can the heavenly ones themselves be, for there must be one complete Church! The city must be walled all round. And if there is one gap in the wall, the city will not be one. Come, then, put your trust in Jesus, that His Church may be one."

The Prayer Offered

Beloved, Christ prays for the unity of His Church, that all saints who have gone to heaven in days gone by, that all saints who live now, that all who ever live may be brought into the unity of the one life in Himself. We do not attach enough importance to the power of Christ's prayer, I fear. We think of Joshua fighting in the valley, but we forget our Moses with hands outstretched upon the hill. We are looking at the wheels of the machine, and we are thinking that this wheel or that or the other is needing more oil or not working exactly to its point. Ah, but let us never forget the engine, that mysterious motive force that is hidden and concealed, upon which the action of the whole depends! Christ's prayer for His people is the great motive force by which the Spirit of God is sent to us, and the whole Church is kept filled with life. And the whole of that force is tending to this one thing—to unity. It is removing everything that keeps us from being one; it is working with all its divine omnipotence to bring us into a visible unity when Christ shall stand in the latter days upon the earth. Beloved, let us have hope for sinners yet unconverted; Christ is praying for them. Let us have hope for the entire body of the faithful; Christ is praying for their unity, and what He prays for must be effected, for He never pleads in vain. He prays that the Church may be one, and it is one. He prays that they may be perfect and complete, and it shall be amidst eternal hallelujahs.

The Result Anticipated

"That the world may believe that thou hast sent me." The effect of the sight of the complete Church upon human minds will be overwhelming. Angels and principalities will look at Christ's perfect Church with awe. They will all exclaim, "What a marvel! What a wonder! What a masterpiece of divine power and wisdom!" When they saw the foundation laid in the precious blood of Christ, they gazed long and wistfully. But when they see the whole Church complete, every spire and pinnacle, and the great topstone brought out with shouting, all built of precious jewels and pearls, fashioned like unto the similitude of a palace, why they will make heaven ring again and again. When the world was made they sang for joy, but how shall the vaults of heaven echo when the Church is all complete and the new creation shall have been perfected!

What will be the effect upon men? Astonishment will be the effect upon angels, but what upon men? Why the world, the wicked world that rejected Christ, that wicked crucifying world that would have none of Him and now will have none of His people, that wicked world that hates His saints and has strived with all its might to pluck down the walls of His Church, will believe, will be compelled to believe, that God has sent His Son. They will bite their tongues with rage, they will gnash their teeth with horror, but there will be no doubt about it. Do not suppose that the world will ever be convinced so as to believe in Christ and to be saved by the unity of the Church. It is not anticipated in John 17 that the whole world ever will be saved. That is not dreamed of the whole chapter through—the world is spoken of as something for which Christ does not pray, whose enlightenment is not anticipated. But that world, though it weeps and wails and curses and abhors, shall be made distinctly to recognize the divinity of Christ's mission when it shall see the entire unity of the Church.

Before my astonished gaze, there seems to me to rise up as from a great sea of confusion a wondrous building. I see the first stone sunk into the depths of that sea dyed with blood, and I see the top of it just emerging above lofty waves of strife and confusion. Now I see other stones built on that, all of them dyed with blood—the first apostles, all of them martyrs. I see stone rising upon stone as age succeeds age. At first, nearly all the foundations are laid in the fair vermilion of martyrdom, but the structure rises. The stones are very different, coming from Asia, Africa, America, and Europe. They are taken from among princes and from among peasants. These stones are very diverse. Perhaps while they were here they scarcely recognized that they belonged to the same building, but there they are, and for thousands of years that building goes on and on and on building, every stone being made ready. We know not how many more years that masterly edifice will take, but at the last, despite all the frowns of hell and all the power of devils, that edifice will be completed, not a single stone being lost, not one elect child of God being absent, and not one of those stones having suffered any injury or been put out of its place. And the whole so fair, so matchless, such a display of power and wisdom and love that even the hateful ones whose hearts are hard as adamant against the Most High will be compelled to say God must have sent Christ. They cannot restrain that confession when all the Church shall be one as the Father is one with Christ. Oh, happy day! Dawn on our eyes and make us to be blessed.

Are We a Part of That Great Unity?

There is the question. It is not, Are you a member of a Christian church? That is a carnal question. You may be very grievously mistaken if that is your argument. But if you can go another way to work and say, "I have received eternal life, for I have believed in the Lord Jesus Christ and I am given of the Father unto Him." Why then, beloved, you come at it directly. Being one with Christ, you are one with His people.

Do not look for a matter that is to be written on sheets of paper, on rolls and books, but look for a bond written on hearts and consciences and souls. Do not be looking for all saints all in one room but in Christ, all living upon heavenly bread and drinking of the wines on the lees well refined that come from Christ Jesus. Look for a spiritual union and you will find it. If you look for the other thing, you will not find it, and if you did find it, it would be a great and awful thing, from which you might pray God to deliver His Church. Spiritual men, look for spiritual unity by first asking whether you are spiritual yourself. Have you been born into the family? Have you been washed with the blood? Have you passed from death to life? If not, even if you could be in the body, you would be as a dead substance in the body working a fester, a gangrene, necessitating pain and suffering. You would be a thing accursed, to be cast away. But are you alive by the life of Christ? Does God dwell in you, and do you dwell in Him? Then give me your hand. Never mind about a thousand differences. If you are in Christ and I am in Christ, we cannot be two; we must be one.

Let us love each other with a pure heart fervently. Let us live on earth as those who are to live together a long eternity in heaven. Let us help each other's spiritual growth. Let us aid each other as far as possible in every holy, spiritual enterprise that is for the promotion of the kingdom of the Lord. Let us chase out of our hearts everything that would break the unity that God has established. Let us cast from us every false doctrine, every false thought of pride, of enmity, of envy, of bitterness, that we whom God has made one may be one before men as well as before the eye of the heart-searching God. May the Lord bless us, dear friend, as a Church, make us one, and keep us so. For it will be the dead stuff among us that will make the divisions. It is the living children of God who make the unity. It is the living ones who are bound together. There will be no fear about that—Christ's prayer takes care of us, that we shall be one. As for those of you who are joined with us in invisible fellowship and are not one with Christ, may the Lord save you with His great salvation, and His shall be the praise. Amen and Amen.

ever

*H*ow shall the chosen get home to the Father? Chariots are provided. Here are the chariots of fire and horses of fire in this prayer. "I will," says Jesus, "that they be with me"; and with Him they must be. There are difficulties in the way—long nights and darkness lie between, and hills of guilt and forests of trouble and bands of fierce temptations. Yet the pilgrims shall surely reach their journey's end, for the Lord's "I will" shall be a wall of fire round about them. In this petition I see both sword and shield for the Church militant. Here I see the eagles' wings on which they shall be upborne till they enter within the golden gates. Jesus says, "I will," and who is he who shall hinder the homecoming of the chosen? He may as well hope to arrest the marches of the stars of heaven.

Chapter Seven

Our Lord's Prayer of Glory

*Father, I will that they also, whom thou hast given me, be with
me where I am; that they may behold my glory, which thou hast
given me: for thou lovedst me before the foundation of the world*
—John 17:24

THE PRAYER OF THE SAVIOR rises as it
proceeds. Jesus asked for His people that they might be preserved
from the world, then that they might be sanctified, and then that
they might be made manifestly one. Now He reaches His crowning
point—that they may be with Him where He is and behold His
glory. It is well when in prayer the spirit takes to itself wings. The
prayer that swings to and fro like a door upon its hinges may admit
to fellowship, but that prayer is more after the divine pattern that,
like a ladder, rises round by round until it loses itself in heaven.

This last step of our Lord's prayer not only is above all the rest
but also is a longer step than any of the others. He here ascends, not
from one blessing that may be enjoyed on earth to another of higher
degree, but He mounts right away from all that is of this present
state into that which is reserved for the eternal future. He quits the
highest peaks of grace, and at a single stride, His prayer sets its foot
in glory: "That they also, whom thou hast given me, be with me
where I am."

There is this to be noticed also concerning this divine prayer,
that not only does it rise as to its subject, but it even ascends as to

the place where the Intercessor appears to occupy. Has it not been so with yourselves in prayer at times that you have hardly known where you were? You might have cried with Paul, "Whether in the body,...or whether out of the body, I cannot tell" (2 Cor. 12:2). Do not these words of our Lord Jesus remind you of this? Was He not carried away by the fervor of His devotion? Where was He when He uttered the words of our text? If I follow the language, I might conclude that our Lord was already in heaven. He says, "Father, I will that they also, whom thou hast given me, be with me where I am; that they may behold my glory." Does He not mean that they should be in heaven with Him? Of course He does. Yet He was not in heaven. He was still in the midst of His apostles, in the body upon earth. He had yet Gethsemane and Golgotha before Him ere He could enter His glory. He had prayed Himself into such an exaltation of feeling that His prayer was in heaven and He Himself was there in spirit. What a hint this gives to us! How readily may we quit the field of battle and the place of agony and rise into such fellowship with God that we may think and speak and act as if we were already in possession of our eternal joy! By the ardor of prayer and the confidence of faith we may be caught up into Paradise and there utter words that are beyond the latitude of earth.

Nor is this all, for still the prayer not only rises as to its matter and place but also, in a very singular way, takes to itself a higher style. Before, our Lord has asked and pleaded. But now He uses a firmer word: He says, "Father, I will." I would not force that word so as to make it bear an imperious or commanding meaning, for the Savior speaks not so to the Father. But still it has a more elevated tone about it than asking. Our Lord here uses the royal manner rather than the tone of His humiliation. He speaks like the Son of God; He addresses the great Father as one who counts it not robbery to be equal with Him but exercises the prerogative of His eternal Sonship. He says, "I will." This is a tone that belongs not to us except in a very modified degree, but it teaches us a lesson.

It is well in prayer, when the Holy Spirit helps us, not only to groan out of the dust as suppliant sinners but also to seek our Father in the spirit of adoption with the confidence of children, and then with the promise of God in our hand, we may with consecrated bravery lay hold upon the covenant angel and cry, "I will not let thee go, except thou bless me" (Gen. 32:26). Importunity is a humble approach to this divine "I will." The will consecrated, educated, and sanctified may and must reveal itself in our more spiritual petitions, just as, with equal correctness, it hides away when the pleading is for temporal things and whispers, "[N]ot as I will, but as thou wilt" (Matt. 26:39). The Lord pours upon His pleading servants at times a kind of inspiration by which they rise into power in prayer and have their will of the Lord. Is it not written: "Delight thyself also in the LORD; and he shall give thee the desires of thine heart" (Ps. 37:4)? We come at last to feel that the desires of our heart are inspired of His Spirit and then that we have the petitions that we have asked of Him.

There is much for our edification in a text like this, which in subject, place, and style rises to such an elevation. It is the apex of this wonderful pyramid of prayer; the last round of the ladder of light. O Spirit of the Lord, instruct us while we behold it!

I have taken this text because it has taken hold on me. A beloved brother, Charles Stanford, has just been taken from our church. I seem to be standing as one of a company of disciples, and my brethren are melting away. My brethren, my comrades, my delights, are leaving me for the better land. We have enjoyed holy and happy fellowship in days of peace, and we have stood shoulder to shoulder in the battle of the Lord, but we are melting way. One has gone; another has gone; before we look round, another will have departed. We see them for a moment, and they vanish from our gaze. It is true they do not rise into the air like the divine Master from Olivet; yet do they rise, I am persuaded of that. Only the poor body descends, and that descent is for a very little while. They rise, to be forever with the Lord. The grief is to us who are left behind. What a gap is left where stood Hugh Stowell Brown! Who is to fill it? What a gap is left where stood Charles Stanford! Who is to fill it? Who among us will go next? We stand like men amazed. Some of us stood next in the rank with those who have been taken.

Why this constant thinning of our ranks while the warfare is so stern? Why this removal of the very best when we so much need the noblest examples? I am bowed down and could best express myself in a flood of tears as I survey the line of graves so newly dug. But I restrain myself from so carnal a mode of regarding the matter and look upon it in a clearer light. The Master is gathering the ripest of His fruit, and well does He deserve them. His own dear hand is putting His apples of gold into His baskets of silver, and as we see that it is the Lord, we are bewildered no longer. His Word, as it comes before us in the text, calms and quiets our spirits. It dries our tears and calls us to rejoicing as we hear our heavenly Bridegroom praying, "Father, I will that they also, whom thou hast given me, be with me where I am." We understand why the dearest and best are going. We see in whose hand is held the magnet that attracts them to the skies. One by one they must depart from this lowland country to dwell in the palace of the King, for Jesus is drawing them to Himself. Our dear babes go home because "he shall gather the lambs with his arm, and carry them in his bosom" (Isa. 40:11). Our ripe saints go home because the Beloved is come into His garden to gather lilies. These words of our Lord Jesus explain the continual homegoing. They are the answer to the riddle that we call death.

The Home Word

The rallying word is *Father*. Observe, our Lord had said, "Holy Father," and toward the close of the prayer, He said, "O righteous Father." But in commencing this particular petition, He uses the word *Father* by itself. This relationship is in itself so dear that it agrees best with the loftiest petition. I like to think of that name "Father" as used in this connection. Is it not the center of living unity? If there is to be a family gathering and reunion, where should it be but in the father's house? Who is at the head of table but the father? All the interests of the children unite in the parent, and he feels for them all.

From the great Father, the Lord Jesus Himself came forth. We do not understand the doctrine of the eternal Trinity—we adore the mystery into which we may not pry. But we know that as our Lord Jesus is God-and-man Mediator, He came forth from the Father, and unto the Father's will He submitted Himself in so doing. As for us, we come distinctly of that Father. It is He that made us and not we ourselves, and of His own will begat He us by the word of truth. We were born a second time from heaven, and from our heavenly Father our spiritual life is derived.

Throughout this chapter I want to show you that it is right that we should part with our brethren and joyfully permit their going home. What can be more right than that children should go home to their Father? From Him they came, to Him they owe their life; should they not always tend toward Him, and should not this be the goal of their being, that they should at last dwell in His presence? To go away from the Father and to live apart from Him is the sorrow of our fallen nature as it plays the prodigal. But the coming back to the Father is restoration to life, to peace, to happiness. Yes, all our hopeful steps are toward the Father. We are saved when by believing in the name of Jesus we receive power to become the sons of God. Our sanctification lies in the bosom of our adoption. Because Jesus comes from the Father and leads us back to the Father, thus there is a heaven for us. Whenever we think of heaven, let us therefore chiefly think of the Father, for it is in our Father's house that there are many mansions. And it is to the Father that our Lord has gone, that He may prepare a place for us.

"FATHER!" Why, it is a bell that rings us home. He who has the spirit of adoption feels that the Father draws him home, and he would fain run after Him. How intensely did Jesus turn to the Father! He cannot speak of the glory wherein He is to be without coupling His Father with it. Brethren, it is in the Father that we live and move and have our being. Is there any spiritual life in the world that does not continually proceed from the life of the great Father? Is it not by the continual outcoming of the Holy Ghost from the Father that we remain spiritual men? And as from Him we live, so for Him we live, if we live aright. We wish so to act as to glorify God in everything. Even our salvation should not be an ultimate end; we should desire to glorify God by our salvation. We look upon the doctrines that we preach and the precepts that we obey as means to the glory of God, even the Father.

This is the consummation that the Firstborn looks for and to which all of us who are like Him are aspiring also, namely, that God may be all in all, that the great Father may be had in honor and may be worshiped in every place. Since, then, we are from Him and of Him and to Him and for Him, this word *Father* calls us to gather at His feet. Shall any one of us lament the process? No; we dare not complain that our choicest brethren are taken up to gladden the great Father's house. Our brother is gone, but we ask, "Where is he gone?" When the answer comes, "He is gone to the Father," all notion of complaint is over. To whom else should he go? When the great Firstborn went away from us, He told His sorrowing followers that He was going to their Father and His Father; and that answer was enough. So, when our friend or our child or our wife or our brother is gone, it is enough that he or she is with the Father. To call any of them back does not occur to us, but rather we each one desire to follow after them all.

> *Father, I long, I faint to see*
> *The place of Thine abode;*
> *I'd leave Thine earthly courts and flee*
> *Up to Thy seat My God.*

A child may be happy at college, but he longs for the holidays. Is it merely to escape his lessons? Ah, no! Ask him, and he will tell you, "I want to go home to see my father." The same is equally true, and possibly more so, if we include the feminine form of parentage. What a home cry is that of "mother!" The sight of that dear face has been longed and hungered for by many a child when far away. Mother and father, they are blended in the great Fatherhood of God. Let it but be said that anyone has gone to his father, and no further question is asked as to the right of his going there. To the father belongs the first possession of the child; should he not have his own child at home? The Savior wipes our tears away with a handkerchief that is marked in the corner with this word—*Father*.

The Home Impetus

The force that draws us home lies in the words, "I will." Jesus Christ, our most true God, veiled in human form, bows His knee and prays, throwing His divine energy into the prayer for the bringing home of His redeemed. This one irresistible, everlastingly almighty prayer carries everything before it. "Father, I will that they also, whom thou hast given me, be with me where I am" is the centripetal force that is drawing all the family of God toward its one home.

How shall the chosen get home to the Father? Chariots are provided. Here are the chariots of fire and horses of fire in this prayer. "I will," says Jesus, "that they be with me"; and with Him they must be. There are difficulties in the way—long nights and darkness lie between, and hills of guilt and forests of trouble and bands of fierce temptations. Yet the pilgrims shall surely reach their journey's end, for the Lord's "I will" shall be a wall of fire round about them. In this petition I see both sword and shield for the Church militant. Here I see the eagles' wings on which they shall be upborne till they enter within the golden gates. Jesus says, "I will," and who is he who shall hinder the homecoming of the chosen? He may as well hope to arrest the marches of the stars of heaven.

Examine the energy of this "I will" for a moment, and you will see, first, that it has the force of *an intercessory prayer.* It is a gem from that wonderful breastplate of jewels that our Great High Priest wore upon His breast when He offered His fullest intercession. I cannot imagine our Lord's interceding in vain. If He asks that we may be with Him where He is, He must assuredly have His request. It is written, that He "was heard in that he feared" (Heb. 5:7). When with strong crying and tears He poured out His soul unto death, His Father granted the requests of His heart. I do not wonder it should be so. How could the best Beloved fail of that which He sought in intercession from His Father God! Mark, then, that the force of irresistible intercession is drawing every blood-bought soul into the place where Jesus is. You cannot hold your dying babe when Jesus asks for it to be with Him. Will you come into competition with your Lord? Surely you will not. You cannot hold your aged father, nor detain your beloved mother, beyond the time appointed. The intercession of Christ has such a force about it that they must ascend even as sparks must seek the sun.

More than intercession is found in the expression "I will." It suggests the idea of *a testamentary bequest and appointment.* The Lord Jesus is making His last will and testament, and He writes, "Father, I will that they also, whom thou hast given me, be with me." No man who makes his will likes to have it frustrated. Our Savior's testament will assuredly be carried out in every jot and tittle, for not only did He die, and thus make His will valid, but He lives again to be His own executor and to carry out His will. When I read in our Lord's testament the words, "Father, I will that they be with me," I ask, "Who is to hold them back?" They must in due time be with Him, for the will of the ever-blessed Savior must be carried out. There can be no standing against a force of that kind.

Nor is this all. Not only do the words read to me like intercession and testamentary decree, but also they show a strong expression of *desire, resolve, and purpose.* Jesus desires it and says, "I will." It is a deliberate desire—a forcible, distinct, resolute, determined purpose. The will of God is supreme law. It does not need that He should speak. He does but will or purpose, and the thing is done. Now read my text: "I will that they be with me." The Son of God wills it. How are the saints to be hindered from what the Lord wills? They must rise from their beds of dust and silent clay; they must rise to be with Jesus where He is, for Jesus wills it. By your anxious care you may seek to detain them. You may sit about their bed and nurse them both night and day, but they must quit these dark abodes when Jesus gives the signal. You may clutch them with affectionate eagerness and even cry in despair, "They shall not go, we cannot bear to part with them"; but go they must when Jesus calls. Would you set at naught His testament? You could not if you would; you would not if you could. Rather be inclined to go with them than think to resist the heavenly attraction that upraises them. If Jesus says, "I will," it is yours to say, "Not as I will, but as You will. They were never so much mine as they are Yours. I never had so much right to them as You have who has bought them. They never so truly could be at home with me as they will be at home with You in Your bosom. So my will dissolves itself into Your will, and I say with steadfast resignation, 'Let them go.'"

Brothers and sisters, you perceive the forces that are bearing away our beloved ones. I see tender hands reaching after us; they are invisible to sense but palpable to faith. Cords of love are being cast about the chosen, and they are being drawn out secretly from their fellows. Would you break those bands asunder and cast those cords from us? I beseech you, think not so. But let the pierced hand that bought the beloved ones seek out its own purchase and bring them home. Should not Jesus have His own? Do we not bow our knee and pray for Jesus, "Thy will be done on earth, as it is in heaven"?

Note the Home Character

"Father, I will that *they also, whom thou hast given me*, be with me where I am." The description is "they also, whom thou hast given me." The Greek is somewhat difficult to translate. There is here a something in the singular as well as persons in the plural. "Father, I will concerning *that* which Thou hast given Me, that *they* may be with Me where I am." Our Lord looked upon those whom the Father gave Him as one—one body, one Church, one bride. He willed that as a whole the Church should be with Him where He is. Then He looked again and saw each of the many individuals of whom the one Church is composed, and He prayed that each, that all of these, might be with Him and behold His glory. Jesus never so prays for the whole Church as to forget a single member. Neither does He so pray for the members individually as to overlook the corporate capacity of the whole. Sweet thought! Jesus wills to have the whole of what He bought with His precious blood with Him in heaven. He will not lose any part. He did not die for a part of a church, nor will He be satisfied unless the entire flock that He has purchased shall be gathered around Him.

But while the Lord looks at those whom His Father gave Him as one body, He looks upon you and me as a part of that great unity, and His prayer is that all of us may be with Him. I believe that He prays as much for the least as for the greatest, as much for Benjamin as for Judah, as much for the despondent as for those who are fully assured. The prayer is one of great breadth and comprehensiveness, but yet it is not the prayer that those who believe in universalism would put into His mouth. He does not pray that those who die unbelievers may be with Him where He is. Neither does He will that souls in hell should one day come out of it and be with Him in glory. There is no trace of that doctrine in holy writ. Those who teach such fables draw their inspiration from some other source. The new purgatory, in which so many have come to believe, is unknown to Holy Scripture. No, our Lord's prayer is distinctly for those whom the Father gave Him—for every one of these, but for no others. His "I will" concerns them only.

I am glad that there is no sort of personal character mentioned here, but only "those whom thou hast given me." It seems as if the Lord in His last moments was not so much looking at the fruit of grace as at grace itself. He did not so much note either the perfections or the imperfections of His people, but noted only the fact that they were His by the eternal gift of the Father. They belonged to the Father: "Thine they were." The Father gave them to Jesus: "Thou gavest them Me." The Father gave them as a love token and a means of His Son's glorification: "Thine they were, and Thou gavest them Me." And now our Lord pleads that because they were the Father's gift to Him, He should have them with Him. Does anybody raise an objection to Christ's right to have those with Him who were His Father's, whom His Father gave Him, and whom He Himself actually took into His own possession? No, they should be with Him, since they are His in so divine a manner.

If I possess a love token that some dear one has given me, I may rightly desire to have it with me. Nobody can have such a right to your wedding ring as you have yourself. And are not Christ's saints, as it were, a signet upon His finger, a token that His Father gave Him of His good pleasure in Him? Should they not be with Jesus where He is, since they are His crown jewels and His glory? We in our creature love lift up our hands and cry, "My Lord, my Master, let me have this dear one with me a little longer. I need the companionship of one so sweet, or life will be misery to me." But if Jesus looks us in the face and says, "Is your right better than Mine?," we draw back at once. He has a greater part in His saints than we can have. O Jesus, Your Father gave them to You of old. They are His reward for the travail of Your soul, and far be it from us to deny You. Though blinded by our tears, we can yet see the rights of Jesus, and we loyally admit them. We cry concerning our best beloved, "[T]he LORD hath taken away; blessed be the name of the LORD" (Job 1:21). Does not the text sweetly comfort us in the taking away of one and another, since it shows how they belong to Christ?

The Home Companionship

Those who are taken away, where are they gone? The text states: "I will that they also whom thou hast given me be with me where I am; that they may behold my glory." By this language we are impressed with *the nearness of the saints to Christ in glory:* "that they may be with me." When our Lord used these words and John took them down, the disciples were with Him. They had left the supper table where they had feasted together. The Master had said, "Arise, let us go hence," and it was in the very midst of them that the Lord Jesus offered this choice prayer. Learn, then, that in heaven the saints will be nearer to Christ than the apostles were when they sat at the table with Him or heard Him pray. That was a nearness that might consist only in place, and their minds might still be, as they often were, far away from Him. But up in heaven we shall be one with Him in sympathy, in spirit, in conscious fellowship. We shall be with Jesus in the closest, clearest, and most complete sense. No fellowship on earth can reach to the plenitude of the communion that we shall enjoy above. "With Him"—"forever with the Lord"—this is heaven. Who would wish to detain from such companionship those whom we love?

Yet do not drop the thought of place lest you refine away the essence of the prayer. Let us see the spiritual clearly, but let us not, on that account, make the sense less real, less matter of fact. To the prayer that His saints may be with Him, our Lord added the words, "may be with Me where I am." Our bodies will rise from the dust, and they *must occupy a place*: That place will be where Jesus is. Even spirits must be somewhere, and that somewhere with us is to be where Jesus is. We are to be, not metaphorically and fancifully but really, truly, literally, with Jesus. We shall enjoy an intense nearness to Him in that blessed place that the Father has prepared for Him and that He is preparing for us. There is a place where Jesus is revealed in all the splendor of His majesty amid angels and glorified spirits. Those whom our Lord's will has taken away from us have not gone into banishment in a mysterious land; neither are they shut up in a house of detention till there is a general jail delivery, but they are with Christ in Paradise. They serve Him, and they see His face. Who would be so cruel as to keep a saint from such a fair country? I would desire all good for my children, my relatives, my friends; and what good is better than to be where Jesus is? Are you not glad to hear of the promotion of those you love? Will you quarrel with God because some of your dearest ones are promoted to the skies? The thought of their amazing bliss greatly moderates our natural grief. We weep for ourselves, but as we remember their companionship with the altogether lovely One, a smile blends with our tears.

Notice the *occupation* of those who are with Jesus: "that they may behold my glory." I do not wonder that Jesus wants His dear ones to be with Him for this purpose, since love always desires for a partner in its joys. When I have been abroad and have been specially charmed with glorious scenery, I have a hundred times felt myself saying, almost involuntary, "How I wish that my dear wife could be here! I should enjoy this a hundred times as much if she could but see it!" It is an instinct of affection to seek fellowship in joy. The Lord Jesus is truly human, and He feels this unselfish desire of every loving human heart and therefore says, "Father, I will that they be with Me where I am, that they may behold My glory." Our Lord graciously permits His disciples to have fellowship with Him in His sufferings, and hence He is all the more desirous that they should participate in His glory. He knows that nothing will be a greater joy to them than to see *Him* exalted. Therefore He would give them this highest form of delight. Was not Joseph delighted when he said to his brethren, "And ye shall tell my father of all my glory in Egypt" (Gen. 45:13), and still more so when he could actually show his father how great was his power, how exalted was his rank. It is joy to Jesus to let us behold His joy, and it will be glory to us to behold His glory. Should not the redeemed ascend to such blessed delights? Would you hinder them?

How unselfish it is on our Lord's part to think Himself not fully glorified till we behold His glory! How unselfish He will make us also, since it will be our glory to see His glory! He does not say that He is going to take us home that *we* may be in glory but that we may behold *His* glory. His glory is better to us than any personal glory. All things are more ours by being His. Glory apart from Him is no glory. Beloved, even as our Lord seems to lose Himself in His people, His people hide themselves away in Him. It is His glory to glorify them, it is their glory to glorify Him, and it will be the glory of glories for them to be glorified together. Who would not go to this heaven? Who would keep a brother out of it an hour?

Observe the fellowship that exists in the glory land. Read the verse: "that *they* may behold *my* glory, which *thou* hast given *me*." What a blending of persons! Where did our Lord's glory come from? "Thou gavest it Me," says Jesus. Hence, it is the Father's glory passed over to the Son. Yet Jesus calls it "*My* glory," for it is truly His own. The saints are to behold this, and it will be their glory to see it. Here we have the Father and the Elder Brother and the many brethren and a wonderful communism of interests and possessions. It is ever so in a loving family. We ask not whose is this or whose is that when we are at home. If you were to go into a stranger's house, you would not think of taking this or that. But as your father's own son, you make yourself at home, and no one inquires, "What are you doing?" Bridegroom and bride do not quarrel about whether property is his or hers. Laws have been made lately to settle different estates for those who are one. This is well enough when love is gone, but true conjugal love laughs at all that can make separate that which God hath joined together. The wife says, "That is mine." "No," saith the lawyer, "it is your husband's." Her answer is, "And therefore it is mine."

In that blessed union into which divine love has admitted us, Christ is ours, and we are Christ's. His Father is our Father. We are one with Him; He is one with the Father. And hence all things are ours, and the Father Himself loves us. All this not only will be true in heaven but also will there be realized and acted on. So when the Lord brings His people home, we shall be one with Him, and He one with the Father, and we also in Him shall be one with the Father so that we shall then find boundless glory in beholding the glory of our Lord and God.

My text has baffled me. I am beaten back by its blaze of light. Forgive me. I had a thought, but I cannot express it. The fire of my text burns with such fervent heat that it threatens to consume me if I draw nearer to it. Easily could I step into heaven—so I feel at this moment.

The Home Atmosphere

None of us can wish our departed friends back from their thrones. Since they have gone to be where Jesus is and to enter so fully into the most blissful fellowship with Him and the Father, we would not have them return even for an instant to this poor country. We only wish that our turn for migration may come soon. We would not be too long divided from our fellows. If some of the birds have gone to the sunny land, let us plume our wings to follow them. There will be only a little interval between our parting and our everlasting meeting. Look at the many who died before we came into the world. Some of them have been in heaven together now for thousands of years. To them it must seem that they were only divided by a moment's interval. Their continents of fellowship have made the channel of death seem but a streak of sea. Soon we shall take the same view of things.

Breathe the home atmosphere. Jesus tells us that the atmosphere of His home is *love:* "thou lovedst me before the foundation of the world." Brethren, can you follow me in a great flight? Can you stretch broader wings than the condor ever knew and fly back into the unbeginning eternity? There was a day before all days when there was no day but the Ancient of Days. There was a time before all time when God only was: the uncreated, the only existent One. The divine three, Father, Son, and Spirit, lived in blessed consort with each other, delighting in each other. Oh, the intensity of the divine love of the Father to the Son! There was no world, no sun, no moon, no stars, no universe, but God alone. The whole of God's omnipotence flowed forth in a stream of love to the Son, while the Son's whole being remained eternally one with the Father by a mysterious essential union.

How came all this that we now see and hear? Why this creation? this fall of Adam? this redemption? this Church? this heaven? How came it all about? It needed not to have been, but the Father's love made Him resolve to show forth the glory of His Son. The mysterious volume that has been gradually unfolded before us has only this one design—the Father would make known His love to the Son and make the Son's glories to appear before the eyes of those whom the Father gave Him. This fall and redemption and the story as a whole, so far as the divine purpose is concerned, are the fruit of the Father's love for the Son and His delight in glorifying the Son. Those myriads, those white-robed myriads, harping to music infinitely deep, what mean they all? They are the Father's delight in the Son. That He might be glorified forever, He permitted that He should bear a human body and should suffer, bleed, and die so that there might come out of Him, as a harvest comes from a dying and buried corn of wheat, all the countless hosts of elect souls, ordained forever to a felicity exceeding bounds. These are the bride of the Lamb, the body of Christ, the fullness of Him who filleth all in all. Their destiny is so high that no language can fully describe it. Only God knows the love of God and all that it has prepared for those who are the objects of it.

Love wraps up the whole in its cloth of gold. Love is both the source and the channel and the end of the divine acting. Because the Father loved the Son, He gave us to Him and ordained that we should be with Him. His love for us is love for the Son. Because of the boundless, ineffable, infinite love of the great Father toward His Son, therefore has He ordained this whole system of salvation and redemption, that Jesus in the Church of His redeemed might everlastingly be glorified. Let our saintly ones go home, beloved, if that is the design of their going. Since all comes of divine love and all sets forth divine love, let them go to Him who loves them—let divine love fulfill its purpose of bringing many sons unto glory. Since the Father once made our Lord perfect by His sufferings, let Him now be made perfectly glorious by the coming up of His redeemed from the purifying bath of His atonement. I see them rise like sheep from the washing, all of them gathering with delight at the feet of that great Shepherd of the sheep.

Beloved, I am lost in the subject now. I breathe that heavenly air. Love surrounds all and conquers grief. I will not cause the temperature to fall by uttering any other words but this: Hold your friends lovingly, but be ready to yield them to Jesus. Detain them not from Him to whom they belong. When they are sick, fast and pray; but when they are departed, do much as David did, who washed his face and ate and drank. You cannot bring them back again. You will go to them; they cannot return to you. Comfort yourselves with the double thought of their joy in Christ and Christ's joy in them. Add the triple thought of the Father's joy in Christ and in them. Let us watch the Master's call. Let us not dread the question—who next, and who next? Let none of us start back as though we hoped to linger longer than others. Let us even desire to see our names in the celestial conscription. Let us be willing to be dealt with just as our Lord pleases. Let no doubt intervene; let no gloom encompass us.

Dying is but going home; indeed, there is no dying for the saints. Charles Stanford is gone! Thus was his death told to me: "He drew up his feet and smiled." Thus will you and I depart. He had borne his testimony in the light, even when blind. He had cheered us all, though he was the greatest sufferer of us all. And now the film has gone from the eyes, the *anguish* is gone from the heart, and he is with Jesus. He smiled. What a sight was that that caused that smile! I have seen many faces of dear departed ones lit up with splendor. Of many I could feel sure that they had seen a vision of angels. Traces of a reflected glory hung about their countenances. O brethren, we shall soon know more of heaven than all the divines can tell us. We will meet with Jesus, where He is, where we shall behold His glory. Some of you cannot do this. Turn from your evil ways. Turn to the right, where stands that cross, and keep straight on, and you will come to Jesus in glory. Blessed be the name of the Lord! Amen.

*P*rayer *was the channel of the Redeemer's comfort, earnest, intense, reverent, repeated prayer. And after each time of prayer, Jesus seems to have grown quiet and to have gone to His disciples with a measure of restored peace of mind. The sight of their sleeping helped to bring back His griefs, and therefore He returned to pray again, and each time He was comforted, so that when He had prayed for the third time, He was prepared to meet Judas and the soldiers and to go with silent patience to judgment and to death. His great comfort was prayer and submission to the divine will, for when He had laid His own will down at His Father's feet, the feebleness of His flesh spoke no more complainingly, but in sweet silence, like a sheep dumb before her shearers, He contained His soul in patience and rest. Dear brothers and sisters, if any of you shall have your Gethsemane and your heavy griefs, imitate your Master by resorting to prayer, by crying to your Father, and by learning submission to His will.*

Chapter Eight

Prayer in Gethsemane

And being in an agony he prayed more earnestly: and his sweat was as it were great drops of blood falling down to the ground
—Luke 22:44

OUR LORD, AFTER HAVING eaten the passover and celebrating the supper with His disciples, went with them to the Mount of Olives and entered the garden of Gethsemane. What induced Him to select that place to be the scene of His terrible agony? Why there in preference to anywhere else would He be arrested by His enemies? May we not conceive that as in a garden Adam's self-indulgence ruined us, so in another garden the agonies of the second Adam should restore us. Gethsemane supplies the medicine for the ills that followed upon the forbidden fruit of Eden. No flowers that bloomed upon the banks of the fourfold river were ever so precious to our race as the bitter herbs that grew hard by the black and sullen stream of Kidron.

May not our Lord also have thought of David, when on that memorable occasion he fled out of the city from his rebellious son, and it is written, "the king also himself passed over the brook Kidron" (2 Sam. 15:23), and he and his people went up barefooted and bareheaded, weeping as they went? Behold, the greater David leaves the temple to become desolate and forsakes the city that had rejected His admonitions, and with a sorrowful heart crosses the foul brook to find in solitude a solace for His woes. Our Lord Jesus, moreover, meant us to see that our sin changed everything about Him into sorrow, it turned His riches into poverty, His peace into travail, His glory into shame, and so the place of His peaceful retirement, where in hallowed devotion He had been nearest heaven in communion with God, our sin transformed into the focus of His sorrow, the center of His woe. Where He had enjoyed most, there He must be called to suffer most. Our Lord may also have chosen the garden because He needed every remembrance that could sustain Him in the conflict and He felt refreshed by the memory of former hours that there had passed away so quietly. He had there prayed and gained strength and comfort. Those gnarled and twisted olives knew Him well. There was hardly a blade of grass in the garden that He had not knelt upon. He had consecrated the spot to fellowship with God. What wonder, then, that He preferred this favored soil? Just as a man would choose in sickness to lie in his own bed, so Jesus chose to endure His agony in His own oratory, where the recollections of former communings with His Father would come vividly before Him.

But probably the chief reason for His resort to Gethsemane was that it was His well-known haunt, and John tell us, "Judas also, which betrayed him, knew the place" (John 18:2). Our Lord did not wish to conceal Himself; He did not need to be hunted down like a thief or searched out by spies. He went boldly to the place where His enemies knew that He was accustomed to pray, for He was willing to be taken to suffering and to death. They did not drag Him off to Pilate's hall against His will, but He went with them voluntarily. When the hour was come for Him to be betrayed, there He was in a place where the traitor could readily find Him, and when Judas would betray Him with a kiss, His cheek was ready to receive the traitorous salutation. The blessed Savior delighted to do the will of the Lord, though it involved obedience unto death.

Having thus come to the gate of the garden of Gethsemane, let us now enter. But first let us put off our shoes from our feet, as Moses did when he also saw the bush that burned with fire and was not consumed. Surely we may say with Jacob, "How dreadful is this place!" (Gen. 28:17). I tremble at the task that lies before me, for how shall my feeble words describe those agonies for which strong crying and tears were scarcely an adequate expression? I desire with you to survey the sufferings of our Redeemer, but oh, may the Spirit of God prevent our minds from thinking even one word that would be derogatory to Him either in His immaculate manhood or His glorious Godhead. It is so easy to describe the divine side in such a manner as to trench upon the human or to depict the human at the cost of the divine. Make me not an offender for a word if I should err. A man would need to be inspired himself or to confine himself to the very words of inspiration to appropriately speak at all times upon the great "mystery of godliness," God manifest in the flesh, and especially when he has to dwell most upon God so manifest in suffering flesh that the weakest traits in manhood become the most conspicuous.

The Cause of Christ's Grief

Meditating upon the agonizing scene in Gethsemane, we are compelled to observe that our Savior there endured a grief unknown to any previous period of His life, and therefore we will begin our study by raising the question, What was the cause of the peculiar grief of Gethsemane? Our Lord was "a man of sorrows, and acquainted with grief" (Isa. 53:3) throughout His whole life, and yet, though it may sound paradoxical, I scarcely think there existed on the face of the earth a happier man than Jesus of Nazareth, for the griefs that He endured were counterbalanced by the peace of purity, the calm of fellowship with God, and the joy of benevolence. This last every good man knows to be very sweet, and all the sweeter in proportion to the pain that is voluntarily endured for the carrying out of its kind designs. It is always joy to do good, cost what it may. Moreover, Jesus dwelt at perfect peace with God at all times. We know that He did so, for He regarded that peace as a choice legacy that He could bequeath to His disciples, and before He died He said to them, "Peace I leave with you, my peace I give unto you" (John 14:27). Jesus was meek and lowly of heart, and therefore His soul had rest. He was one of the meek who inherit the earth; one of the peacemakers who are and must be blessed. I think I mistake not when I say that our Lord was far from being an unhappy man.

But in Gethsemane all seems changed. His peace is gone, His calm is turned to tempest. After supper our Lord had sung a hymn, but there was no singing in Gethsemane. Down the steep bank that led from Jerusalem to the Kidron, He talked very cheerfully, saying, "I am the vine, ye are the branches" (John 15:5), and that wondrous prayer that He prayed with His disciples after that discourse is very full of majesty: "Father, I will that they also, whom thou hast given me, be with me where I am" (John 17:24) is a very different prayer from that inside Gethsemane's walls, where He cries, "O my Father, if it be possible, let this cup pass from me" (Matt. 26:39).

Notice that all His life long you scarcely find Him uttering an expression of grief, and yet here He says, not only by His sighs and by His bloody sweat but also in so many words, "My soul is exceeding sorrowful, even unto death" (Matt. 26:38). In the garden the Sufferer could not conceal His grief and does not appear to have wished to do so. Backward and forward thrice He ran to His disciples, letting them see His sorrow and appealing to them for sympathy. His exclamations were very piteous, and His sighs and groans were, I doubt not, very terrible to hear. Chiefly did that sorrow reveal itself in bloody sweat, which is a very unusual phenomenon, although I suppose we must believe those writers who record instances somewhat similar. The old physician Galen gives an instance in which, through extremity of horror, an individual poured forth a discolored sweat, so nearly crimson as at any rate to appear to have been blood. Other cases are given by medical authorities. We do not, however, on any previous occasion observe anything like this in our Lord's life. It was only in the last, grim struggle among the olive trees that our Champion resisted unto blood, agonizing against sin. What ailed You, O Lord, that You should be so sorely troubled just then?

We are clear that His deep sorrow and distress were not occasioned by any bodily pain. Our Savior had doubtless been familiar with weakness and pain, for He took our sicknesses, but He never in any previous instance complained of physical suffering. Neither at the time when He entered Gethsemane had He been grieved by any bereavement. We know that on the occasion when Jesus wept, it was because His friend Lazarus was dead. But here there was no funeral, nor sick bed, nor particular cause of grief in that direction. Nor was it the revived remembrance of any past reproaches that had lain dormant in His mind. Long before, this "reproach hath broken my heart" (Ps. 69:20), and He had known to the full the vexations of abuse and scorn. They had called Him "a gluttonous man, and a winebibber" (Luke 7:34), and they had charged Him with casting out devils by the prince of the devils (Matt. 12:24). They could not say more, and yet He had bravely faced it all. It could not be possible that He was now sorrowful unto death for such a cause. There must have been something sharper than pain, more cutting than reproach, more terrible than bereavement that at this time grappled with the Savior and made Him "sorrowful and very heavy" (Matt. 26:37).

Do you suppose it was the fear of coming scorn or the dread of crucifixion? Was it terror at the thought of death? Is not such a supposition impossible? Every man dreads death, and as man, Jesus could not shrink from it. When we were originally made, we were created for immortality, and therefore to die is strange and uncongenial work to us, and the instincts of self-preservation cause us to start back from it. But surely in our Lord's case, that natural cause could not have produced such specially painful results. It does not make even such poor cowards as we are sweat great drops of blood. Why, then, should it work such terror in Him? It is dishonoring to our Lord to imagine Him less brave than His own disciples, yet we have seen some of the very feeblest of His saints triumphant in the prospect of departing. Read the stories of the martyrs, and you will frequently find them exultant in the near approach of the most cruel sufferings. The joy of the Lord has given such strength to them that no coward thought has alarmed them for a single moment, but they have gone to the stake or to the block with psalms of victory upon their lips. Our Master must not be thought of as inferior to His boldest servant. It cannot be that He should tremble where they were brave. Oh, no; the noblest spirit among yon martyr band is the Leader Himself, who in suffering and heroism surpassed them all. None could so defy the pangs of death as the Lord Jesus, who, for the joy that was set before Him, endured the cross, despising the shame.

I cannot conceive that the pangs of Gethsemane were occasioned by any extraordinary attack from Satan. It is possible that Satan was there and that his presence may have darkened the shade, but he was not the most prominent cause of that hour of darkness. This much is quite clear, that our Lord at the commencement of His ministry engaged in a very severe duel with the prince of darkness, and yet we do not read concerning that temptation in the wilderness a single syllable as to His soul's being exceeding sorrowful, neither do we find that He was "sore amazed, and very heavy" (Mark 14:33), nor is there a solitary hint at anything approaching to bloody sweat. When the Lord of angels condescended to stand foot to foot with the prince of the power of the air,

He had no such dread of him as to utter strong cries and tears and fall prostrate on the ground with threefold appeals to the great Father. Comparatively speaking, to put His foot on the old serpent was an easy task for Christ and did but cost Him a bruised heel, but this Gethsemane agony wounded His very soul even unto death.

What is it, then, that so peculiarly marks off Gethsemane and the griefs thereof? We believe that now the Father put Him to grief for us. It was now that our Lord had to take a certain cup *from the Father's hand.* Not from the Jews, not from the traitor Judas, not from the sleeping disciples, not from the devil came the trial now. It was a cup filled by One whom He knew to be His Father but who nevertheless He understood to have appointed Him a very bitter potion, not a cup to be drunk by His body and to spend its gall upon His flesh but a cup that specially amazed His soul and troubled His inmost heart. He shrank from it, and therefore be assured that it was a draught more dreadful than physical pain, since from that He did not shrink. It was a potion more dreadful than reproach, from that He had not turned aside, more dreadful than Satanic temptation, for *that* He had overcome. It was a something inconceivably terrible, amazingly full of dread, that came from the Father's hand. This removes all doubt as to what it was, for we read: "Yet it pleased the LORD to bruise him; he hath put him to grief: when thou shalt make his soul an offering for sin" (Isa. 53:10). "[T]he LORD hath laid on him the iniquity of us all" (Isa. 53:6). The Lord had made Him to be sin for us though He knew no sin (2 Cor. 5:21). This, then, is that which caused the Savior such extraordinary depression. He was now about to "taste death for every man" (Heb. 2:9), to bear the curse that was due to sinners, because He stood in the sinner's place and must suffer in the sinner's stead. Here is the secret of those agonies that it is not possible for me to set forth in order before you, so true is it that

> 'Tis to God, and God alone,
> That His griefs are fully known.

Yet I would exhort you to consider these griefs awhile, that you may love the Sufferer. He now realized, perhaps for the first time, what it was to be a sin bearer. As God, He was perfectly holy and incapable of sin, and as man, He was without original taint and spotlessly pure. Yet He had to bear sin, to be led forth as the scapegoat bearing the iniquity of Israel upon His head, to be taken and made a sin offering, and as a loathsome thing (for nothing was more loathsome than the sin offering) to be taken without the camp and utterly consumed with the fire of divine wrath. Do you wonder that His infinite purity started back from that? Would He have been what He was had it not been a very solemn thing for Him to stand before God in the position of a sinner? Yea, and as Luther would have said it, to be looked upon by God as if He were all the sinners of the world and as if He had committed all the sin that ever had been committed by His people, for it was all laid on Him, and on Him must the vengeance due for it all be poured. He must be the center of all vengeance and bear away upon Himself what should have fallen upon the guilty sons of men.

To stand in such a position, when once it was realized, must have been very terrible to the Redeemer's holy soul. Now also the Savior's mind was intently fixed upon the dreadful nature of sin. Sin had always been abhorrent to Him, but now His thoughts were engrossed with it. He saw its worse than deadly nature, its heinous character, and horrible aim. Probably at this time, beyond any former period, He had, as a man, a view of the wide range and all-pervading evil of sin and a sense of the blackness of its darkness and the desperateness of its guilt as being a direct attack upon the throne, yea, and upon the very being of God. He saw in His own person to what lengths sinners would go and how they would sell their Lord, like Judas, and seek to destroy Him, as did the Jews. The cruel and ungenerous treatment He had Himself received displayed man's hate of God, and, as He saw it, horror took hold upon Him, and His soul was heavy to think that He must bear such an evil and be numbered with such transgressors, be wounded for their transgressions, and be bruised for their iniquities. Neither the wounding nor the bruising distressed Him so much as the sin itself, and that utterly overwhelmed His soul.

Then, too, no doubt the penalty of sin began to be realized by Him in the garden—first the sin that had put Him in the position of a suffering Substitute, and then the penalty that must be borne because He was in that position. I dread to the last degree that kind of theology that seeks to depreciate and diminish our estimate of the sufferings of our Lord Jesus Christ. Brethren, that was no trifling suffering that made recompense to the justice of God for the sins of men. I am never afraid of exaggeration when I speak of what my Lord endured. All hell was distilled into that cup, of which our

God and Savior Jesus Christ was made to drink. It was not eternal suffering, but since He was divine, He could in a short time offer unto God a vindication of His justice that sinners in hell could not have offered had they been left to suffer in their own person forever. The woe that broke over the Savior's spirit, the great and fathomless ocean of inexpressible anguish that dashed over the Savior's soul when He died, is so inconceivable that I must not venture far lest I be accused of a vain attempt to express the unutterable. But this I will say, the very spray from that great tempestuous deep as it fell on Christ baptized Him in a bloody sweat. He had not yet come to the raging billows of the penalty itself, but even standing on the shore, as He heard the awful surf breaking at His feet, His soul was sore amazed and very heavy. It was the shadow of the coming tempest. It was the prelude of the dread desertion that He had to endure when He stood where we should have stood and paid to His Father's justice the debt that was due from us. It was this that laid Him low. To be treated as a sinner, to be smitten as a sinner, though in Him was no sin—this it was that caused Him the agony of which our text speaks.

The Character of the Grief Itself

I shall trouble you as little as possible with the Greek words used by the evangelists. I have studied each of them to try to find out the shades of their meaning, but it will suffice if I give you the results of my careful investigation. What was the grief itself? How was it described? This great sorrow assailed our Lord some four days before He suffered. If you turn to John 12:27, you find that remarkable utterance: "Now is my soul troubled." We never knew Him to say that before. This was a foretaste of the great depression of spirit that was so soon to lay Him prostrate in Gethsemane. "Now is my soul troubled; and what shall I say? Father, save me from this hour: but for this cause came I unto this hour." After that we read of Him in Matthew 26:37 that He "began to be sorrowful and very heavy." The depression had come over Him again. It was not pain, it was not a palpitation of the heart or an aching of the brow; it was worse than these. Trouble of spirit is worse than pain of body. Pain may bring trouble and be the incidental cause of sorrow, but if the mind is perfectly untroubled, how well a man can bear pain. And when the soul is exhilarated and lifted up with inward joy, pain of body is almost forgotten, the soul conquering the body. On the other hand, the soul's sorrow will create bodily pain, the lower nature sympathizing with the higher. Our Lord's main suffering lay in His soul. His soul sufferings were the soul of His sufferings. "A wounded spirit who can bear?" (Prov. 18:14). Pain of spirit is the worst of pain, sorrow of heart is the climax of griefs. Let those who have ever known sinking spirits, despondency, and mental gloom attest to the truth of what I say!

This sorrow of heart appears to have led to a very deep depression of our Lord's spirit. In Matthew 26:37 you find it recorded that He was *very heavy*, and that expression is full of meaning. The word in the original is a very difficult one to translate. It may signify the abstraction of the mind and its complete occupation by sorrow to the exclusion of every thought that might have alleviated the distress. One burning thought consumed His whole soul and burned up all that might have yielded comfort. For a while His mind refused to dwell on the result of His death, the consequent joy that was set before Him. His position as a sin bearer and the desertion by His Father that was thereby necessitated engrossed His contemplations and hurried His soul away from all else. Some have seen in the word a measure of distraction, and though I will not go far in that direction, yet it does seem as if our Savior's mind underwent agitations and convulsions widely different from His usual calm, collected spirit. He was tossed to and fro as upon a mighty sea of trouble that was wrought to tempest, carrying Him away in its fury. "We did esteem him stricken, smitten of God, and afflicted" (Isa. 53:4). As the psalmist said, innumerable evils compassed Him about so that His heart failed Him (Ps. 40:12). His heart was melted like wax in the midst of His bowels with sheer dismay.

He was very heavy. Some consider the word to signify at its root "separated from the people," as if He had become unlike other men, even as one of whose mind is staggered by a sudden blow or pressed with some astounding calamity. Mere onlookers would have thought our Lord to be a man distraught, burdened beyond the limits of men, and borne down by a sorrow unparalleled among men. Epaphroditus' sickness, whereby he was brought near to death, is called by the same word (Phil. 2:26). So that, we see, that Christ's soul was sick and fainted. Was not His sweat produced by exhaustion? The cold, clammy sweat of dying men comes through faintness of body, but the bloody sweat of Jesus came from an utter faintness and prostration of soul. He was in an awful soul swoon and suffered an inward death, whose accompaniment was not watery tears from the eyes but a weeping of blood from the entire man. Many of you, however, know in your measure what it is to be very heavy without my multiplying words in explanation, and if you do not know by personal experience, all explanations must be vain. When deep despondency comes on, when you forget everything that would sustain you and your spirit sinks down, down, down, then can you sympathize with your Lord. Others think you foolish, call you nervous, and bid you rally yourself, but they know not your case. If they understood it, they would not mock you with such admonitions, impossible to those who are sinking beneath inward woe. Our Lord was *very heavy*, very sinking, very despondent, overwhelmed with grief.

Mark tells us next that our Lord was *sore amazed* (Mark 14:33). The Greek word does not merely import that He was astonished and surprised, but it suggests that His amazement went to an extremity of horror, such as men fall into when their hair stands on end and their flesh trembles. As the delivery of the law made Moses exceedingly fear and quake, and as David said, "My flesh trembleth for fear of thee" (Ps. 119:120), so our Lord was stricken with horror at the sight of the sin that was laid upon Him and the vengeance that was due on account of it. The Savior was first *sorrowful*, then depressed and *heavy*, and lastly *sore amazed* and filled with amazement. Even He as a man could scarce have known what it was that He had undertaken to bear. He had looked at it calmly and quietly and felt that whatever it was, He would bear it for our sake. But when it actually came to the bearing of sin, He was utterly astonished and taken aback at the dreadful position of standing in the sinner's place before God, of having His holy Father look upon Him as the sinner's representative, and of being forsaken by that Father with whom He had lived on terms of amity and delight from old eternity. It staggered His holy, tender, loving nature, and He was *sore amazed* and was *very heavy*.

We are further taught that He was surrounded, encompassed, and overwhelmed by an ocean of sorrow, for the thirty-eighth verse of Matthew 26 contains the word *perilupos*, which signifies an encompassing around with sorrows. In all ordinary miseries, there is generally some loophole of escape, some breathing place for hope. We can generally remind our friends in trouble that their case might be worse, but in our Lord's griefs, worse could not be imagined. He could say with David, "The pains of hell gat hold upon me" (Ps. 116:3). All God's waves and billows went over Him. Above Him, beneath Him, around Him, without Him, and within all, all was anguish, neither was there one alleviation or source of consolation. His disciples could not help Him—they were all but one sleeping, and he who was awake was on the road to betray Him. His spirit cried out in the presence of the Almighty God beneath the crushing burden and unbearable load of His miseries. No griefs could have gone further than Christ's, and He Himself said, "My soul is *exceeding sorrowful*," or surrounded with sorrow "even unto death." He did not die in the garden, but He suffered as much as if He had died. He endured death intensively, though not extensively. It did not extend to the making His body a corpse, but it went as far in pain as if it had been so. His pangs and anguish went up to the mortal agony and only paused on the verge of death.

Luke, to crown all, tells us in our text, that our Lord was *in an agony*. The expression *agony* signifies a conflict, a contest, a wrestling. With whom was the agony? With whom did He wrestle? I believe it was with Himself. The contest here intended was not with His God. No, "not as I will but as thou wilt" does not look like wrestling with God. It was not a contest with Satan, for, as we have already seen, He would not have been so sore amazed had that been the conflict. But it was a terrible combat within Himself, an agony within His own soul. Remember that He could have escaped from all this grief with one resolve of His will, and naturally the manhood in Him said, "Do not bear it!" and the purity of His heart said, "Oh, do not bear it, do not stand in the place of the sinner." The delicate sensitiveness of His mysterious nature shrank altogether from any form of connection with sin. Yet infinite love said, "Bear it, stoop beneath the load." And so there was agony between the attributes of His nature, a battle on an awful scale in the arena of His soul.

The purity that cannot bear to come into contact with sin must have been very mighty in Christ, while the love that would not let His people perish was very mighty, too. It was a struggle on a titanic scale, as if a Hercules had met another Hercules. Two tremendous forces strove and fought and agonized within the bleeding heart of Jesus. Nothing causes a man more torture than to be dragged hither and thither with contending emotions. As civil war is the worst and most cruel kind of war, so a war within a man's soul when two great passions in him struggle for the mastery, and both noble passions, too, causes a trouble and distress that none but he who feels it can understand. I marvel not that our Lord's sweat was as it were great drops of blood, when such an inward pressure made Him like a cluster trodden in the winepress. I hope I have not presumptuously looked into the ark or gazed within the veiled holy of holies. God forbid that curiosity or pride should urge me to intrude where the Lord has set a barrier. I have brought you as far as I can and must again drop the curtain with the words I used just now: *'Tis to God, and God alone, That His griefs are fully known.*

What Was Our Lord's Solace?

Jesus sought help in human companionship, and very natural it was that He should do so. God has created in our human nature a craving for sympathy. We do no wrong when we expect our brethren to watch with us in our hour of trial. But our Lord did not find that men were able to assist Him. However willing their spirit might be, their flesh was weak. What, then, did He do? He resorted to prayer, and especially to prayer to God under the character of Father. I have learned by experience that we never know the sweetness of the fatherhood of God so much as when we are in very bitter anguish. I can understand why the Savior said, "Abba, Father." It was anguish that brought Him down as a chastened child to appeal plaintively to a Father's love. In the bitterness of my soul I have cried, "If, indeed, You are my Father, by the bowels of Your fatherhood have pity on Your child." And here Jesus pleads with His Father as we have done and finds comfort in that pleading.

Prayer was the channel of the Redeemer's comfort, earnest, intense, reverent, repeated prayer. And after each time of prayer, Jesus seems to have grown quiet and to have gone to His disciples with a measure of restored peace of mind. The sight of their sleeping helped to bring back His griefs, and therefore He returned to pray again, and each time He was comforted, so that when He had prayed for the third time, He was prepared to meet Judas and the soldiers and to go with silent patience to judgment and to death. His great comfort was prayer and submission to the divine will, for when He had laid His own will down at His Father's feet, the feebleness of His flesh spoke no more complainingly, but in sweet silence, like a sheep dumb before her shearers, He contained His soul in patience and rest. Dear brothers and sisters, if any of you shall have your Gethsemane and your heavy griefs, imitate your Master by resorting to prayer, by crying to your Father, and by learning submission to His will.

I shall conclude by drawing two or three inferences from the whole subject. May the Holy Spirit instruct us.

The first is this: Learn *the real humanity of our Lord Jesus Christ.* Do not think of Him as God merely, though He is assuredly divine, but feel Him to be near of kin to you, bone of your bone, flesh of your flesh. How thoroughly can He sympathize with you! He has been burdened with all your burdens and grieved with all your griefs. Are the waters very deep through which you are passing? Yet they are not deep compared with the torrents with which He was buffeted. Never a pang penetrates your spirit to which your covenant Head was a stranger. Jesus can sympathize with you in all your sorrows, for He has suffered far more than you have ever suffered and is able therefore to succor you in your temptations. Lay hold on Jesus as your familiar friend, your brother born for adversity, and you will have obtained a consolation that will bear you through the uttermost deeps.

Next, *see the intolerable evil of sin.* You are a sinner, which Jesus never was, yet even to stand in the sinner's place was so dreadful to Him that He was sorrowful even unto death. What will sin one day be to you if you should be found guilty at the last! Oh, if we could tell the horror of sin, there is not one among us who would be satisfied to remain in sin for a single moment. I believe there would go up a weeping and a wailing such as might be heard in the very streets if men and women who are living in sin could really know what sin is, and what the wrath of God is that rests upon them, and what the judgments of God will be that will shortly surround them and destroy them. O soul, sin must be an awful thing if it so crushed our Lord. If the very imputation of it fetched bloody sweat from the pure and holy Savior, what must sin itself be? Avoid it, pass not by it, turn away from the very appearance of it, walk humbly and carefully with your God that sin may not harm you, for it is an exceeding plague, an infinite pest.

Learn next, *the matchless love of Jesus,* that for your sakes and mine He would not merely suffer in body but consented even to bear the horror of being accounted a sinner and coming under the wrath of God because of *our* sins. Though it cost Him suffering unto death and sore amazement, yet sooner than that we shall perish, the Lord suffered as our surety. Can we not cheerfully endure persecution for His sake? Can we not labor earnestly for Him? Are we so ungenerous that His cause shall know a lack while we have the means of helping it? Are we so base that His work shall flag while we have strength to carry it on? I charge you by Gethsemane, if you have a part and lot in the passion of your Savior, love Him much who loved you so immeasurably, and spend and be spent for Him.

Again looking at Jesus in the garden, we learn the *excellence and completeness of the atonement.* How black I am, how filthy, how loathsome in the sight of God. I feel myself only fit to be cast into the lowest hell, and I wonder that God has not long ago cast me there. But I go into Gethsemane, and I peer under those gnarled olive trees, and I see my Savior. I see Him wallowing on the ground in anguish and hear such groans come from Him as never came from human breast before. I look upon the earth and see it red with His blood while His face is smeared with gory sweat, and I say to myself, "My God, my Savior, what troubles You?" I hear Him reply, "I am suffering for your sin," and then I take comfort, for while I would have spared my Lord such an anguish, now that the anguish is over I can understand how Jehovah can spare me, because He smote His Son in my place.

Now I have hope of justification, for I bring before the justice of God and my own conscience the remembrance of my bleeding Savior, and I say, "Can You twice demand payment, first at the hand of Your agonizing Son and then again at mine?" Sinner as I am, I stand before the burning throne of the severity of God and am not afraid of it. "Can You scorch me, O consuming fire, when You have not only scorched but utterly consumed my Substitute?" Nay, by faith, my soul sees justice satisfied, the law honored, the moral government of God established, and yet my once guilty soul absolved and set free. The fire of avenging justice has spent itself, and the law has exhausted its most rigorous demands upon that person of Him who was made a curse for us, that we might be made the righteousness of God in Him. Oh, the sweetness of the comfort that flows from the atoning blood! Obtain that comfort and never leave it. Cling to your Lord's bleeding heart and drink in abundant consolation.

Last of all, *what must be the terror of the punishment that will fall upon those who reject the atoning blood* and who will have to stand before God in their own proper persons to suffer for their sins. I will tell you with pain in my heart what will happen to those of you who reject my Lord. Jesus Christ my Lord and Master is a sign and prophecy to you of what will happen to you. Not in a garden, but on that bed of yours where you have so often been refreshed, you will be surprised and overtaken, and the pains of death will get hold upon you. With an exceeding sorrow and remorse for your misspent life and for a rejected Savior you will be made very heavy. Then will your darling sin, your favorite lust, like another Judas, betray you with a kiss. While yet your soul lingers on your lips, you will be seized and taken off by a body of evil ones and carried away to the bar of God, just as Jesus was taken to the judgment seat of Caiaphas. There shall be a speedy, personal, and somewhat private judgment, by which you shall be committed to prison where, in darkness and weeping and wailing, you shall spend the night before the great inquest of the judgment morning.

Then shall the day break and the resurrection morning come, and as our Lord then appeared before Pilate, so will you appear before the highest tribunal, not that of Pilate, but the dread judgment seat of the Son of God, whom you have despised and rejected. Then will witnesses come against you, not false witnesses, but true, and you will stand speechless, even as Jesus said not a word before His accusers. Then will conscience and despair buffet you, until you will become such a monument of misery, such a spectacle of contempt, that men shall look at you and say, "Behold the man and the suffering that has come upon him, because he despised his God and found pleasure in sin." Then shall you be condemned. "Depart, ye cursed," shall be your sentence, even as "let Him be crucified" was the doom of Jesus. You shall be taken away by the officers of justice to your doom. Then like the sinner's Substitute you will cry, "I thirst," but not a drop of water shall be given you. You shall taste nothing but the gall of bitterness. You shall be executed publicly, with your crimes written over your head that all may read and understand that you are justly condemned. And then will you be mocked as Jesus was, especially if you have been a professor of religion and a false one. All who pass by will say, "He saved others, he preached to others, but himself he cannot save." God Himself will mock you. Nay, think not I dream, has He not said it: "I also will laugh at your calamity; I will mock when your fear cometh" (Prov. 1:26)?

Cry unto your gods that you once trusted in! Get comfort out of the lusts you once delighted in! To your shame and to the confusion of your nakedness shall you who have despised the Savior be made a spectacle of the justice of God forever. It is right it should be so; justice rightly demands it. Sin made the Savior suffer an agony; shall it not make you suffer? Moreover, in addition to your sin, you have rejected the Savior. You have said, "He shall not be my trust and confidence." Voluntarily, presumptuously, and against your own conscience you have refused eternal life. And if you die rejecting mercy, what can come of it but that first your sin and second your unbelief shall condemn you to misery without limit or end. Let Gethsemane warn you, let its groans and tears and bloody sweat admonish you. Repent of sin, and believe in Jesus. May His Spirit enable you, for Jesus' sake. Amen.

*P*erhaps you are among the least observed by anybody, who is yet noticed by the Savior, for He sees not as man sees but observes most those whom man passes over as beneath his regard. Nobody knows you, nobody cares for you. Your peculiar trouble is quite unknown, and you would not reveal it for the world. You feel quite alone. There is no solitude like that which is to be found in a dense throng, and you are in that solitude now. Be not, however, quite despairing, for you have a friend left. There is far more joy in the fact that as our Master observed most the least observed one on that Sabbath in the synagogue, so we trust He will do this day, and His eye shall light on you, even you. He will not pass you by but will deal out a special Sabbath blessing to your weary heart. Though by yourself accounted to be among the last, you shall now be put upon the first by the Lord's working a notable miracle of love upon you. In the hope that this may be so, we will proceed, by the help of the Holy Spirit, to look into the gracious deed that was done to this poor woman.

Chapter Nine

Prayer for the Bowed Down

And he was teaching in one of the synagogues on the sabbath.
And, behold, there was a woman which had a spirit of infirmity
eighteen years, and was bowed together, and could in no wise lift
up herself. And when Jesus saw her, he called her to him, and said
unto her, Woman, thou art loosed from thine infirmity. And he
laid his hands on her: and immediately she was made straight,
and glorified God—Luke 13:10–13.

I BELIEVE THAT THE infirmity of this
woman was not only physical but also spiritual. Her outward
appearance was the index of her deep and long-continued depression of mind. She was bent double as to her body, and she was
bowed down by sadness as to her mind. There is always a sympathy between body and soul, but it is not always so plainly seen as
in her case. Many sad sights would meet us on all hands if it were
so. Imagine for a moment what would be the result if our outward
forms were to set forth our inward states. If someone had an eye
like that of the Savior and could gaze upon us now and see the
inward in the outward, what would be the appearance? Very
deplorable sights would be seen, for in many cases, a dead person
would be sitting, looking forth from the glassy eyes of death, bearing the semblance of life and a name to live, but all the while being
dead as to spiritual things. My friend, you would shudder as you
found yourself placed next to a corpse. Alas, the corpse would not

shudder but would remain as insensible as ungodly persons usually are, though the precious truth of the gospel rings in their ears—ears that hear but hear in vain. A large number of souls will be found in all congregations "dead in trespasses and sins" (Eph. 2:1) and yet sitting as God's people sit and not to be discerned from the living in Zion.

Even in those cases in which there is spiritual life, the aspect would not be altogether lovely. Here we should see a man blind, and there another maimed, and a third twisted from perfect uprightness. Spiritual deformity assumes many forms, and each form is painful to look upon. A paralyzed man with a trembling faith, set forth by a trembling body, would be an uncomfortable neighbor, and a person subject to fits of passion or despair would be equally undesirable if his body suffered from fits also. How sad it would be to have around us persons with a fever upon them, hot and cold by turns, burning almost to fanaticism at one moment and then chilled as with a northern wind with utter indifference. I will not try to sketch in further detail the halt, lame, blind, and impotent folk who would assemble. Surely if the flesh were shaped according to the spirit, our own church would be turned into a hospital, and each man would flee from his fellow and wish to run from himself. If to any of us our inward ailments were to be set forth upon our brow, I warrant you we would not linger long at the mirror or scarcely dare to think upon the wretched objects that our eyes would behold. Let us quit the imaginary scene with this consoling thought, that Jesus is among us notwithstanding that we be sick folk, and although He sees nothing to delight His eye if He judges us according to the law, yet, since His mercy delights to relieve human misery, there is abundant scope for Him here in the midst of our ailing souls.

In that synagogue on the Sabbath, this poor woman described in the text must have been one of the least observed. Her particular disease would render her very short in stature. She was dwarfed to almost half her original height, and consequently, like other very short persons, she would be almost lost in a standing crowd. A person so bent down as she was might have come in and gone out and not have been noticed by anyone standing upon the floor of the meeting place. But I can imagine that our Lord occupied a somewhat elevated position, as He was teaching in the synagogue, for He had probably gone to one of the higher places for the greater convenience of being seen and heard, and for this reason He could more readily see her than others could. Jesus always occupies a place from which He can spy out those who are bowed down. His quick eye did not miss its mark. She, pour soul, was naturally the least observed of all the people in the company, yet was she the most observed, for our Lord's gracious eye glanced over all the rest, but it lighted upon her with fixed regard. There His tender look remained till He had wrought the deed of love.

Perhaps you are among the least observed by anybody, who is yet noticed by the Savior, for He sees not as man sees but observes most those whom man passes over as beneath his regard. Nobody knows you, nobody cares for you. Your peculiar trouble is quite unknown, and you would not reveal it for the world. You feel quite alone. There is no solitude like that which is to be found in a dense throng, and you are in that solitude now. Be not, however, quite despairing, for you have a friend left. There is far more joy in the fact that as our Master observed most the least observed one on that Sabbath in the synagogue, so we trust He will do this day, and His eye shall light on you, even you. He will not pass you by but will deal out a special Sabbath blessing to your weary heart. Though by yourself accounted to be among the last, you shall now be put upon the first by the Lord's working a notable miracle of love upon you. In the hope that this may be so, we will proceed, by the help of the Holy Spirit, to look into the gracious deed that was done to this poor woman.

The Bowing Down of the Afflicted

We read of this woman that "she had a spirit of infirmity...and was bowed together, and could in no wise lift up herself." Upon which we remark first that *she had lost all her natural brightness*. I can imagine that when she was a girl, she was light of foot as a young roe, that her face was dimpled with many a smile, and that her eyes flashed with childlike glee. She had her share of the brightness and beauty of youth and walked erect like others of her race, looking up to the sun by day and to the sparkling stars at night, rejoicing in all around her and feeling life to be a joy. But there gradually crept over her an infirmity that dragged her down, probably a weakness of the spine. Either the muscles and ligatures began to tighten so that she was drawn more and more toward herself and toward the earth, or else the muscles commenced to relax so that she could not retain the perpendicular position and her body dropped forward more and more. I suppose either of these conditions might cause her to be bowed together so that she could not lift herself up. At any rate, for eighteen years she had not gazed upon the sun; for eighteen years no star of night had gladdened her eye; her face was drawn downward toward the dust, and all the light of her life was dim. She walked about as if she were searching for a grave, and I do not doubt she often felt that it would have been gladness to have found one. She was as truly fettered as if bound in iron and as much in prison as if surrounded by stone walls. Alas, we know certain of the children of God who are at this moment in much the same condition. They are perpetually bowed down, and though they recollect happier days, the memory only serves to deepen their present gloom. They sometimes sing in the minor key:

They seldom enter into communion with God now; seldom or never behold the face of the Well-Beloved. They try to hold on by believing, and they succeed; but they have little peace, little comfort, little joy. They have lost the crown and flower of spiritual life, though that life still remains. I feel certain that I am addressing readers who are in such a plight at this moment, and I pray the Comforter to bless my word to them.

This poor woman was *bowed toward herself* and toward that which was depressing. She seemed to grow downward; her life was stooping; she bent lower and lower and lower as the weight of years pressed upon her. Her looks were all earthward; nothing heavenly, nothing bright could come before her eyes; her views were narrowed to the dust and to the grave. So there are some of God's people whose thoughts sink evermore like lead, and their feelings run in a deep groove, cutting evermore a lower channel. You cannot give them delight, but you can readily cause them alarm. By a strange art they squeeze the juice of sorrow from the clusters of Eshcol. Where others would leap for joy, they stoop for very grief, for they draw the unhappy inference that joyous things are not meant for the like of them. Cordials expressly prepared for mourners they dare not accept, and the more comforting they are, the more are they afraid to appropriate them. If there is a dark passage in the Word of God, they are sure to read it and say, "That applies to me." If there is a thundering portion in a sermon, they recollect every syllable of it, and although they wonder how the preacher knows them so well, yet they are sure that he aimed every word at them. If anything occurs in Providence, either adverse or propitious, instead of reading it as a token for good, whether they might rationally do so or not, they manage to translate it into a sign of evil. "All these things are against me," say they, for they can see nothing but the earth and can imagine nothing but fear and distress.

We have known certain prudent but somewhat unfeeling persons to blame these people and chide them for being low spirited. That brings us to notice next *that she could not lift up herself.* There was no use in blaming her. There may have been a time, perhaps, when her older sisters said, "Sister, you should keep yourself more upright; you are getting quite out of figure." Dear me, what good advice some people can give! Advice is usually given gratis, and this is very proper, since in most cases, that is its full value. Advice given to persons who become depressed in spirit is usually unwise and causes pain and aggravation of spirit. I sometimes wish that those who are so ready with their advice had themselves suffered a little, for then, perhaps, they would have the wisdom to hold their tongues. Of what use is it to advise a blind person to see or to tell one who cannot lift up herself that she should be upright and not look so much upon the earth? This is a needless increase of misery. Some persons who pretend to be comforters might more fitly be classed with tormentors.

A spiritual infirmity is as real as a physical one. When Satan binds a soul, it is as truly bound as when a man binds an ox. It cannot get free; it is of necessity in bondage. And that was the condition of this poor woman. I may be speaking to some who have bravely attempted to rally their spirits. They have tried a change of scenery, they have gone into godly company, they have asked Christian people to comfort them, they have frequented the house of God, and they have read consoling books. But still they are bound, and there is no disputing it. As one who pours vinegar upon soda, so is he who sings songs to a sad heart (Prov. 25:20). There is an incongruity about the choicest joys when forced upon broken spirits. Some distressed souls are so sick that they abhor all manner of meat and draw near unto the gates of death. Yet, if any of my readers is in this plight, may they not despair, for Jesus can lift up those who are most bowed down.

The worst point, perhaps, about the poor woman's case was that *she had borne her trouble for eighteen years,* and therefore her disease was chronic and her illness confirmed. Eighteen years! It is a long, long time. Eighteen years of happiness!—the years fly like Mercuries, with wings to their heels: They come, and they are gone. But eighteen years of pain, eighteen years of being bowed down to the earth, eighteen years in which the body approximated rather to the fashion of a brute than to that of a human, what a period this must be! Eighteen long years—each with twelve dreary months dragging like a chain behind it! She had been eighteen years under the bond of the devil. What a woe was this! Can a child of God be eighteen years in despondency? I am bound to answer yes. Similar instances are well known to those familiar with religious biographies. Individuals have been locked up for many years in the gloomy den of despair and yet, after all, have been singularly brought out into joy and comfort. Eighteen years' despondency must be a frightful affliction, and yet there is an escape out of it, for though the devil may take eighteen years to forge a chain, it does not take our blessed Lord eighteen minutes to break it. He can soon set the captive free. Build, build your dungeons, O fiend of hell, and lay the foundations deep and place the courses of granite so fast together that none can stir a stone of your fabric. But when He comes, Your Master who will destroy all your works, He does but speak, and like the unsubstantial fabric of a vision, your bastille vanishes into thin air. Eighteen years of melancholy do not prove that Jesus cannot set the captive free; they only offer Him an opportunity for displaying His gracious power.

Note further about this poor woman, that bowed down as she was both in mind and body, *she yet frequented the house of prayer.* Our Lord was in the synagogue, and there was she. She might very well have said, "It is very painful for me to go into a public place. I should be excused." But no, there she was. Dear child of God, the devil has sometimes suggested to you that it is vain for you to go anymore to hear the Word. Go all the same. He knows you are likely to escape from his hands as long as you hear the Word, and therefore if he can keep you away, he will do so. It was while in the house of prayer that this woman found her liberty, and there *you* may find it. Therefore, still continue to go up to the house of the Lord, come what may.

All this while, too, she was a daughter of Abraham. The devil had tied her up like an ox, but he could not take away her privileged character. She was still a daughter of Abraham, still a believing soul trusting in God by humble faith. When the Savior healed her, He did not say, "Thy sins be forgiven thee." There was no particular sin in the case. He did not address her as He did those whose infirmity had been caused by sin. For notwithstanding her being thus bowed down, all she needed was comfort, not rebuke. Her heart was right with God. I know it was, for the moment she was healed, she began to glorify God, which showed that she was ready for it and that the praise was waiting in her spirit for the glad opportunity. In going up to the house of God, she felt some measure of comfort, though for eighteen years she was bowed down. Where else should she have gone? What good should she have gained by staying at home? A sick child is best in its father's house, and she was best where prayer was to be made.

Here, then, is a picture of what may still be seen among the sons of men and may possibly be your case, dear reader. May the Holy Spirit bless this description to your heart's encouragement.

The Hand of Satan in This Bondage

We should not have known it if our Lord had not told us that it was Satan who had bound this poor woman for eighteen years. *He must have bound her very cunningly to make the knot hold all that time*, for he does not appear to have possessed her. You notice in reading the evangelists that our Lord never laid his hand on a person possessed with a devil. Satan had not *possessed* her, but he had fallen upon her once upon a time eighteen years before and bound her up as men tie a beast in its stable, and she had not been able to get free all that while. The devil can tie in a moment a knot that you and I cannot unloose in eighteen years. He had in this case so securely fastened his victim that no power of herself or others could avail. In the same way, when permitted, he can tie up any one of God's own people in a very short time and by almost any means. Perhaps one word from a preacher that was never meant to cause sadness may make a heart wretched; one single sentence out of a good book or one misunderstood passage of Scripture may be quite enough in Satan's cunning hand to fasten up a child of God in a long bondage.

Satan had bound the woman to herself and to the earth. There is a cruel way of tying a beast that is somewhat after the same fashion. I have seen a poor animal's head fastened to its knee or foot, and somewhat after that fashion, Satan had bound the woman downward to herself. So there are some children of God whose thoughts are all about themselves. They have turned their eyes so that they look inside and see only the transactions of the little world within themselves. They are always lamenting their own infirmities, always mourning their own corruptions, always watching their own emotions. The one and only subject of their thoughts is their own condition. If they ever change the scene and turn to another subject, it is only to gaze upon the earth beneath them, to groan over this poor world with its sorrows, its miseries, its sins, and its disappointments. Thus they are tied to themselves and to the earth and cannot look up to Christ as they should or let the sunlight of His love shine full upon them. They go mourning without the sun, pressed down with cares and burdens. Our Lord uses the figure of an ox or an ass tied up, and He says that even on the Sabbath its owner would loose it for watering.

The poor woman was restrained from what her soul needed. She was like an ox that cannot get to the trough to drink. She knew the promises, she heard them read every Sabbath day, she went to the synagogue and heard of Him who comes to loose the captives, but she could not rejoice in the promise or enter into liberty. So are there multitudes of God's dear people who are fastened to themselves and cannot get to watering, cannot drink from the river of life or find consolation in the Scriptures. They know how precious the gospel is and how consolatory are the blessings of the covenant, but they cannot enjoy the consolations or the blessings. Oh, that they could! They sigh and cry, but they feel themselves to be bound.

There is a saving clause here. Satan had done a good deal to the poor woman, but *he had done all he could do.* You may rest assured that whenever Satan smites a child of God, he never spares his strength. He knows nothing of mercy, neither does any other consideration restrain him. When the Lord delivered Job into Satan's hand for a time, what destruction and havoc Satan made with Job's property. Satan did not save Job chick or child, or sheep or goat or camel or ox, but he smote him right and left and caused ruin to his whole estate. When, under a second permit, Satan came to touch Job in his bone and in his flesh, nothing would satisfy the devil but covering him from the sole of his foot to the crown of his head with sore boils and inflammations. He might have pained him quite sufficiently by torturing one part of his body, but this would not suffice; he must glut himself with vengeance. The devil would do all he could, and therefore he covered him with running sores. Yet, as in Job's case, there was a limit, so was there here. Satan had bound this woman, but he had not killed her. He might bend her toward the grave, but he could not bend her into it. He might make her droop over till she was bent double, but he could not take away her poor feeble life. With all his infernal craft he could not make her die before her time. Moreover, she was still a woman, and he could not make a beast of her, notwithstanding that she was thus bowed down into the form of the brute.

Even so, the devil cannot destroy you, O child of God. He can smite you, but he cannot slay you. He worries those whom he cannot destroy and feels a malicious joy in so doing. He knows there is no hope of your destruction, for you are beyond shot of his gun. But if he cannot wound you with the shot, he will frighten you with the powder if he can. If he cannot slay, he will bind as if for the slaughter. Ay, and he knows how to make a poor soul feel a thousand deaths in fearing one. But all this while, Satan was quite unable to touch this poor woman as to her true standing: She was a daughter of Abraham eighteen years before when first the devil attacked her, and she was a daughter of Abraham eighteen years afterward, when the fiend had done his worst. And you, dear heart, if you should never have a comfortable sense of the Lord's love for eighteen years, are still His beloved. If never once He should give you any token of His love that you could sensibly enjoy, and if by reason of bewilderment and distraction you should keep on writing bitter things against yourself all this while, yet still your name is on the hands of Christ, where none can erase it. You belong to Jesus, and none shall pluck you out of His hands. The devil may bind you fast, but Christ has bound you faster still with cords of everlasting love that must and shall hold you to the end.

That poor woman was being prepared, even by the agency of the devil, to glorify God. Nobody in the synagogue could glorify God as she could when she was at last set free. Every year out of the eighteen gave emphasis to the utterance of her thanksgiving. The deeper her sorrow, the sweeter her song. I should like to have been there that morning, to have heard her tell the story of the emancipating power of the Christ of God. The devil must have felt that he had lost all his trouble, and he must have regretted that he had not let her alone all the eighteen years, since he had only been qualifying her thereby to tell out more sweetly the story of Jesus' wondrous power.

The Liberator at His Work

We have seen the woman bound by the devil, but here comes the Liberator, and the first thing we read of Him is that *He saw her.* His eyes looked round, reading every heart as he glanced from one to another. At last He saw the woman. Yes, that was the very one He was seeking. We are not to think that He saw her in the same way as I see one of you, but He read every line of her character and history, every thought of her heart, every desire of her soul. Nobody had told Him that she had been eighteen years bound, but He knew all about it—how she came to be bound, what she had suffered during the time, how she had prayed for healing, and how the infirmity still pressed upon her. In one minute He had read her history and understood her case. He saw her, and what meaning there was in His searching glance. Our Lord had wonderful eyes. All the painters in the world will never be able to produce a satisfactory picture of Christ because they cannot copy those expressive eyes. Heaven lay calmly reposing in His eyes. They not only were bright and penetrating but also were full of a melting power, a tenderness irresistible, a strength that secured confidence. As He looked at the poor woman, I doubt not the tears started from our Lord's eyes, but they were not tears of unmingled sorrow, for He knew that He could heal her, and He anticipated the joy of doing so.

When He had gazed upon her, *He called her to Him.* Did He know her name? Oh, yes, He knows all our names, and His calling is therefore personal and unmistakable. "I have called thee by thy name," says He; "thou art mine" (Isa. 43:1). See, there is the poor creature, coming up the aisle; that pitiful mass of sorrow, though bowed to the earth, is moving. Is it a woman at all? You can hardly see that she has a face, but she is coming toward Him who called her. She could not stand upright, but she could come *as she was*—bent and infirm as she was. I rejoice in my Master's way of healing people, for He comes to them where they are. He does not propose to them that if they will do somewhat He will do the rest, but He begins and ends. He bids them approach Him as they are and does not ask them to mend or prepare.

When the woman came, *the great Liberator said to her,* "*Woman, thou art loosed from thine infirmity.*" How could that be true? She was still as bent as she was before. He meant that the spell of Satan was taken from her, that the power that had made her thus to bow herself was broken. This she believed in her inmost soul, even as Jesus said it, though as yet she was not at all different in appearance from her former state. Oh, that some of you who are God's dear people would have power to believe that the end of your gloom has come—power to believe that your eighteen years are over and that your time of doubt and despondency is ended. I pray that God may give you grace to know that when this morning's sun first gilded the east, light was ordained for you. Behold, I come today to publish the glad message from the Lord. Come forth, ye prisoners, leap ye captives, for Jesus comes to set you free today. The woman was liberated, but she could not actually enjoy the liberty, and I will tell you why directly. Our Lord proceeded to give her full enlargement in His own way: *He laid His hands on her*. She suffered from lack of strength, and I conceive that the Lord, by putting His hands upon her, poured His life into her. The warm stream of His own infinite power and vitality came into contact with the lethargic stream of her painful existence and so quickened it that she lifted up herself. The deed of love was done: Jesus had done it. Beloved mourners, if we could get you away from thinking about yourselves to thinking about our Lord Jesus and from looking down upon your cares to thinking of Him, what a change would come over you. If His hands could be laid upon you—those dear pierced hands that bought you, those mighty hands that rule heaven and earth on your behalf, those blessed hands that are outstretched to plead for sinners, those dear hands that will press you to His bosom forever—if you could feel them by thinking of Him, then you would soon recover your early joy and renew the elasticity of your spirit, and the bowing dream of your soul would pass away like a night dream, to be forgotten forever. O Spirit of the Lord, make it to be so.

The Loosing of the Bound

She was made straight, we are told, and that at once. Now, what I want you to notice is this, that she must have lifted herself up—that was her own act and deed. No pressure or force was put upon her; she lifted up herself, and yet she was *made straight*. She was passive in that much as a miracle was wrought upon her, but she was active, too, and, being enabled, she lifted up herself. What a wonderful meeting there is here of the active and the passive in the salvation of men. The Arminian says to the sinner, "Now, sinner, you are a responsible being; you must do this and that." The Calvinist says, "Truly, sinner, you are responsible enough, but you are also unable to do anything of yourself. God must work in you both to will and to do." What shall we do with these two teachers? We will let both speak and believe what is true in both their testimonies. Is it true what the Arminian says, that there must be an effort on the sinner's part or he will never be saved? Unquestionably it is. As soon as ever the Lord gives spiritual life, there is spiritual activity. Nobody is ever lugged into heaven by his ears or carried there asleep on a feather bed. God deals with us as with responsible, intelligent beings. That is true, and what is the use of denying it?

Now, what has the Calvinist to say? He says that the sinner is bound by the infirmity of sin and cannot lift up himself, and when he does so, it is God that does it all, and the Lord must have all the glory of it. Is not that true, too? "Oh," says the Arminian, "I never denied that the Lord is to have the glory. I will sing a hymn with you to the divine honor, and I will pray the same prayer with you for the divine power." It is most true that Jesus alone saves the sinner and equally true that the sinner believes unto salvation. The Holy Ghost never believed on behalf of anybody: A man must believe for himself and repent for himself or be lost. But yet there never was a grain of true faith or true repentance in this world except it was produced by the Holy Ghost. I am not going to explain these difficulties, because they are not difficulties except in theory. They are plain facts of practical everyday life. The poor woman knew at any rate where to put the crown. She did not say, "I straightened myself." But she glorified God and attributed all the work to His gracious power.

The most remarkable fact is that *she was made straight immediately*, for there was something beyond her infirmity to be overcome. Suppose that any person had been diseased of the spine or of the nerves and muscles for eighteen years, even if the disease that occasioned his being deformed could be entirely removed, what would be the effect? Why, that the result of the disease would still remain, for the body would have become set through long continuance in one posture. In this case, the bond that held the poor bowed body was taken away, and at the same time, the consequent rigidity was removed, and she in a moment stood up straight. This was a double display of miraculous power. O my poor tried friend, if the Lord will visit you, He will take away not only the first and greatest cause of your sadness but also the very tendency to melancholy.

The long grooves that you have worn shall be smoothed, the ruts in the road of sorrow that you have worn by long continuance in sadness shall be filled up, and you shall be strong in the Lord and in the power of His might.

The cure being thus perfect, *up rose the woman to glorify God.* I wish I had been there. I should have liked to have seen that hypocritical ruler of the synagogue when he made his angry speech. I should have liked to have seen him when the Master silenced him so thoroughly. But especially I should have rejoiced to have seen this poor woman standing upright and to have heard her praise the Lord. What did she say? It is not recorded, but we can well imagine. It was something like this: "I have been eighteen years in and out among you. You have seen me and know what a poor, miserable, wretched object I was. But God has lifted me up all in a moment. Blessed be His name, I have been made straight." What she spoke with her mouth was not half of what she expressed. No reporter could have taken it down. She spoke with her eyes, she spoke with her hands, she spoke with every limb of her body. I suppose she moved about to see whether she was really straight and to make sure that it was not all a delusion. She must have been all over a living mass of pleasure, and by every movement, she praised God from the sole of the foot to the crown of the head. Never was there a more eloquent woman in the universe. She was like one newborn, delivered from a long death, joyous with all the novelty of a fresh life. Well might she glorify God.

She made no mistake as to how the cure was wrought. She traced it to a divine power, and that divine power she extolled. Brother, sister, cannot you glorify Christ that He has set you free? Though bound so long you need not be bound any longer. Christ is able to deliver you. Trust Him, believe Him, be made straight, and then go and tell your kinsfolk and acquaintances, "You knew how depressed I was, for you cheered me in my sorrow as best you could, but now I have to tell you what the Lord has done for my soul."

Expecting the Lord Jesus
to Do the Same Thing Today

What was His reason for setting this woman free? According to His own statement it was, first of all, *human kindness*. He says, "When you have your ox tied up and you see that it is thirsty, you untie the knot and lead the poor creature away down to the river to water. None of you would leave an ox tied up to famish." This is good reasoning and leads us to believe that Jesus will help sorrowing ones. Tried soul, would you not loose an ox if you saw it suffering? And do you think the Lord will not loose you? Have you more mercy than the Christ of God? Come, come, think not so meanly of my Master. If your heart would lead you to pity an animal, do you think His heart will not lead Him to pity you? He has not forgotten you: He remembers you still. His tender humanity moves Him to set you free.

More than that, there was *special relationship*. He tells this master of the synagogue that a man would loose *his* ox. Perhaps he might not think it his business to go and loose that which belonged to another man, but it is his own ox, and he will loose him. And do you think, dear heart, that the Lord Jesus will not loose you? He bought you with His blood, His Father gave you to Him, He has loved you with an everlasting love: Will He not loose you? You are His property. Do you not know that He runs over hill and dale to find His lost sheep? Will He not liberate His captive daughter? Assuredly He will. Are you a daughter of Abraham, a child of faith, and will He not set you free? Depend upon it, He will.

Next, there was a *point of antagonism* that moved the Savior to act promptly. He says, "This woman being a daughter of Abraham, whom Satan hath bound." Now, if I knew the devil had tied anything up, I am sure I would try to unloose it, would not you? We may be sure some mischief is brewing when the devil is working, and therefore, it must be a good deed to undo his work. But Jesus Christ came into the world on purpose to destroy the works of the devil; and so when He saw the woman like a tied-up ox, He said, "I will unloose her if for nothing else but that I may undo what the devil has done." Now, dear tried friend, inasmuch as your sorrow may be traced to Satanic influence, Jesus Christ will prove in your case more than a match for the devil, and He will set you free.

Then think of *her sorrowful condition*. An ox tied up to the manger without water would soon be in a very sad plight. Pity it, poor thing. Hear the lowing of the ox as hour after hour its thirst tells upon it. Would you not pity it? And do you think the Lord does not pity His poor, tried, tempted, afflicted children? Those tears, shall they fall for nothing? Those sleepless nights, shall they be disregarded? That broken heart that would but cannot believe the promise, shall that forever be denied a hearing? Has the Lord forgotten to be gracious? Has He in anger shut up the bowels of His mercy? Ah, no, He will remember your sorrowful estate and hear your groanings, for He puts your tears into His bottle.

Last of all, there was this reason to move the heart of Christ, that *she had been eighteen years in that state*. "Then," said He, "she shall be loosed at once." The ruler of the synagogue would have said, "She has been eighteen years bound, and she may well wait till tomorrow, for it is only one day." "Nay," says Christ, "if she has been bound eighteen years, she shall not wait a minute. She has had too much of it already. She shall be set free at once." Do not, therefore, argue from the length of your despondency that it shall not come to an end, but rather argue from it that release is near. The night has been so long it must be so much nearer the dawning. You have been scourged so long that it must be so much nearer the last stroke, for the Lord does not afflict willingly nor grieve the children of men. Therefore take heart and be of good courage. Oh, that my divine Master would now come and do what I fain would do but cannot, namely, make every child of God to leap for joy.

I know what this being bound up by Satan means. The devil has not tied me up for eighteen years at a stretch, and I do not think he ever will, but he has brought me into sad bondage many a time. Still, my Master comes and sets me free and leads me out to watering. And what a drink I get at such times? I seem as if I could drink up the Jordan at a draught when I get to His promises and swallow my fill of His sweet love. I know by this that He will lead other poor souls out to the watering. And when He does so to any of you, I pray you drink like an ox. You may be tied up again; therefore drink as much as you can of His grace and rejoice while you may. Eat that which is good and let your soul delight in fatness. Be glad in the Lord, you righteous, and shout for joy all you who are upright in heart, for the Lord looses the prisoners. May He loose you now. Amen.

God also may find a reason for allowing His saints to be tempted of Satan, and that reason may have more relation to others than to themselves. They may have to be tested for other people's good. The testing of their faith is "more precious than of gold that perisheth, though it be tried with fire" (1 Pet. 1:7), and part of its preciousness is its usefulness. The child of God under temptation, behaving himself grandly, will become a standing example to those who are around him. "Ye have heard of the patience of Job" (James 5:11), but you never would have heard of the patience of Job if Satan had not sifted him. This great treasury of instruction, the book of Job, and all the truth taught us by Job's example come to us through God's having permitted Satan to put forth his hand and to press the patriarch so sorely. We also may be afflicted not so much for ourselves as for others, and this may be remarkably the case in the instances of those of you whom God makes useful to a large circle of friends. You live for others, and therefore suffer for others. The whole of your lives will be accounted for not by yourselves but by your surroundings. As a minister, I may have to be tempted because temptation is one of the best books in a minister's library. As a parent, you may need affliction because a father without a trial can give no counsel to a tempted child. Public workers have to be tried in ways that to a private Christian are unnecessary. Let us accept remarkable discipline if thereby we are qualified for remarkable service. If by the roughness of our own road we are trained to conduct the Lord's sheep along their difficult pathway to the pastures on the hilltops of glory, let us rejoice in every difficulty of the way. If apostles and men like Peter had to be put into Satan's sieve while they were being trained for their lifework, we may not hope to escape.

Chapter Ten

Jesus' Prayer for Peter

And the Lord said, Simon, Simon, behold, Satan hath desired to have you, that he may sift you as wheat: But I have prayed for thee, that thy faith fail not: and when thou art converted, strengthen thy brethren—Luke 22:31–32.

PETER WAS TO BE SIFTED, so our Lord warned him, and Satan was to operate with the sieve. Satan had an intense desire to destroy Peter. Indeed, Satan would like to destroy all the chosen of God. Therefore, Satan desired to sift Peter as wheat in the hope that he would be blown away with the husks and the chaff. To see a child of God perish would bring to the evil one a malicious joy, for he would have wounded the heart of God. If ever the fallen spirit can be happy, he would derive happiness from defeating the grace of God and robbing the Lord Jesus of those whom He bought with His blood. "Satan hath desired to have you." It would be a satisfaction to him to have a believer in his power. He was anxious to get Peter into his clutches, to give him as tremendous a shaking as he could manage.

If Satan knows, as he no doubt does, concerning any one believer that he cannot quite destroy him, he is especially anxious to worry him. If he cannot devour the chosen, he would at least defile them. If he cannot ruin their souls, he would break their quiet. As the Revised Version puts it, Satan even asks of God to have them that he may sift them as wheat. This is a curious statement, for it seems from it that the devil can pray and that his petition may be granted him. The margin has it: "Satan hath obtained you by asking." The Lord may grant the request of the devil himself, and yet He would not prove thereby that He had any love toward him. The Lord's wisdom may grant Satan's desire and in the very act overthrow his evil power. Let us not, then, stake our faith in the Lord's love upon His giving us the precise answer we desire, for what He gives to Satan He may see fit to deny to those whom He loves, and He may do so because He loves them.

It is a fact that the evil one is permitted to test the precious metal of God's treasury. The story in the book of Job is no fiction or piece of imagination. It is, even so, that Satan desires to have choice ones of God put into his power that he may test them, that he may torment them, that he may, if possible, destroy them. The Lord may permit this, as He did in the case of Job and as He did in the case of the apostles, and specially in the case of Peter. He may grant the tempter's request and allow him to touch our bone and our flesh and see whether we will hold to our God in mortal agony.

We are not bound to know God's reasons for what He does or permits. It is sometimes sinful to inquire into those reasons. What the Lord does is right; let that be enough for us who are His children. But we can see sometimes a reason why the saints should be sifted as wheat, for *it is customary for wheat to be sifted.* Sifting brings a desirable result with it: It is *for the saints' good* that they should be tried. Satan doubtless wishes that he may let the good seed fall to the ground and be destroyed. But God overrules it to separate the chaff from the wheat and to make the wheat into clean grain, fit for storage in the King's granary. Satan has often done us a good turn when he has meant to do us a bad one.

God also may find a reason for allowing His saints to be tempted of Satan, and that reason may have more relation to others than to themselves. They may have to be tested *for other people's good.* The testing of their faith is "more precious than of gold that perisheth, though it be tried with fire" (1 Pet. 1:7), and part of its preciousness is its usefulness. The child of God under temptation, behaving himself grandly, will become a standing example to those who are around him. "Ye have heard of the patience of Job" (James 5:11), but you never would have heard of the patience of Job if Satan had not sifted him. This great treasury of instruction, the book of Job, and all the truth taught us by Job's example come to us through God's having permitted Satan to put forth his hand and to press the patriarch so sorely. We also may be afflicted not so much for ourselves as for others, and this may be remarkably the case in the instances of those of you whom God makes useful to a large circle of friends. You live for others, and therefore suffer for others. The whole of your lives will be accounted for not by yourselves but by your surroundings. As a minister, I may have to be tempted because temptation is one of the best books in a minister's library. As a parent, you may need affliction because a father without a trial can give no counsel to a tempted child. Public workers have to be tried in ways that to a private Christian are unnecessary. Let us accept remarkable discipline if thereby we are qualified for remarkable service. If by the roughness of our own road we are trained to conduct the Lord's sheep along their difficult pathway to the pastures on the hilltops of glory, let us rejoice in every difficulty of the way. If apostles and men like Peter had to be put into Satan's sieve while they were being trained for their lifework, we may not hope to escape.

Observe what came before the sifting and went out with the sifting. Note well that blessed "but." *"But I have prayed for thee."* Jesus, that master in the art of prayer, that mighty pleader who is our Advocate above, assures us that He has already prayed for us. "I have prayed for thee" means: "Before the temptation, I have prayed for you. I foresaw all the danger in which you would be placed, and concerning that danger I have exercised my function as High Priest and Intercessor." What a divine comfort is this to any who are passing through deep waters! You only go where Jesus has gone before you with His intercession. Jesus has made provision for all your future in a prayer already presented. "I *have* prayed for thee." You may be much comforted by the prayers of a Christian who has power with God, but what are all such intercessions compared with the praying of your Lord? It were well to have Noah, Samuel, and Moses praying for us but better far to have Jesus say, "I have prayed for thee." Blessed be God, Satan may have his sieve, but as long as Jesus wears His breastplate, we shall not be destroyed by Satan's tossings.

Notice that the principal object of the prayer of our Lord was *"that thy faith fail not."* Jesus knows where the vital point lies, and there He holds the shield. As long as the Christian's faith is safe, the Christian's self is safe. I may compare faith to the head of the warrior. O Lord, you have covered my head in the day of battle, for you have prayed for me that my faith fail not. I may compare faith to the heart, and the Lord holds His shield over the heart that we may not be injured where a wound would be fatal. "I have prayed for thee, that thy faith fail not." Faith is the standard-bearer in every spiritual conflict, and if the standard-bearer fall, then it is an evil day. Therefore our Lord prays that the standard-bearer may never fail to hold up his banner in the midst of the fray: If faith fails, courage fails, patience fails, hope fails, love fails, joy fails. Faith is the root-grace; and if this be not in order, the leafage of the soul, which shows itself in the form of other graces, will soon begin to wither. "I have prayed for thee, that thy faith fail not."

Learn from this—that you take care to commend your faith to your God. Do not begin to doubt because you are tempted: That is to lay bare your breast. Do not doubt because you are attacked: That is to loosen your harness. Believe still. "I had fainted," said David, "unless I had believed" (Ps. 27:13). We are either believing or fainting. Which shall it be? "Above all, taking the shield of faith" (Eph. 6:16), not only taking it so that it may cover all but also making this the vital point of holy carefulness. Watch in all things, but specially guard your faith. If you are careful about one thing more than another, above all be careful of your faith. "I have prayed for thee, that thy faith fail not." Our Savior's pleading goes to the point, and thus it teaches us where to direct our own desires and our own prayers. He asks for us far more wisely than we shall ever learn to ask for ourselves. Let us copy His petitions.

Therefore it follows because of Christ's prayer that though Peter may be very badly put to it, yet he shall be recovered, for Christ speaks of it as of an assured fact: "*When thou art converted.*" It is as much as to say, "When you come back to your old life and your old faith, exercise yourself usefully for your Lord." Jesus speaks of Peter's restoration as if it were quite sure to be. And is it not quite sure to be? If Jesus, the Beloved of the Father, prays for His people, shall He not win His suit with God? He will win it! He will uplift Peter from among the siftings where Satan has thrown him. We are sure He will, for in prospect thereof He sets him a loving and suitable task: "When thou art converted, strengthen thy brethren." The establishment and confirmation of all the rest are to hinge upon the setting up in his place of poor, thrice-denying Peter.

I may be addressing a number of people who believe on the

Lord Jesus Christ as Peter did but have fallen into a bad state and need a new conversion. I am very sorry for you, but I am by no means staggered at the sight of you, for you belong to a numerous class. I am constantly counseling backsliders, who come back very sincerely and very truly and are pleased to find a Christian home again. I meet with many who have been outside in the world, some of them for years, attending the house of God very irregularly and seldom or never enjoying the light of God's countenance. They have wandered so that none can tell whether they are the Lord's or not, except the Lord Himself, and He always knows those who are His. I bear happy witness that the Lord brings His own back again. Though the Lord's sheep stray, yet the Good Shepherd finds them. Though the Lord's children go into the far country, yet they each one in due time say, "I will arise and go to my father" (Luke 15:18). It is not every prodigal who returns, but only the prodigal *son*. In due time, the son returns to the Father's house. The Lord will find His own even though Satan tries to prevent the gracious discovery.

It may be that you have wandered into error. May you be brought back very speedily; and if you are, we say to you, "Strengthen your brethren." Possibly there has been a general decay in grace within your soul; you have lost your joy, your peace, your love, your zeal. May the Lord restore you in answer to the prayer of Him who redeemed you. And then, when you are converted, seek to recover your brethren from the decay of their graces that has also injured them. You will not be converted in quite the same sense as you were at first, but yet you will be turned again to your old life and hope, and then you are to strengthen your brethren by aiming at the restoration to their first love and earliest zeal.

Perhaps you have been neglectful. I find that many who were good Christian people in the country, always at the house of prayer and walking near to God, will come up to this wicked London to live, and the change is a serious injury to them. They get lost to Christian society, and by degrees they become deteriorated by the ungodliness of this modern Sodom. Nobody in the street wherein they live ever goes to a place of worship, and they do not know anybody at the church, and so they give up going to public worship and fall into the ways and habits of the ungodly world. They are not happy. God's children never are happy when they leave their Father. If you have ever eaten the white bread of heaven, you will never rest content with the black ashes of earth. If the flavor of Christ's love has once been in your mouth, you are spoiled for a worldling. You will not make an expert sinner now, for your hand is out of it. Once converted, you must be a child of God, or nothing. You are ruined for this world; and if the world to come is not yours, where are you? The devil himself will not like you long; you are not of his sort. There is a something about you that will not suit Satan any more than Jonah suited the whale. The whale was quite as glad to part with Jonah as Jonah was to be set free from the whale. I see arrangements for your coming home again. The Lord devises means that His banished shall not perish. Those tokens of disquiet, those startings in your sleep, those horrible forebodings, those inward hungerings, are all pulling at you to come home. You have been trying to feed upon the dust that is ordained to be the serpent's meat, and if the Lord had not loved you, you would have done so. A deceived heart has turned you aside, but in love to your soul, the Lord has made you aware of it, and your cry is, "I will go and return to my first husband, for then it was better with me than now." These are tokens by which I am assured that the Lord will bring His own back. I rest confident that He will turn them, and they shall be turned. And I am going to talk to backsliders about what they are to do when they do come back again.

We are going to take it for granted that they will come back and to speak to them now about what it is their privilege to attempt under such gracious circumstances. "When thou art converted, strengthen thy brethren."

His Duty

He has gone astray, and he has been brought back; what better can he do than to strengthen his brethren? *He will thus help to undo the evil that he has wrought.* Peter must have staggered his brethren. Some of them must have been quite frightened at him. John soon looked after him, but then they were not all Johns. Full of love, John soon hunted up Peter, but the others must have felt that he was a mere reed shaken by the wind. It must have staggered the faith of the weaker sort to see that Peter, who had been such a leader among them, was among the first to deny his Lord. Therefore, Peter, you must build what you have thrown down and bind up what you have torn! Go and talk to these people again and tell them how foolish and weak you were. Warn them not to imitate your example. You must henceforth be more bold than anybody else, that you may in some measure undo the mischief that you have done.

Now, do think of this, any of you who have been cold toward the Lord. You have wasted months, and even years, in backsliding. Try to recover lost ground. It will be almost impossible for you to do it, but do at least make a serious attempt. If anybody has been staggered by your backsliding, look after him, and try to bring him back, and strengthen him. Ask his pardon and beg him to recover the strength of which you helped to rob him. This is the least that you can do. If almighty love has drawn you back again after sad wanderings, lay yourself out with all your heart to do good to those who may have been harmed by your sad turnings aside. Am I asking more of you than simple justice demands?

Besides, *how can you better express your gratitude to God* than by seeking to strengthen your weak brethren when you have been strengthened yourself? After our first conversion, you and I were found seeking earnestly after sinners like ourselves. We had been newly brought out of the house of bondage, and we longed to lead other slaves into the liberty wherewith Christ makes men free. This, I say, we should do when first brought to Jesus' feet. But if, to our disgrace, we have turned aside and have backslidden, and if, to God's infinite glory, He has restored our souls and made us strong again, we renew our zeal for the salvation of others, and we should have a special eye to backsliders like ourselves. We should say, "Lord, I will show how much I thank You for restoring me by endeavoring to find any who have been overtaken in a fault, that I may restore such in the spirit of meekness, remembering myself also, since I have been tempted and have not stood against temptation." Those of you whom the Good Shepherd has restored should have a quick eye for all the sickly ones of the flock and watch over them with a sympathetic care. You should say, "This is the field that I shall try to cultivate. Because in my spiritual sickness the Lord has been pleased to deal so graciously with me, I would therefore lay myself out to cherish others who are diseased in soul."

Do you not think, too, that this becomes our duty because *doubtless it is a part of the divine design*? Never let us make a mistake by imagining that God's grace is given to a man simply with an eye to himself. Grace neither begins with man nor ends with him with an object confined to the man's own self. When God chose His ancient people Israel, it was not merely that Israel might enjoy the light but that Israel might preserve the light for the rest of the nations. When God saved you, He did not save you for your own sake but saved you for His own name's sake, that He might through you show forth His mercy to others. We are windows through which the light of heavenly knowledge is to shine upon multitudes of eyes. The light is not for the windows themselves but for those to whom it comes through the windows. Have you ever thought enough about this? When the Lord brings you back from your backsliding, it is decidedly with this view—that you may be qualified to sympathize with others and wisely guide them back to the fold. All your history, if you read it aright, has a bearing upon your usefulness to your fellowmen. If you have been permitted in an hour of weakness to grow cold or turn aside, and if the Lord in unspeakable compassion has restored you to His ways, surely this must be His motive—that you may afterward strengthen your brethren.

By the way, the very wording of the text seems to suggest the duty: We are to strengthen our "brethren." We must do it *so that we may manifest brotherly love and thus prove our sonship toward God.* What a blessed thing it is when we come back to God and feel that we are still in the family! That was the point we debated with ourselves: We feared that we were not the Lord's. It is not a bad thing to try yourself and see whether your faith is gold or dross. To have a question about your position in the heavenly family is a very painful thing and should not be endured one moment if it is in our power to solve the doubt. But if the Lord has brought you back as His child, you now know that you belong to the family, and it will be suggested at once to you to do something for *the brethren.* Naturally, you will look around to see whether there is any child of God to whom you can show favor for his Father's sake. You have injured all by your backsliding; and hence it is your duty, when restored to the family, to benefit them all by special consecration and double earnestness. Let it be your delight as well as your duty to strengthen your brethren. Prove that you are a brother by acting a brother's part. Claim your privilege as a child and exercise it as a child should by helping another child who is in need. I think that the text within itself contains this argument.

Let us see to it, dear friends, if we have been restored, that we try to look after our weak brethren, *that we may show forth a zeal for the honor and glory of our Lord.* When we went astray, we dishonored Christ. If any of these others go astray, they will do the same. Therefore, let us be watchful that if we can, we may prevent their being as foolish as we have been. Let us learn tenderness from our own experience and feel a deep concern for our brethren. If one member of this church sins, we all suffer—in our reputation, at any rate; and, specially, the best known among us have to bear a great deal because of the inconsistency of this person and of that. Do you want us to be wounded through you? Alas, Christ Himself suffers! His worst wounds are those He receives in the house of His friends. Peter, if you ever denied your Master, mind you look well to others who are growing presumptuous as you were before your great sin. If you meet anyone who is beginning to say, "I will go with you to prison and to death," give him a gentle jog and say, "Mind, brother, you are going near a nasty hole into which I once fell. I pray you take warning from me." If you speak from experience, you will have no cause to boast, but you will find your own sin a reason why you should tenderly guard your brethren lest they should cause like dishonor to that dear name that is more precious, I hope, to you than life itself. "When thou art converted, strengthen thy brethren." It is your duty.

He Has a Qualification for It

This Peter is the man who, when he is brought back again, can strengthen his brethren. He can strengthen them by telling them of *the bitterness of denying his Master.* He went out and wept bitterly. It is one thing to weep; it is another thing to weep bitterly. There are sweet tears as well as salt tears, but oh, what weeping a sin costs a child of God! I recall a minister speaking very unguardedly that the child of God lost nothing by sin except his comfort. And I thought, "Oh, dear me! And is that nothing?" It is such a loss of comfort that if that were all, it would be the most awful thing in the world. The more God loves you and the more you love God, the more expensive will you find it to sin. An ordinary sinner sins cheaply; the child of God sins very dearly. If you are the King's favorite, you must mind your manners, for He will not take from you what He will take from an enemy. The Lord your God is a jealous God because He is a loving God. He has such love for His own chosen that if they turn aside, His jealousy burns like coals of juniper. May God keep us from ever provoking His sacred jealousy by wandering at any time into any kind of sin. Peter, because he could tell of the bitterness of backsliding, was the man to go and speak to anyone who was about to backslide: "Do not so, my brother, for it will cost you dear."

Peter was the man to tell another of *the weakness of the flesh,* for he could say to him, "Do not trust yourself. Do not talk about never going aside. Remember how I talked about it. I used to be very lofty in my talk and in my feelings, but I had to come down. I felt so sure that I loved my Lord and Master that I put great confidence in myself and could not think that I should ever wander from Him. But see, see how I fell. I denied Him thrice ere the time called cock-crowing." Thus, you see, Peter was wonderfully qualified, by having known the bitterness of sin and by feeling the weakness of his own flesh, to go and strengthen others in these important points.

Peter was also qualified to bear his personal witness to *the power of his Lord's prayer.* He could never forget that Jesus had said to him, "I have prayed for thee." He would say to any brother who had grown cold or presumptuous, "The Lord Jesus prayed for me, and it was because of His prayer that I was preserved from going further, so that I was led back and delivered from the sieve of the evil one." Do you not think that this would strengthen any trembling one when Peter mentioned it? It is wonderful how men and women are helped by those who have had a similar experience to themselves. Theory is all very well, but to speak from experience has a singular power about it. How one can comfort the bereaved if one has been bereaved himself! But how little can the young and inexperienced yield of consolation to those who are greatly tried, even though they are anxious to do so! And so, brethren, if the Lord has blessed you and remembered you in His great mercy and you know the power of the prayer of the great Intercessor, you can strengthen your brethren by reminding them of the perseverance of the Savior's love.

And could not Peter speak about *the love of Jesus to poor wanderers?* The Lord turned and looked upon Peter, and that look broke Peter's heart, and afterward the Lord spoke to Peter by the sea and said to him, "Feed my sheep" (John 21:16). O beloved, Peter would always remember that, and he would speak of it to any whom he found in a sad and weary condition. He would say, "My Lord was very good to me and was willing to receive me back. Nay, He did not wait until I came back, but He came after me. He sent after me, saying, 'Go tell my disciples *and Peter;*' and when He saw that I was penitent, He never rebuked me except in such a gentle way that I was rather comforted than rebuked by what He said." O you who have wandered and Christ has restored you, comfort the wanderers when you see their tears! When you hear any word of doubt or anything like despair from them, tell them that there is no truth in the suggestion of Satan that Christ is unwilling to forgive. Beseech them not to slander that dear heart of love, which is infinitely more ready to melt toward the penitent than the penitent's heart is to melt toward it. You know it. You know that you can speak not only what you have read in the Bible but also what you have felt in your own heart. You are qualified, therefore, to strengthen your brethren.

And could not Peter fully describe *the joy of restoration?* "Oh," he would say, "do not wander. There is no good in it. Do not go away from Jesus. There is no profit to be found there. Come back to Him. There is such peace, such rest with Him. Never, never go away again." Peter ever afterward in his epistles—and we are sure that it must have been the same in his spoken ministry—would testify to the love and goodness of Christ and urge the saints to steadfastness in the faith. I would appeal to any child of God whether he ever gained anything by going away from Christ. No, the old proverb says that honesty is the best policy, but I will turn it to a higher use and say, "Holiness is the best policy." Communion with Christ is the happiest life. If you gained all the world and did not lose your soul but only lost the light of Christ's countenance for a few days, you would make a poor bargain. There is heaven in every glance of His eye. There is infinite joy in every word of His mouth when He speaks comfortably to His servants. Go not away from Him. Be like Milton's angel, who lived in the sun. Abide in Christ, and let His words abide in you. Closer, closer, closer, this is the way to spiritual wealth. To follow afar off and live at a distance from Christ, even if it does not make your soul to perish, yet it will wither up your joys and make you feel an unhappy man, an unhappy woman. Therefore, all those who have tried it should bear their witness and put their experience into the scale as they thus strengthen their brethren.

It Will Be Such a Benefit to Himself

Continually and heartily strengthen your brethren, for thus you will be *made to see your own weakness.* You will see it in those whom you comfort. As you see how they doubt or grow cold or become lukewarm, you will say to yourself, "These are men of like passions with myself. I see which way I shall drift unless the grace of God sustains me." It will lead you to throw out another anchor and get a fresh hold as you see how they yield to the tide. One man is wonderfully like another man, only that other men are better than we are; and when we are trying to strengthen them, we are not to look upon ourselves as superior beings but rather as inferior beings and say, "He fell yesterday, I may fall today; and if I do not fall today, I may tomorrow." All the weaknesses and follies you see in others, believe that they are in yourself, and that will tend to humble you. I think that a true minister is often excited to better work by what he sees of weakness in his people because he says to himself, "Am I feeding this flock well?" Perhaps he thinks to himself, "If I had properly tended them, they would not have shown all these weaknesses." And then he will begin to blame his own ministry and look to his own heart, and that is a good thing for us all. We very seldom, I think, blame ourselves too much, and it is a benefit to us to see our own failings in others.

But what *a comfort* it must have been to Peter *to have such a charge committed to him!* How sure he must have felt that Jesus had forgiven and restored him to His confidence, when the Lord, having asked him, "[L]ovest thou me?" said to him, "Feed my lambs" (John 21:15). Peter is all right again, or else Christ would not trust lambs to him. It is a grand proof of our being fully restored to the divine heart when the Lord entrusts us with work to do for His own dear children. If you and I are made the means of strengthening our brethren, what a comfort it will be to our hearts! I know that it is not the highest form of comfort, for Jesus would say of it, "In this rejoice not...but rather rejoice, because your names are written in heaven" (Luke 10:20). But still to a loving child of God, it is no small consolation to find that God is using him. I know, for my own part, that when I go to see our friends who are ill and near to death, it is a supreme consolation to see how calm they always are, without any exception. Yes, and how joyful they are and triumphant in the departing hour! Then I say to myself, "Yes, my Master has owned my ministry." The seals of fresh conversions are very precious, but the surest seals are these dying saints who have been nurtured in the gospel that we have preached. They prove the truth of it, for if they do not flinch when they stand looking into eternity, but even rejoice in the prospect of meeting their Lord, then what we preach is true, and our Master has not left us without witness. So you see that it is a great benefit to a man to strengthen his brethren because it becomes a comfort to his own soul.

And whenever you lay yourself out to strengthen weak Christians, as I pray you may, *you will get benefit from what you do in the holy effort*. Suppose you pray with them. Well, then, you will pray a little more than if you only prayed for yourself, and anything that adds to your prayerfulness is a clear gain. I wish that you had the habit of making everybody pray with you who comes to your house, saying to them, "Now we have done our little business, let us have a word or two of prayer." Even some of God's people would look at you. It will do them good to look at you and learn from you the blessed habit. With regard to those who are strangers to divine things, there will often occur opportunities in which you have put them under an obligation, or they have come to you in trouble to ask advice, and then you may boldly say, "Do not let us part till we have prayed." We used to have an old member of our church who used to pray in very extraordinary places. Two women were fighting, and he knelt down between them to pray, and they stopped their fighting directly. Before a door when there has been a noise in the house, he has begun to pray. He was better than a policeman, for his prayer awed the most obstinate. They could not understand it. They thought it a strange thing, and they did not care to put themselves into direct opposition to the man of God. There is a wonderful power in prayer to bless ourselves besides the blessing that it will bring upon others. Pray with the weak ones, and you will not be a weak one yourself.

Well, then, your example. If you use your example to strengthen the weak—if you carefully say to yourself, "No, I shall not do that because, though I may do it, I may do injury to some weak one"—this will do you good. If you hesitate, if you draw back from your own rights and say, "No, no, no. I am thinking of the weak ones," you will get good from that self-denial. If the poor, trembling wandering backslider is much upon your mind, you will often be very tender how you act. You will look to see where your foot is going down next time for fear of treading upon somebody or other. And in that way, you will be winning for yourself the great gain of a holy carefulness of walk and conversation—no small gain to you.

And again, suppose that in trying to strengthen these weak ones, you begin to quote Scripture to them—quote a promise to them—this will bless you. Some of you do not know which promise to quote. You do not even know where to find it in the Word. But if you are in the habit of studying Scripture with a view to strengthening the weak, you will understand it in the best way, for you will get it in a practical form and shape. You will have the Bible at your fingertips. Moreover, one of these days, the text that you looked up for old Mary will suit yourself. How often have we paid Paul with that which we meant to give to Peter! We have ourselves fed on the milk we prepared for the babes. Sometimes what we have laid up for another comes in handy for ourselves. We strangely find that we have been fed while we were feeding others, according to that promise, "[H]e that watereth shall be watered also himself" (Prov. 11:25).

I have said all this to you who have wandered and come back, and I want to say it directly to you. May the Holy Spirit speak to your inmost souls. You know who you are and how far all this applies to you. The Lord bless you.

But if you have not wandered, if the Lord has kept you these twenty years close to Him and given you the light of His countenance all that time, I think that you and I and any of us of that sort ought to strengthen our brethren still more. Oh, what we owe to sovereign grace! To be kept from wandering—what a blessing is that! Let us feel that instead of having a small debt to pay, we have a greater debt to acknowledge. Let us wake up to strengthen our brethren.

And then, once more, if all this should be done to those who are in the family, what ought we not to do for those outside—for those who have no Christ and no Savior? If you are converted yourself, seek the salvation of your children, of your own brothers and sisters, and of all your household. Try to bring in your neighbors to hear the Word. Get them, if you can, under the sound of the gospel.

Tarry here just a minute to recollect that the angels also are, according to your measure and degree, at your call. You have but to pray to God, and angels shall bear you up in their hands lest you dash your foot against a stone. We do not think enough of these heavenly beings, yet they are all ministering spirits sent forth to minister to those who are heirs of salvation. Like Elijah's servant, if your eyes were opened, you would see the mountain full of horses of fire and chariots of fire round about the servants of God. Let us learn from our Master to reckon upon forces invisible. Let us not trust in that which is seen of the eye and heard of the ear, but let us have respect to spiritual agencies that evade the senses but are known to faith. Angels play a far greater part in the affairs of Providence than we realize. God can raise us up friends on earth, and if He does not do so, He can find us abler friends in heaven. There is no need to pluck out the sword with which to cut off men's ears, for infinitely better agencies will work for us. Have faith in God, and all things shall work for your good. The angels of God think it an honor and a delight to protect the least of His children.

Chapter Eleven

Jesus Declining the Legions

*Thinkest thou that I cannot now pray to my Father, and he shall
presently give me more than twelve legions of angels? But how
then shall the scriptures be fulfilled, that thus it must be?*
                                    —Matthew 26:53–54

IT IS THE GARDEN of Gethsemane. Here
stands our Lord, and yonder is the betrayer. He is foremost of the
multitude. You know his face, the face of that son of perdition, even
Judas Iscariot. He comes forward, leaving the men with the staves
and the swords and the torches and the lanterns, and he proceeds
to kiss his Master. It is the token by which the officers are to know
their victim. You perceive at once that the disciples are excited: One
of them cries, "Lord, shall we smite with the sword?"(Luke 22:49).
Their love for their Master has overcome their prudence. There are
but eleven of them, a small band to fight against the cohort sent by
the authorities to arrest their Master. But love makes no reckoning
of odds. Before an answer can be given, Peter has struck the first
blow, and the servant of the high priest has narrowly escaped having his head cleft in twain; as it is, his ear is cut off.

One is not altogether surprised at Peter's act; for in addition to
his headlong zeal, he had most likely misunderstood the saying of
his Lord at supper: "[H]e that hath no sword, let him sell his garment, and buy one" (Luke 22:36). There was not time for our Lord
to explain, and they were so accustomed to His concrete style of

speech that they should not have misunderstood Him; but they did so. He had simply told them that the days of peace, in which they could freely go in and out among the people, had now come to an end. For as He Himself, who had once been in favor with all the people, would now be "reckoned among the transgressors" (Luke 22:37), so would the disciples be counted among the offscouring of all things. Now they could no longer reckon on the hospitality of a friendly people but must carry their own purse and scrip. Instead of feeling safe wherever they went, they must understand that they were in an enemy's country and must travel through the world like men armed for self-defense. They were now to use their own substance, to not hope for cheerful entertainment among a grateful people, and would need to be on their guard against those who in killing them would think that they were doing God service.

They took His language literally and therefore replied, "Lord, behold, here are two swords" (Luke 22:38). I think He must have smiled sadly at their blunder as He answered, "It is enough." He could never have thought of their fighting that He might not be delivered to the Jews, since for that purpose two swords were simply ridiculous. They had missed His meaning, which was simply to warn them of the changed circumstances of His cause. But they caught at the words that He had used and exhibited their two swords. Possibly, as some have supposed, these were two long sacrificial knives with which they had killed the Paschal Lamb. But, indeed, the wearing of weapons is much more general in the East than with us. Our Lord's disciples were largely Galileans, and as the Galileans were more of a fighting sort than other Jews, the wearing of swords was probably very general among them. However, two of the apostles had swords, not that they were fighting men, but probably because it was the fashion of their country, and they had thought it needful to wear them when passing through a dangerous district. At any rate, Peter had a sword and instantly used it. He smites the first man he could reach. I wonder he had not smitten Judas, as one might have excused him if he had. But it is a servant of the high priest who bears the blow and loses his ear.

Then the Savior comes forward in all His gentleness, as self-possessed as when He was at supper, as calm as if He had not already passed through an agony. Quietly He says, "Suffer ye thus far" (Luke 22:51). He touches the man's ear and heals it, and in the lull that followed, when even the men who came to seize Him were spellbound by this wondrous miracle of mercy, He propounds the great truth, that those who take the sword shall perish by the sword, and He bids Peter put up his weapon. Then He utters these memorable words: "Thinkest thou that I cannot now pray to my Father, and he shall presently give me more than twelve legions of angels? But how then shall the scriptures be fulfilled, that thus it must be?" And He also said what John alone appears to have heard: "[T]he cup which my Father hath given me, shall I not drink it?" (John 18:11).

The wound of Malchus served a gracious purpose, for it enabled our Lord to work a new miracle, the like of which He had never wrought before, namely the restoration of a member maimed or cut off by violence. The blunder of the apostles was also over-ruled to answer a very instructive purpose. You wonder that the Lord should, even in appearance, encourage His disciples to have swords and then forbid them to use them. Follow me in a thought that is clear to my own mind. For a man to abstain from using force when he has none to use is no great virtue. But for a man to have force ready to his hand and then abstain from using it is a case of self-restraint, and possibly of self-sacrifice, of a far nobler kind. Our Savior had His sword at His side that night, though He did not use it. "What!" say you, "how can that be true?" Our Lord says, "Can I not now pray to my Father, and he will give me twelve legions of angels?" Our Lord had the means of self-defense. Something far more powerful than a sword hung at His side, but He refused to employ the power within His reach. His servants could not bear this test, as they had no self-restraint, and the hand of Peter is on His sword at once.

The failure of the servants in this matter seems to me to illustrate the grand self-possession of their Master. "Alas," He seems to say, "you cannot be trusted even with swords, much less could you be entrusted with greater forces. If you had the angelic bands at your command, down they would come streaming from the sky to execute works of vengeance and so mar my great lifework of love." Brethren, we are better without swords and other forms of force than with them, for we have not yet learned, like our Lord, to control ourselves. Admire the glorious self-restraint of our Lord Jesus Christ, who, armed not with a sword but with the embattled hosts of "helmeted cherubim and sworded seraphim," yet refused even by a prayer to bring them down to His relief. Peter's passionate use of the sword illustrates the happy self-control of his Lord, and this is the use of the incident.

Our Lord's Grand Resource

"Thinkest thou that I cannot now pray to my Father?" Our Lord is surrounded by His adversaries, and there are none about Him powerful enough to defend Him from their malice. What can He do? He says, "I can pray to my Father." This is our Lord's continual resource in the time of danger, yea, even in that time of which He said, "[T]his is your hour, and the power of darkness" (Luke 22:53). He can even now pray to His Father.

First, Jesus had no possessions on earth, but *He had a Father.* I rejoice in His saying, "Thinkest thou that I cannot now pray to my Father?" He is a betrayed man, given up into the hands of those who thirst for His blood, but He has a Father almighty and divine. If our Lord had merely meant to say that God could deliver Him, He might have said, "Thinkest thou not that I can pray to Jehovah?" But He uses the sweet expression "my Father," both here and in that text in John, where He says, "[T]he cup which my Father hath given me, shall I not drink it?" (John 18:11).

O brethren, remember that we have a Father in heaven. When all is gone and spent, we can say, "Our Father." Relatives are dead, but our Father lives. Supposed friends have left us, even as the swallows leave in our wintry weather. But we are not alone, for the Father is with us. Cling to that blessed text: "I will not leave you comfortless: I will come to you" (John 14:18). In every moment of distress, anxiety, perplexity, we have a Father in whose wisdom, truth, and power we can rely. Your dear children do not trouble themselves much, do they? If they have a need, they go to their father; if they are puzzled, they ask their father; if they are ill-treated, they appeal to their father. If but a thorn is in their finger, they run to their mother for relief. Be it little or great, the child's sorrow is the parent's care. This makes a child's life easy. It would make ours easy if we could but act as children toward God. Let us imitate the Elder Brother, and when we, too, are in our Gethsemane, let us, as He did, continue to cry, "My Father, my Father." This is a better defense than shield or sword.

Our Lord's resource was to approach His Father with prevailing prayer. "Can I not now pray to my Father?" Our Lord Jesus could use that most marvelous weapon of all—prayer, which is shield and sword and spear and helmet and breastplate, all in one. When you can do nothing else, you can pray. If you can do many things besides, it will still be your wisdom to say, "Let us pray!" But I think I hear you object that our Lord had been praying, and yet His griefs were not removed. He had prayed Himself into a bloody sweat with prayer, and yet He was left unprotected, to fall into His enemies' hands. This is true, and yet it is not all the truth, for He had been strengthened, and power for deliverance was at His disposal. He had only to press His case to be rescued at once. The Greek word here is not the same word that sets forth ordinary prayer. The Revised Version puts it, "Thinkest thou that I cannot *beseech* my Father?" We make a great mistake if we throw all prayer into one category and think that every form of true prayer is alike. We may pray and plead, and even do this with extreme earnestness, and yet we may not use that mode of beseeching that would surely bring the blessing. Hitherto our Lord had prayed, and prayed intensely, too; but there was yet a higher form of prayer to which He might have mounted if it had been proper so to do. He could so have besought that the Father must have answered, but He would not.

O brethren, you have prayed a great deal, perhaps, about your trouble, but there is a reserve force of beseeching in you yet. By the aid of the Spirit of God, you may pray after a higher and more prevailing rate. This is a far better weapon than a sword. I was speaking to a brother yesterday about a prayer that my Lord had remarkably answered in my own case, and I could not help saying to him, "But I cannot always pray in that fashion. Not only can I not so pray, but I would not dare to do so even if I could." Moved by the Spirit of God, we sometimes pray with a power of faith that can never fail at the mercy seat. But without such an impulse, we must not push our own wills to the front. There are many occasions upon which, if a man had all the faith that could move mountains, he would most wisely show it by saying nothing beyond, "Nevertheless not as I will, but as thou wilt." Had our Lord chosen to do so, He had still in reserve a prayer power that would have effectually saved Him from His enemies. He did not think it right so to use it, but He could have done so had He pleased.

Notice that our Lord *felt that He could even then pray*. Matters had not gone too far for prayer. When can they do so? The word *now* practically occurs twice in our version, for we get it first as *now*, and then as *presently*. It occurs only once in the original, but as its exact position in the verse cannot easily be decided, our translators, with a singular wisdom, have placed it in both the former and the latter part of the sentence. Our Savior certainly meant: "I am come now to extremities. The people are far away whose favor formerly protected me from the Pharisees, and I am about to be seized by armed men. But even now I can pray to my Father." Prayer is an ever open door. There is no predicament in which we cannot pray. If we follow the Lamb wherever He goes, we can now pray effectually to our Father, even as He could have done. Do I hear you say, "The fatal hour is near"? You may now pray. "But the danger is imminent!" You may now pray. If, like Jonah, you are now at the bottom of the mountains and the weeds are wrapped about your head, you may even now pray. Prayer is a weapon that is usable in every position in the hour of conflict. The Greeks had long spears, and these were of grand service to the battalion so long as the rank was not broken; but the Romans used a short sword, and that was a far more effectual weapon at close quarters. Prayer is both the long spear and the short sword. Yes, brother, between the jaws of the lion you may even now pray. We glory in our blessed Master, that He knew in fullness of faith that if He would bring forth His full power of prayer, He could set all heaven on the wing. As soon as His beseeching prayer would reach the Father's ear, immediately, like flames of fire, angels would flash death upon His adversaries.

Our Lord's resort was not to the carnal weapon but to the mighty engine of supplication. Behold, my brethren, where our grand resort must always be. Look not to the arm of flesh but to the Lord our God. Church of God, look not piteously to the state, but fly to the mercy seat. Church of God, look not to the ministry, but resort to the throne of grace. Church of God, depend not upon learned men, but beseech God in supplicating faith. Prayer is the tower of David built for an armory. Prayer is our battle-ax and weapons of war. We say to our antagonist, "Think that I cannot now pray to my Father?" Let this suffice to display our Savior's grand resource in the night of His direst distress.

Our Lord's Undiminished Power in Heaven

Jesus says, when about to be bound and taken away to Caiaphas, "I can presently call down twelve legions of angels from the skies." He had influence in heaven with the Father, the great

Lord of angels. He could have of the Father all that the Father possessed. Heaven would be emptied if needful to satisfy the wish of the Beloved Son. The man Christ Jesus who is about to be hung upon the cross has such power with the Father that He has but to ask and to have. The Father would answer Him at once: "He shall *presently* send me twelve legions of angels." There would be no delay, no hesitation. The Father was ready to help Him, waiting to deliver Him. All heaven was concerned about Him. All the angelic bands were waiting on the wing, and Jesus had but to express the desire and instantaneously the garden of Gethsemane would have been as populous with shining ones as the New Jerusalem itself.

Our Lord speaks of angels that His Father would send Him. We may interpret it that the Father would at once put at His disposal the glorious inhabitants of heaven. Think of seraphs at the disposal of the Man of Sorrows! He is despised and rejected of men, and yet angels that excel in strength are at His beck and call. Swift of wing and quick of hand and wise of thought, they are charmed to be the messengers of the Son of Man, the servitors of Jesus. Think of this, beloved, when you bow before the throne-crowned head and when you gaze upon the nailed hands and feet. Remember that angels and principalities and powers, and all the ranks of pure spirits by whatsoever name they are named, were all at the beck of Jesus when He was newly risen from His agony and was about to be led away to the high priest. He is our Lord and God, even at His lowest and weakest.

Jesus speaks of the twelve legions. I suppose he mentions the number twelve as a legion for each one of the eleven disciples and for Himself. They were only twelve, and yet the innumerable hosts of heaven would make forced marches for their rescue. A legion in the Roman army was six thousand men at the very lowest. Twelve times six thousand would come in answer to a wish from Jesus. Nay, He says, "more" than twelve legions. There can be no limit to the available resources of the Christ of God. Thousands of thousands would fill the air if Jesus willed it. The band that Judas led would be an insignificant squad to be swallowed up at once if the Savior would but summon His allies. Behold, dear brethren, the glory of our betrayed and arrested Lord. If He was such then, what is He now, when all power is given Him of His Father! Bear in your minds the clear idea that Jesus in His humiliation was nevertheless Lord of all things, and especially of the unseen world, and of the armies that people it. The more clearly you perceive this, the more will you admire the all-conquering love that took Him to the death of the cross.

Tarry here just a minute to recollect that the angels also are, according to your measure and degree, at your call. You have but to pray to God, and angels shall bear you up in their hands lest you dash your foot against a stone. We do not think enough of these heavenly beings, yet they are all ministering spirits sent forth to minister to those who are heirs of salvation. Like Elijah's servant, if your eyes were opened, you would see the mountain full of horses of fire and chariots of fire round about the servants of God. Let us learn from our Master to reckon upon forces invisible. Let us not trust in that which is seen of the eye and heard of the ear, but let us have respect to spiritual agencies that evade the senses but are known to faith. Angels play a far greater part in the affairs of Providence than we realize. God can raise us up friends on earth, and if He does not do so, He can find us abler friends in heaven. There is no need to pluck out the sword with which to cut off men's ears, for infinitely better agencies will work for us. Have faith in God, and all things shall work for your good. The angels of God think it an honor and a delight to protect the least of His children.

Our Lord's Perfect Willingness in Suffering

Our Lord would be betrayed into the hands of sinners, but He would go with them willingly. He had not shunned the garden, though Judas knew the place. No part of our Lord's sufferings came upon Him by the necessity of His nature. Neither as God nor as sinless man was He bound to suffer. There was no necessity that Christ should endure any of the inflictions laid upon Him except the necessity of His fulfilling the Scriptures and performing the work of mercy that He came to do. He must die because He became the great sacrifice for sin, but apart from that, no necessity of death was on Him. They scourged Him, but they could not have lifted the thong if He had not permitted it. He thirsted on the cruel tree, but all the springs of water in the world He makes and fills, and therefore He needed not to have thirsted if He had not chosen to submit thereto. When He died, He did not die through the failure of His natural strength. He died because He had surrendered Himself to death as our great propitiation. Even in His expiring moment, our Lord cried with a loud voice to show that His life was in Him still.

He "gave up the ghost," freely parting with a life that He might have retained. He voluntarily surrendered His spirit to God. It was not snatched from Him by a force superior to His own will. He willingly bore our sins and died as our Substitute. Let us love and bless the willing Sufferer.

Indeed, our Lord was not merely submissive to the divine will, but if I may use the words in a paradoxical manner, I would say that He was actively submissive. A single prayer would have brought our Lord deliverance from His enemies. But He exercised force upon Himself and held in His natural impulse to beseech the Father. He held in check the noblest of spiritual gifts, that choicest of all forms of power—the power of prayer. One would have thought that a good man might always exercise prayer to the full of his bent, and yet Jesus laid His hand upon His prayer power as if it had been a sword, and He put it back into its sheath. "He saved others; himself he cannot save" (Mark 15:31). He prayed for others; but in this instance, for Himself He would not pray as He might have done. He would do nothing, even though it were to pray a prayer that even in the slightest degree would oppose the will of the Father. He was so perfectly submissive, yea, so eager to accomplish our salvation, that He would not pray to avoid the cruelty of His enemies and the bitterness of death. He sees it is the Father's will, and therefore He will not have a wish in opposition to it. "The cup which my Father hath given me, shall I not drink it?"(John 18:11). Remember that He needed not to commit any wrong thing to prevent His being taken and slain. A good thing, namely, a prayer, would do it, but He will not pray. He has undertaken the work of redemption, and He must and will go through with it. He has such a desire for your salvation and for mine, such a thirst to honor and glorify His Father in the work that He had engaged to do, that He will not even prevent His sufferings by a prayer.

Wonderful is that question, "How then shall the scriptures be fulfilled?" It is as much as to say, "Who else can drink that cup? Who else can tread the winepress of Almighty wrath? No, I must do it. I cannot lay this load upon any other shoulders." Therefore, for the joy that was set before Him, He endured the cross, despising the shame. He was willing from beginning to end to be our suffering Savior. He was willing to be born at Bethlehem, to work at Nazareth, to be mocked at Jerusalem, and at last to die at Calvary. At any one point, He could have drawn back. No constraint was upon Him but that of a love stronger than death.

I want you to draw the inference that Jesus is willing to save. A willing Sufferer must be a willing Savior. If He willingly died, He must with equal willingness be ready to give to us the fruit of His death. If any of you would have Jesus, you may surely have Him at once. He freely delivered Himself up for us all. If He was so willing to become a sacrifice, how willing must He be that the glorious result of His sacrifice should be shared in by you and by all who come to God by Him! If there be unwillingness anywhere, you are unwilling. He rejoices to be gracious. I wish the charm of this truth would affect your heart as it does mine. I love Him greatly because I see that at any moment He might have drawn back from redeeming me, and yet He would not. A single prayer would have set Him free, but He would not pray it, for He loved us so!

> *This was compassion like a God,*
> *That when the Saviour knew*
> *The price of pardon was His blood,*
> *His pity ne'er withdrew.*

Do not grieve Him by thinking that He is unwilling to forgive, that He is unwilling to receive a sinner such as you. Has He not said, "[H]im that cometh to me I will in no wise cast out" (John 6:37)? You will delight Him if you come to Him, whoever you are. If you will but draw near to Him by simple trust, He will see in you the purchase of His agony. All the merit of His death shall flow out freely to you. Come.

Our Lord's Great Respect for Holy Scripture

Notice, that our Lord believed in *the divinity of Scripture*. He says, "How then shall the scriptures be fulfilled?" But if the Scriptures are only the writings of men, there is no necessity that they should be fulfilled. If they are merely the fallible utterances of good men, I see no particular necessity that they should be fulfilled. Our Lord Jesus Christ insisted upon it that the Scriptures must be fulfilled, and the reason was that they are not the word of man but the Word of God. The Scriptures were evidently the Word of God to our Lord Jesus Christ. He never trifles with them, nor differs from them, nor predicts that they will vanish away. It is He who says, "Think not that I am come to destroy the law, or the prophets: I am not come to destroy, but to fulfil. For verily I say unto you, Till heaven and earth pass, one jot or one tittle shall in no wise pass from the law, till all be fulfilled" (Matt. 5:17–18).

He believed in the divine origin of the Scriptures and also in *their infallibility.* "How then shall the scriptures be fulfilled, that thus it must be?" He does not hint that the Scriptures might be a little mistaken. He does not argue, "I will bring the twelve legions of angels down to deliver Myself, and it is no matter to Me that then the Scriptures will be made void." Oh, no! The Scriptures must be true, and they must be fulfilled, and therefore He must be betrayed into the hands of men. He settles it as a matter of necessity that Scripture must infallibly be verified, even to its jots and tittles.

See, brethren, *the priceless worth* of Scripture in the estimation of our Lord. In effect He says, "I will die rather than any Scripture shall be unfulfilled. I will go to the cross rather than any one word of God should not be carried out." The prophet Zechariah has written, "Awake, O sword, against my shepherd, and against the man that is my fellow, saith the LORD of hosts: smite the shepherd, and the sheep shall be scattered" (Zech. 13:7). The fulfillment of that prophecy fell due that night, and the Son of God was prepared to be submitted as the Shepherd of the sheep rather than the Word of the Father should fall to the ground. "Skin for skin, yea, all that a man hath will he give for his life" (Job 2:4), but Jesus would give His life for the Scriptures. Brethren, it were worthwhile for the whole Church to die rather than any truth of Scripture should be given up. Let all our thousands be consumed upon the altar as one great holocaust sooner than the Scriptures should be dishonored. The Word of the Lord must live and prevail whether we die or not. Our Lord teaches us to prize it beyond liberty or life.

The force of our Lord's language goes further yet. Let me repeat the words and then enlarge upon them. "How then shall the scriptures be fulfilled, that thus it must be?" Holy Scripture is the transcript of the secret decree of God. We do not believe in fate, but we believe in predestination, the settled purpose of a wise and loving Father. The book of fate is cruel reading, but the book of divine foreordination is full of charming sentences, and those lines out of it that are written in the Scriptures we joyfully choose to have fulfilled. It is the will of our Father who is in heaven that settles the things that must be, and because of this, we cheerfully yield ourselves up to predestination. Once being assured that God has appointed it, we have no struggles, nay, we will not even breathe a wish to have the matter otherwise. Let the will of the Father be the supreme law. It should be so. We find a depth of comfort in saying, "It is the Lord; let Him do what seems Him good."

The prophecies of Scripture were to the Lord Christ the revelation of the predestination of God that so it must be, and He cheerfully, joyfully, even without a prayer against it, gives Himself up at once to that which must be because God has appointed it. If any of you do not believe in the predestination of God, you will, probably, in some hour of depression, ascribe your sorrows to a cruel fate. The human mind, somehow or other, is driven at last to this decision, that some things are beyond the control of man and of his will and that they are fixed by necessity. How much better to see that God has fixed them! There is the wheel revolving surely and unalterably. Would it not comfort you to believe that it is full of eyes and that it is moving according to the settled purpose of the Lord? That man who says, "It is my Father's will" is the happy man. Predestination is as sure and as certain as fate, but there is at the back of it a living and loving personality, ordering all things. To this we cheerfully yield ourselves.

Beloved, let us value Scripture as much as Christ did. I was going to say, let us value it even more, for if our Lord valued unfulfilled Scripture, how much more should we value it, to whom the Scriptures are fulfilled in a large degree because the Christ has suffered and has done even as it was written of Him by the prophets of God!

Our Lord's Lessons to Each of Us

The first lesson is this: Desire no other forces for God's work than God Himself ordains to use. Do not desire that the government should come to your rescue to support your church. Do not desire that the charms of eloquence should be given to ministers, that they may therewith command listening ears and so maintain the faith by the wisdom of words. Do not ask that learning and rank and prestige may come upon the side of Christianity, and so religion may become respectable and influential. Means that God has not chosen to use should not be looked upon by us with covetous eyes. Has He not said, "Not by might, nor by power, but by my spirit, saith the LORD of hosts" (Zech. 4:6)? Jesus has all those squadrons of angels at His disposal; do you not wish that He would use them? What a glorious vision is before us as we see their serried ranks and mark their glittering splendor! But Jesus bids them stand still and see the salvation of God wrought out without their interposition. To them He has not put in subjection the new world. They must not meddle with the redemption of men. The conflict for truth is to be a spiritual battle between man and the serpent: Nothing but spiritual force is to be employed, and that not by angels but by men. Man must overcome sin by spiritual means only. Put up the sword, Peter! Jesus does not want its keen edge. Keep your swords in your sheaths, ye seraphim! Jesus does not want even your blades of celestial temper. His weakness has done more than human or angelic strength. His suffering and death have done the deed that all the hierarchy of angels could never have accomplished. The truth is to win the fight. The Spirit is to subdue the powers of evil. Brethren, do not ask anybody else to interfere. Let us have this fight out on the ground that God has chosen. Let us know that God is omnipotent in the realm of mind and that by His truth and Spirit He will overcome. He holds back all forces other than those of argument and persuasion and enlightenment by His Spirit. Do not let us even wish to put our hand to any force other than He ordains to use.

Next, take care that when other forces are within reach, you do not use them for the promotion of the heavenly kingdom. When you are in argument for the truth, do not grow angry, for this would be to fight the Lord's battles with the devil's weapons. Do not wish to oppress a person whose views are erroneous or even blasphemous. The use of bribes for the propagation of opinions is mean, and the refusal of charities to those who differ from us in sentiment is detestable. Let no threat escape your lip, nor bribe pollute your hand. It is not thus that the battles of truth are to be fought. If you ever feel inclined to shut a man's mouth by wishing him banishment or sickness or any sort of ill, be grieved with yourself that so unchristly a thought should have entered your head. Desire only good for the most perverse of men. Fighting for Christ would be wounding Him sorely. The Lord Jesus desires you to fight for Him by your faith, by your holy life, by your confidence in truth, by your reliance upon the Spirit of God. But whenever your hand begins to itch for the sword-hilt, then may you hear Him say, "Put up thy sword into its sheath." He will conquer by love, and by love alone. If at this present moment I could take this church and endow it with all the wealth of the establishment and gather into its midst all the wisdom and talent and eloquence that now adorns society, and if I could do this by one single prayer, I should long hesitate to offer the petition. These might prove idols and provoke the living God to jealousy. Infinitely better for us to be poor and weak and devoid of that which is highly esteemed among men, and then to be baptized into the Holy Ghost, than to become strong and be left of our God. We shall war this warfare with no unsanctified weapons, with no instrument other than God appoints. Speaking the truth in the power of the Spirit of God, we are not afraid of the results. Surely this is what Christ means: "I could pray to My Father and receive at once a bodyguard of angels, but I will do nothing of the kind, for by other means than these must My kingdom come."

And the next lesson is, never attempt to escape suffering at the expense of truth. "How then shall the scriptures be fulfilled?"says Christ. "I can escape being taken, and bound, and made a felon of, but then how are the Scriptures to be fulfilled?" Would you like to be throughout life screened from all affliction? I think I hear a great many say, "I should." Would you? Would you be always free from sickness, poverty, care, bereavement, slander, persecution? How, then, could that word be true, "I have chosen thee in the furnace of affliction" (Isa. 48:10)! What would that text mean, "[W]hat son is he whom the father chasteneth not" (Heb. 12:7)? Are you to be an exception to the rule? Do not kick against suffering, for in so doing you may be fighting against God. When Peter drew his sword, he was unconsciously fighting to prevent our redemption. When we struggle against tribulation or persecution, we may be warring against untold benefit. Do you desire to ride through the world like princes? Do not desire such a dangerous fate, for how then could the Scriptures be fulfilled, that the disciple is not above his Lord? Bow your spirit before the majesty of Scripture and patiently endure all things for the elect's sake.

Again, never tremble when force is on the wrong side. You see they are coming, Pharisees and priests and those sent by the authorities to arrest the Savior; but He is not afraid. Why should He be? He could command twelve legions of angels to beat off the foe. The man who knows he has a reserve behind him may walk into an ambush without fear. The multitudes think that there stands before them a mere man, a feeble man, strangely red as with bloody sweat. Ah, they know neither Him nor His Father! Let Him give a whistle, and from behind the olives of the grove and from the walls of the garden and from every stone of the Mount of Olives would spring up warriors mightier than those of Caesar. One of these mighties of God slew of Sennacherib's army one hundred and eighty-five thousand men in a single night (2 Kings 19:35); another smote all the firstborn of Egypt (Ex. 12:29). Think, then, what more than twelve legions of them could accomplish! Brethren, all these holy, heavenly beings are on our side.

"Oh, but there are so many against us!" Yes, I know there are; but more are they who are for us. All the myriads of heaven are our allies. See the legions waiting for the summons? Who wants to give the word of command till our great Commander in Chief decides that the hour is come? Let us patiently wait till He shall descend from heaven with a shout, with the voice of the archangel and the trump of God (1 Thess. 4:16). Then will the reserves pour forth from heaven's gate, and all the holy angels shall swell the pomp of the great appearing. Till that moment, wait! In your patience possess ye your souls! The Lord Jesus waited; His angels waited; His Father waited. They are all still waiting. Heaven's long-suffering still runs like a silver thread through the centuries. Jesus will come with His angels in all the glory of the Father, but dream not that He must come tomorrow, or else be charged with being slack concerning His promise. Desire that He may come in your lifetime and look for Him, but if He tarries, be not dismayed. If He tarry for another century, do not be weary. If another thousand years should intervene between us and the bright millennial day, yet stand fast in your place, fearing nothing, but setting up your banners in the name of the Lord. "The LORD of hosts is with us; the God of Jacob is our refuge" (Ps. 46:7). We have no lack of strength; it is only that God wills that it be not put forth and that our weakness for the present should be the instrument of His most majestic conquests. Lord, we are content to trust in You and wait patiently for You. But leave us not, we beseech You. Amen.

I feel so glad to think our Lord spoke out His feelings when He was passing through this inward conflict. It is instructive that He should have done so, for with His strength of mind He was quite capable of preserving a self-contained attitude and keeping His agony to Himself. Yet you notice that neither here, in which case He spoke so that others heard Him, nor at Gethsemane, in which case He took three of His disciples to be with Him, nor even on the cross, in which case He cried aloud, "My God, my God, why hast thou forsaken me?" did He endeavor to conceal His emotion from others. It may be that by this He intended to teach us wisdom. He would show us by His own example that it is well for us not to be too much shut up within ourselves. Smother not your sorrow, tell it out, or it may gather an ungovernable heat. That is the worst of grief that cannot weep or moan. Give a vent to pent-up feelings. Even if it is but a child who hears your tale, it will relieve your mind to tell it. Anything is better than banking up the fires and concentrating all the heat within the soul. Act not the stoic's part. Be not ashamed to let it be known that you are human and can grieve and be troubled even as others.

Chapter Twelve

A Golden Prayer

Father, glorify thy name—John 12:28.

IN THE FIRST PART OF this chapter I shall strictly keep to the words of our Lord Jesus Christ and endeavor to show what they teach us with regard to Him. These are His own words, and it would be robbery to borrow them until first we have seen what they meant as they fell from His lips. Their most golden meaning must be seen in the light of His sacred countenance. Then, in the second part of the chapter, I shall try to point out how the petition before us may be used. I pray that divine grace may be given us that it may be engraven upon our hearts and that each of us may be taught by the Holy Spirit daily to say, "Father, glorify Your name." I would suggest that these words should be to all the Lord's people as their prayer throughout life. It is as fitting for the beginner in grace as the veteran believer; it will be proper both at the wicket-gate of faith and at the portals of glory. Like a lovely rainbow, let Jesus' prayer "Father, glorify thy name" overarch the whole period of our life on earth. I cannot suggest a better petition for the present moment, nor indeed for any moment of our pilgrimage. As for the past, "Father, glorify Your name"; in the present, fulfill this desire to Your servants; and in the future, do it yet more abundantly.

In Respect to Our Lord Jesus Christ

The prayer occurs in the following connection. Jesus had wrought a notable miracle in the raising of Lazarus from the dead. The fame of the miracle had attracted many to hear Him. Enthusiastic crowds had gathered, and He had become so extremely popular that the Pharisees said, "[T]he world is gone after him" (John 12:19). The people were willing to have made Him a king, and a great concourse met Him with branches of palm trees and cried, "Hosanna: Blessed is the King of Israel that cometh in the name of the Lord" (John 12:13). Our Lord passed in royal but humble pomp through the streets of Jerusalem, riding upon a colt, the foal of an ass. This public manifestation, the renown of the miracle, and the general talk of the populace led to strangers hearing of Him and inquiring about Him. Certain Greeks of a very respectable order—their mode of address to Philip shows their superior behavior—were present who asked to be introduced to Him. They "would see Jesus" (John 12:21), not, of course, merely *see* Him in the street, for that they could do if they pleased without applying to Philip. But they would have an interview with Him and learn more about His teaching and His claims.

I suppose that the sight of these Greeks greatly gladdened the heart of the Savior, for He delighted to see men coming into the light. He seemed to say within Himself, "Behold the nations come to Me; the Gentiles arise and seek their Savior." He saw in those Greeks the advance guard of the Gentile world. He looked upon the strangers with delight, regarding them as representative men, the first of myriads who from the ends of the earth and the islands of the sea should come flocking to Him to behold the glory of God in the face of Jesus Christ. Our Lord rejoiced in spirit; His heart was glad within Him, and He began to address Himself to the people round about and to the Greeks who mingled with the throng. At that very moment, the thought flashed across the Savior's mind: "But these nations who are to be born unto Me and to be saved by Me cannot be so born without birthpangs or saved except I endure unspeakable suffering as their Redeemer." This fact came vividly before our Lord's mind, and it rushed over His spirit like a raging torrent. He saw that He could not become the seed corn of a great harvest unless first of all He should fall into the ground and die. He was the one grain of wheat upon whom all depended, and He must lose comfort and life and be buried in the earth, or else He would abide alone and bring forth no fruit (John 12:24). He saw the vicarious suffering that lay in His way.

Do not imagine that our Savior dreaded death in itself. He was far superior in sacred courage and strength of mind to any of His servants, and yet many of them have welcomed death, and others of them, such as the martyrs, have endured it in its most terrible forms, without fear, even expressing a holy delight in glorifying the name of God by their mortal agony. Our Lord was not less brave than these in the prospect of His departure. But never let it be forgotten that the death of Christ was a very peculiar one, and in fact stands by itself alone. His death was the vindication of justice, it was the death of the sin bearer, it was a sacrificial, substitutionary, expiatory death, and this is very different from the death of a pardoned and justified believer, who passes out of the world resting on the atonement and supported by a sense of having been reconciled to God by the great Sacrifice. Our Lord was called to bear the enormous load of man's transgressions. Over His holy soul the dark shadow of human guilt must pass, and on His sensitive spirit must be made to meet the iniquity of us all. His saints' deaths are blessed in the sight of the Lord, but He must be made a curse for us that we might be blessed in Him. And as the mind of Christ perceived this clearly lying in the way of that triumph among the Gentiles that gave Him joy, there was a struggle in His soul, and before the assembled people, that struggle was manifested.

The Greeks desired to see Jesus, and they did see Him in a very remarkable manner, so that they must have been astounded at the sight. If they expected to see a king, they did indeed behold a royal soul, but they saw Him in such grief as falls not to the lot of common men. If they wished to see somewhat of His greatness of spirit and power of mind, they did see it, but it was a power that did not transfigure His face with glory but filled it with an agony marring all its beauty.

I shall not be too bold if I say that Gethsemane was rehearsed in public upon the occasion before us. Our Lord's soul was troubled, so He says (John 12:27). He felt a sort of foreshadowing of that midnight among the olives, in which His soul was "exceeding sorrowful, even unto death" (Matt. 26:38). It was out of that conflict that our text came. In fact, our text is to His suffering in the midst of the crowd what "nevertheless not as I will, but as thou wilt" was to the agony of Gethsemane (Matt. 26:39) or what "It is finished" was to the passion upon Calvary (John 19:30). It was the culminating point, the climax, and the conquest of a great mental battle. When He had thus spoken, He seemed to shake Himself clear of the agony and to emerge from it with the memorials of it still upon Him, but with His face set like a flint to go forward to the bitter and the glorious end, this being now His watchword, "Father, glorify thy name."

I call your attention first to *the trouble of the Redeemer's soul*. I always tremble within myself when I try to speak of the inner conflicts of our blessed Lord, for it is so easy to make a mistake and darken counsel by words without knowledge. His person is complex, and therefore we readily confuse, yet He is but one, and it is equally dangerous to make overnice distinctions. Loving jealousy of our Lord's honor makes us feel that we scarcely know how to speak of Him. I remember an earnest admirer of art who in pointing with his walking stick to the beauties of a famous picture pushed his cane through the canvas and ruined it. It is possible that in our enthusiasm to point out the beauties and points of interest in the life and death of our Lord, we may spoil it all. I fear lest in my ignorance I should make sorrow for myself by dishonoring Him for whose honor I would gladly lay me down and die. Help me, O divine Spirit!

This much is clear, that our Savior's heart was full of trouble. He who could still the sea and bid the storms retreat was tempest-tossed in His own soul and cast about Him for anchorage. He who could drive the fever from its lair or send a legion of demons into the deep was nevertheless troubled in spirit and cried, "[W]hat shall I say?" (John 12:27). Master of all worlds, supreme among the angels, and adored at His Father's right hand, yet He confesses, "Now is my soul troubled." Lord of all, yet learned He obedience by the things that He suffered. How near akin it makes Him to us! How human! How compassed with infirmity! You worship Him, and rightly so, but still He is a man and a mourner. You call Him Master and Lord, and you do well, yet not only did He wash His disciples' feet, but His own feet trembled in the rough places of the way. He felt those same commotions of spirit that make our hearts sad within us and cause us to pour out our souls within us.

Do not think of the Lord Jesus as other than a dear brother born for adversity or a faithful husband sharing all our lot, being bone of our bone and flesh of our flesh. Did you cry out in anguish, "Now is my soul troubled"? Then remember that your Lord has used the same words. Are you half distracted? Are you tossed to and fro in your thoughts? Do you ever ask, "What shall I say?" Jesus also understands by sympathy what it is you mean. Do you look around you and feel that you know not what to do, and does your trembling heart suggest that you should pray, "Father, save me from this hour"? In all this you may see the Well-Beloved's footprints. You are not upon a new and strange track. He leads you through no darker rooms than He went through before. With the like afflictions He has been afflicted. There is nothing in them novel or surprising to His sympathetic heart.

Beloved, let me invite you to consider that not only did our Lord thus suffer, but it is joyful to reflect that He suffered all this without sin. Hence it follows that mental conflict is not in itself sinful. Even the shrinking back of the flesh from suffering is not necessarily evil. The question What shall I say? and the apparent distraction of the spirit for the moment as to what shall be its course are not in themselves criminal. There could be no sin in the Lord Jesus, and consequently there is not of necessity sin in our inward struggles, though I am far from venturing to hope that in any one of them we are quite clear of fault. Our Lord's nature was so pure that however much it was stirred, it remained clear. But in our case, though the stirring is not sinful, it sets in motion the sin that dwells in us, and we are defiled.

Yet I do not believe that all those depressions of spirit that come of sickness, all those wanderings of mind in the heat of fever, all those shrinkings and drawings back from pain, which are essential to our humanity, are by our heavenly Father set down as sin, though sin is doubtless mixed with them. If they are sinful, yet surely they are blotted out as soon as written down, for "as a father pitieth his children, so the LORD pitieth them that fear him" (Ps. 103:13). He pities rather than censures or condemns. You do not judge your children harshly for what they say when they are racked with pain or prostrated by weakness. Neither can I think that our heaven Father would have us doubt our interest in Christ because in our semi-delirium we could not realize His love, nor would He have us question the grace that is in us because our feverish thoughts were near to despair. When the true heart struggles to love and trust and obey but the poor brain is tortured with dark thoughts, the conflict is not all sinful, nor any of it necessarily so. There may be an awful struggle in the soul and yet the Father may be glorified. The sin lies not in the conflict but in the defeat, if defeat there be. The guilt is not in the shrinking from pain but in permitting that natural feeling to hinder us from duty or lead us to rebel against chastisement. "If it be possible, let this cup pass from me" is not a sinful utterance if it is followed by "nevertheless not as I will, but as thou wilt."

I feel so glad to think our Lord spoke out His feelings when He was passing through this inward conflict. It is instructive that He should have done so, for with His strength of mind He was quite capable of preserving a self-contained attitude and keeping His agony to Himself. Yet you notice that neither here, in which case He spoke so that others heard Him, nor at Gethsemane, in which case He took three of His disciples to be with Him, nor even on the cross, in which case He cried aloud, "My God, my God, why hast thou forsaken me?" did He endeavor to conceal His emotion from others. It may be that by this He intended to teach us wisdom. He would show us by His own example that it is well for us not to be too much shut up within ourselves. Smother not your sorrow, tell it out, or it may gather an ungovernable heat. That is the worst of grief that cannot weep or moan. Give a vent to pent-up feelings. Even if it is but a child who hears your tale, it will relieve your mind to tell it. Anything is better than banking up the fires and concentrating all the heat within the soul. Act not the stoic's part. Be not ashamed to let it be known that you are human and can grieve and be troubled even as others.

In speaking out, our Lord gives us full permission to speak, too. We might have said, "No, I will not tell what is going on within lest my weakness should seem to dishonor God." We know that our Lord did not dishonor the Father by saying, "Now is my soul troubled," and by revealing the inward conflict of His soul. Neither will the fact of our speaking out our grief necessarily dishonor our God. Jesus wept, and we may weep. Jesus told out His sorrows to His friends, and you may do the same.

In thus speaking, our Lord affords us the best of help, for His fellow-feeling is a grand support. Did He say, "Now is my soul troubled"? and did He scarce know what to ask? But did He at the last still triumph and resign Himself into the Father's hands. Then we may take hold of the selfsame power when we also encounter the same sorrow after our measure. Even though in the triumph there should be clear evidence of our personal weakness, yet we will not regret it, since by that means our God shall be the more surely glorified by the more distinct revelation of *His* power.

I will say no more about the trouble of our Redeemer because I would now ask you to fix your thoughts for a minute upon *the firm resolve* that the text sets forth. There is a battle, but from the very first moment to the last of it, there is really no question in the Savior's mind about what He means to do. His purpose was settled beyond disturbance. The surface of His mind was ruffled, but deep down in His heart the current of the Redeemer's soul flowed on irresistibly in the ordained channel. He was even distressed till He had been baptized with the appointed baptism (Luke 12:50). Observe the question raised, and see how really it was answered in His heart before He asked it. "Now is my soul troubled; and what shall I say? Father, save me from this hour" (John 12:27). Must men be unsaved and Jesus be delivered from the lowering storm? If so, yonder Greeks need not ask to see Him, for there will be no "life in a look" at Him. The disciples round about need not cling to Him as their helper, for there is no help in Him unless He dies to redeem the sons of men. Shall men, then, be unredeemed? Shall the blood of atonement be unspilt and no man be ransomed from going down to the pit? Shall He remain alone, the grain of wheat unsown? If He does, He will be happy enough and glorious enough, for heaven is all His own. Does He need men to make Him blessed? Should He remain alone, He will still be God and Lord. But shall the death penalty be left to be borne by men, guilty men, who deserve to bear it? Shall there be no cross, no Calvary, no open tomb, no resurrection, no gates of heaven set wide open for coming souls? There is the question, and you see in the text how resolutely Jesus had settled it. He says in effect: "Father, glorify Your name by My death. For this purpose have I come to this hour, that by My agony and bloody sweat, by My cross and passion, I may redeem the sons of men. Redeemed they must and shall be, cost Me what it may. I have resolved to bear the penalty and magnify Your law, and I will perform it, though hell itself be let loose against Me and all its waves of fire dash over Me. I will endure the cross and despise the shame, to honor You, My Father."

Observe that the text indicates *the deep intent* that steadied our Lord's resolve. Why is Christ resolved to die? Is it to save men? Yes, but not as the chief reason. His first prayer is "Father, glorify thy name." The glory of God was the chief end and object of our Savior's life and death. It is that the Father's name may be illustrious that Jesus would have souls redeemed. His passion had for its main intent the exhibition of the attributes of God. And how completely He has glorified Jehovah's name! Upon the cross we see the divine justice in the streaming wounds of the great Substitute, for the Son of God must die when sin is laid upon Him. There also you behold infinite wisdom, for what but infallible wisdom could have devised the way whereby God might be just and yet the justifier of him who believes (Rom. 3:26). There, too, is love—rich, free, boundless love—never so conspicuous as in the death of man's Redeemer. In the atonement, the divine attributes are all so perfectly glorified that no one crowds out the other. Each one has its full display without in the least degree diminishing the glory of any other. Our blessed Lord, that the Father might be glorified, pushed on to the end that He had set before Him. Whatever conflict might be within His spirit, His heart was fixed upon bearing to the death our load and upon suffering to the end our penalty.

Now, I will detain you here with but one other thought—it is this, *the grand result* that came of it was that God was in very deed glorified, and to this fact special testimony was given. A voice was heard out of heaven saying, "I have both glorified it, and will glorify it again" (John 12:28). That voice speaks of the past: The incarnation of Christ had glorified the name of God. I am unable to describe to you how much of luster the love of God receives from the fact of the Word being made flesh and dwelling among us. It is the mystery of mysteries, the marvel of all marvels, that the Creator should espouse the nature of His creature and that He should be found in fashion as a man. O Bethlehem, you have exceedingly magnified the condescension of God. Angels might well sing, "Glory to God in the highest, and on earth peace, good will toward men" (Luke 2:14). Nor Bethlehem alone, but Nazareth and the thirty years that our Lord spent on earth all illustrate the condescension, the pity, the long-suffering of God. Did God dwell among us thirty years? Did He abide in humility in the carpenter's shop for the best part of that time, and did He afterward come forth to be a poor man, a teacher of peasants, a friend of sinners, a man of sorrows, despised and rejected of men (Isa. 53:3)? Could the holy and the just, the infinite and the glorious thus, as it were, compress infinity into so small a space and marry Deity to such poverty and shame? It was so. Then tune your harps anew, ye seraphs, to tell the amazing love and condescension of "Emmanuel,...God with us" (Matt. 1:23). Well spake that voice, "I have glorified it." But hearken yet again, for it adds, "and will glorify it again." To my mind that word *again* sounds like certain voices I have heard in the Alps. The horn is sounded and then follows an echo; nay, twice, thrice, and perhaps fifty times the music is distinctly repeated, the voices following each other in gradually melting strains. The metaphor is not complete, for in this case the echoes increase in volume.

Lo, Jesus hangs upon the cross and dies, and God is glorified, for justice has its due. He lies in the grave till the third morning, but He bursts the bonds of death. Lo, God's great name is glorified again, since the divine power, truth, and faithfulness are all seen in the resurrection of Christ. Yet a few more days and He ascends into heaven, and a cloud hides Him from our sight—He has glorified the Father's name again by leading captivity captive. Then comes Pentecost and the preaching of the gospel among the heathen, and then is the name of God glorified by the outpouring of the Spirit. Every conversion of a sinner and every sanctification of a believer is a fresh glorifying of the name of the Father. Every reception of a perfected one in heaven—and surely they are entering heaven every day, troops of them climbing the celestial hills, drawn upward by Almighty love—glorifies Jehovah's name again. And, brethren, by and by, when the whole earth shall be filled with His glory, then will the Father glorify His own name again. When in His own time the Lord shall descend from heaven with a shout, with the voice of the archangel and the trump of God (1 Thess. 4:16), and when He shall reign among His ancients gloriously (Isa. 24:23), and we shall hear the gladsome acclamation, "Hallelujah, hallelujah, the Lord God omnipotent reigneth" (Rev. 19:6), and when comes the end, and He shall be all in all (1 Cor. 15:24, 28)— then shall the eternal echoes roll along the glories of the great Father God. The glorious name of the one Jehovah shall through all space and all eternity be magnified, and the prayer of our once suffering but now exalted Savior shall be fully answered: "Father, glorify thy name."

In Reference to Ourselves

I pray that this text may be our prayer from this time forth: "Father, glorify thy name." Have you ever prayed this prayer? I trust I am addressing many to whom it is a very familiar desire, and yet I question if any ever present it so earnestly as those from whom it has been forced by suffering and grief. God's birds often sing best in cages; at any rate, when they have been loose a little while and their notes grow somewhat dull, He tunes their pipes again if He puts them away awhile and clips their wings.

Now this text, as far as we are concerned, whenever we can use it, indicates *conflict ended*. Sometimes we are in such a condition that we do not know which way to turn. We are in great affliction. It may not be so much outward trouble as distress of mind, which is worst of all. The water has leaked *into* the ship, and that is worse than an ocean outside. The vessel begins to fill, you use the pumps but cannot keep it under. At such times you cry, "What shall I do? What shall I say? Where can I look? I am oppressed and overwhelmed." But there is an end of the conflict when you turn round and cry, "Father! Father!" A child may have lost its way and may be sobbing its heart out in its distress, but the moment it sees its father, it is lost no longer; it has found its way and is at rest. Though there may be no difference in your position or change in your circumstances, yet if you catch a sight of your heavenly Father, it is enough; you are a lost child no more. When you can pray, "Father, glorify Your name," there is no more question about "What shall I say?" You have said the right thing, and there let it end.

I wish great happiness to you, but nobody can be confident that life will be free from trouble. On the contrary, you may be pretty confident that it will not be so, for man is born to trouble as the sparks fly upward. We have loved ones we long to be with forever, but remember each of these may be an occasion of sorrow, for we have neither an immortal child, nor an immortal husband, nor an immortal wife, nor an immortal friend. Moreover, the comforts with which we are surrounded may take to themselves wings at any time. Earthly joys are as if they were all made of snow; they melt even as the hoar frost and are gone before we conclude our thanksgiving for their coming. Perhaps you may even face death.

Shall we grow gloomy and desponding? Shall we wish we had never been born or ask that we may die? By no means. Shall we on the other hand grow frivolous and laugh at all things? No, that were ill-becoming an heir of God. What shall we do? We will breathe this prayer, "Father, glorify Your name." That is to say, if I must lose my property, glorify Your name by my poverty; if I must be bereaved, glorify Your name in my sorrows; if I must die, glorify Your name in my departure. When you pray in that fashion, your conflict is over, no outward fright nor inward fear remains. If that prayer rises from the heart, you have now cast aside all gloomy forebodings, and you can thoughtfully and placidly pursue your way into the unknown tomorrow. Pass on, O caravan, into the trackless desert! Still proceed into the wilderness of the future, which no mortal eye has seen, for yonder fiery cloudy pillar leads the way, and all is well. "Father, glorify Your name" is our pillar of cloud, and protected by its shade, we shall not be smitten by the heat of prosperity. It is our pillar of fire by night, nor shall the darkness of adversity destroy us, for the Lord shall be our light. March on, you pilgrims, without a moment's delay because of fear. Tarry not for a single instant, this being your banner and your watchword: "Father, glorify Your name." Torturing doubts and forebodings of the future all end when the glorious name is seen over all.

Our text also breathes a spirit that is *the surrender of self*. When a man can truly say, "Father, glorify Your name," he begins to understand that saying of our Savior concerning the corn of wheat falling into the ground and dying, for that prayer means, "Lord, do what You will with me. I will make no stipulations, but I leave all to You. Remember that I am dust and deal tenderly with me, but still glorify Your name. Do not spare me, if thereby You would be less glorious. Act not according to my foolish wishes or childish desires, but glorify Your name in me by any means and by all means." The prayer means that I am willing to be made nothing of so that God's will may be done. I am willing to be as one dead and buried, forgotten, and unknown if God may be magnified. I am ready to be buried and sown because I believe that this is the way by which I shall grow and bring forth fruit to His praise.

This surrender includes obedient service, for our great Master goes on to say, "If any man serve me, let him follow me" (John 12:26). True self-renunciation shows itself in the obedient imitation of Christ. "Father, glorify Your name" means waiting for the Lord's bidding and running in His ways. If the petition is written out at length, it runs thus: "Help me to copy my Savior's example, help me to follow in His blessed footsteps! This is my desire to honor my heavenly Father by bearing His will and to glorify Him by doing His will. Lord, help me to do both of these, and never let me be forgetful that I am not my own but wholly my Lord's."

The prayer appears to me to be most properly used when it is made a personal one: "Father, glorify Your name *in me*. I am the recipient of so much mercy, get some glory out of me, I pray You." Beloved, I think you must have noticed in this world that the man who really lives is the man who more than his fellows has learned to live for others and for God. You do not care for the preacher whose object is to display his own powers of oration. But if any man shall only desire your soul's good and God's glory, you will put up with much eccentricity from him and bear with many infirmities, because instinctively you love and trust the man who forgets himself. What you thus see in preachers I beg you to try to consider in yourselves. If any of you are living for yourselves, you will be unlovable. But if you will love for love's sake, if you will seek to be Christlike, if you will lay yourselves out to glorify God, to increase His kingdom, and to bless your fellowmen, you will live in the highest and noblest sense. Seek not your own greatness, but labor to make Jesus great, and you will live. Christians live by dying. Kill self, and Christ shall live in you, and so shall you most truly live. The way upward in true life and honor is to go downward in self-humiliation. Renounce all, and you shall be rich; have nothing, and you shall have all things. Try to be something, and you shall be nothing; be nothing, and you shall live. That is the great lesson that Jesus would teach us but which we are slow to learn. "Father, glorify Your name" means let the corn of wheat be buried out of sight, to lose itself in its outgrowth. O self, you are a dead thing, be laid deep in the sepulchre. You rotten carcass, you are an offense to me! Away with you! Do not poison my life, mar my motives, spoil my intents, hinder my self-denials, and defile the chastity of my heart. Away with you. "Father, glorify Your name."

In our text, in the next place, *a new care is paramount*. The man has forgotten self, and self is buried like a grain of wheat, but now he begins to care for God's glory. His cry is, "Father, glorify thy name." Oh, if you can get rid of self, you will feel at your heart a daily intensified longing to have the name of God glorified. Do you not sometimes feel sick at heart as you gaze upon this present generation? My soul is pained within me often when I see how everything is out of joint. Everything is now denied that from our youth we have regarded as sacred truth. The infallibility of Scripture is denied, the authenticity of one portion is challenged, and the inspiration of another is called in question; and the good old Book is torn to pieces by blind critics. Eternal verities against which only blaspheming infidels used to speak are now questioned by professed ministers of Christ. Doctrines that our sires never thought of doubting are now trailed in the mire, and that by those who profess to be teachers of God's Word. "Father, glorify Your name" comes leaping to our lip because it is burning in our heart—burning there in holy wrath against the treachery of men. Indignation arises from our jealousy, and our eager spirits cry, "Oh, that God would glorify His name!" To many of us this is our heaviest care.

Brethren, we desire the Lord to glorify that name in ourselves by preventing our impatience in suffering and keeping us from faintness in labor. We beseech our heavenly Father to destroy our selfishness, to cast out our pride, and to overcome every evil propensity that would prevent His getting glory out of us. Our soul is even as the clusters of the vine that belong to the owner of the vineyard. Our whole nature is as the fruit for which the great Vinedresser waits. Here fling me into the wine vat; let every cluster and every grape be gathered and pressed. Great Lord, cast me into the wine vat of Your service, and then express from me every drop of the essence of life. Let my whole soul flow forth to You. Let the ruddy juice burst forth on the right and on the left. And when the first rich liquor of my life is gone, then even to the utmost lees let me be pressed, till the last drop of the living juice that may bring glory to You shall have come forth of me. Fling all away that will not turn into Your glory, but use all that can be used.

Now, see how *that care is divested of all sorrow* by our casting it upon God. The prayer is not "Father, help me to glorify Your name," but it is "Father, glorify Your name." Your glory is too much for me to compass, but glorify Your own self. In Your Providence so arrange my position and condition as to glorify Your name. By Your grace so sustain me and sanctify me, that I may glorify You. I cannot do it, but You can, and the care that I was glad to feel I am glad also to bring by faith to You. "Father, glorify Your name."

And now, if you can pray in that fashion, *your confidence will come back to you.* If you have been greatly distracted, calm peace will visit you again, for now you will say, "I will bear the Lord's will and be content. I cannot quarrel with my Master's dealings anymore, for I have asked Him to glorify His name, and as I know that He is doing it I cannot murmur. How can I struggle against that which is really glorifying my Father? Your heart will cease to question and to quake and will nestle down beneath the eternal wings in deep and happy peace. Filled with patience, you will take the cup that stood untasted and grasp it with willingness, if not with eagerness. "It is to glorify God," you say. "Every drop of this cup is for His glory." Therefore, you put the chalice to your lip and drink straight on, and on, and on till you have drained the last drop and find that "it is finished." I know you will not fail to do this if your soul has really felt the power of this prayer: "Father, glorify thy name."

Surely he is the grandest creature God has made who glorifies Him most. And who is he? Not the tall archangel of whom Milton sings, whose wand might make a mast for some great admiral, but the most insignificant nobody who has long laid upon her bed of weariness and there has praised the Lord by perfect patience—she, though apparently the least, may be the greatest glorifier of the Father. Perhaps the tiniest creature God has made will bring Him more glory than Leviathan, which makes the deep to be hoary and causes the waters to boil like a pot. That which most thoroughly yields itself to God, that which most completely annihilates itself into the eternal All—is most glorifying to Him. May God of His infinite mercy bring us to this self-annihilation, this care for His glory only. Strive after it, beloved, by the power of the Holy Ghost.

Jesus said, "If any man will come after me, let him deny himself, and take up his cross daily, and follow me" (Luke 9:23). But mark you, the day will come when those who were willing to suffer for Christ will be counted to be the only sane persons who ever lived, and when those who cared for self and disregarded God and faith in Christ and love for their fellowmen will be regarded as having been mere idiots. Hear this parable. It is springtime, and yonder is a farmer walking the furrows and sowing his seed. Those who know nothing of husbandry mock him for his wastefulness with his grain. He is the wise man, is he not, who locks his granary door and preserves his corn? Why should he go and fling it into the cold, thankless ground? Wait till the end of June, when the bloom is on the wheat. Wait till July and August have brought the months of harvest, and you shall see that he who gave his wheat to die shall, amidst the shouts of "Harvest home," be reckoned to have been wise and prudent. He who kept the door of his granary bolted through his sluggishness and selfishness shall then be seen to be fit only for Bedlam, for he has no harvest save a mass of tangled weeds. Scatter your lives for others! Give yourself up to Jesus.